The Black Church in the Twenty-first

The Black Church in the Twenty-first Century

Edited by

Joe Aldred
Keno Ogbo

DARTON · LONGMAN + TODD

First published in 2010 by
Darton, Longman and Todd Ltd.
1 Spencer Court
140 – 142 Wandsworth High Street
London SW18 4JJ

ISBN 938-0-232-52792-6

Phototypeset by Kerrypress Ltd, Luton, Bedfordshire
Printed and bound by Thomson Litho, East Kilbride, Scotland

Contents

List of Figures

List of Tables

Introduction

Joe Aldred and Keno Ogbo

This anthology provides a fresh and exciting look at, and represents a bold attempt to scope and analyse, the key issues facing the Black Church in Britain at the close of the first decade of the twenty-first century. Both the Black Church and the issues it faces are complex multidimensional forces that would be impossible to scope in any one book. However, this collection of essays provides an array of insightful Black British commentators whose personal perspectives on their particular subjects do matter. This is not the traditional outsider's view of the Black Church, it is very much a book of insiders' critical analyses of their beloved institution, the challenges it faces and what response options are preferable in an increasingly secular and plural society.

The 'Black Church' is the term we have used for the book title and as suffix for each chapter of this collection. In so doing we are fully aware of the potential for controversy. However, dispensing with suffixes like 'led' and 'majority' after black permits a certain clarity of identity. 'Church' is always a compound term and in this case the Black Church refers to that multi-denominational Christian tradition that has been established in Britain by people from the Caribbean and Africa and that draws support largely from those communities in Britain, and advocates and agitates on their behalf. In the midst of a government led community cohesion philosophy it is more, not less, important that the Black community has a clear advocate that can speak prophetically to and for it. The Black Church as potentially the most powerful element within the Black community needs an uncluttered identity that makes its role of advocacy undeniable.

If, however, the Black Church is to achieve its spiritual and political potential, its whole must constitute more than the sum of its parts. Marcia Dixon, who writes on the subject weekly in *The Voice* newspaper, describes the Black Church as, 'the most stable, prosperous and influential institution within Britain's African and Caribbean community' (*Black UK Christian Directory 2008*). This is a self-evident truth, and yet as the contents of this book demonstrate it has a long way to go to realise its potential. Imagine what might be were the Black Church to punch its weight by maximising its corporate strength spiritually, socially, economically and politically! And so one of the implicit calls of this book is for greater unity of purpose in the Black Church. This can be achieved without uniformity in organisation, but not without a commitment to unity in diversity.

The organs of unity already exist. At grassroots Black Christians associate across denominational lines as never before. Black leaders associate with one another now more than ever before. Black Church agencies collaborate now, mainly to present a united front to government, more than anything ever known before. And it is our hope that the newly formed Black Christian Leaders Forum will provide the framework for greater cohesion and effectiveness for Black Church united action. For the sake of the next generation, this generation simply must attain a greater unity than hitherto has been achieved to build a lasting legacy that gives hope of a better future for all in this land.

This book points a way forward for the Black Church in the twenty-first century in the words of experts, practitioners and artisans. These are first and foremost personal reflections on the issues and each is written in the image of the writer. Some authors are practised writers, for others this is their first substantive piece, but they bring to it vast experience. Patrick Kalilombe (1999) writing from Malawi and Clemens Sedmak (2007) writing from Austria both affirm the crucial role 'local' practitioners play in doing what Kalilombe calls 'theology at the grassroots' and Sedmak, 'local theology'. Each of our contributors is rooted in a local context and from there offers a perspective to the nation and the world. The order in which the chapters appear is simply as decided by the editors, and does not refer to any order of importance.

Chapter 1 is a reminder that whatever else it does, the task before the Black Church is a theological one. David Muir argues that the Black

Church in today's society is an expression of the consciousness of the diasporian reality. He further explores the Pentecostal 'tribal mark' of initial evidence, going on to examine the political 'Dread Theology' of Robert Beckford, before ending with his 'Theology of Ascent' as a viable way forward for the Black Church. In Chapter 2, Jonathan Oloyede takes the reader on an exciting ecumenical journey. He unpacks the DNA of the Black Church, and the kinds of life-supporting relationships to which it is attracted. Oloyede identifies some of the individuals who hold the key to addressing the challenges, particularly the relationship between Black and White Christians and churches. True unity, he insists, is about taking gutsy, difficult, discomforting but loving steps towards reconciliation for the sake of reaching out to humanity.

Chapter 3 addresses what is the heartbeat of the Black, mostly Pentecostal, Church; namely the Holy Spirit. Joe Aldred examines how the Black Church's pneumatology might act as a catalyst for better relationship between Black and White Pentecostals and how a subtle shift could open the door to better relations with non-Pentecostals also. He argues that the current Pentecostal position on glossolalia as 'initial evidence' has not always been as it is now and calls for a better understanding of the Pentecostal impulse as a gift to the whole Church, not just Pentecostals. In Chapter 4, Juliet Fletcher pours her heart out in a plea for Gospel Music to be better embraced by the Black Church and become a paid profession for its practitioners. She argues passionately that although the most recognised, replicated, and redeeming feature of the Black Church; admired and coveted by others, the Black Church has yet to recognise the value of the music it has. She takes the reader from the Caribbean to Britain and shows that Gospel Music can be the language of protest and liberation, and if the vision and sacrifice of the early trailblazers can be built upon, contemporary and future artistes will have hope of support from their chosen ministry.

In Chapter 5, Julia Smith and Carl Ryan illustrate that disputes happen in churches as any other community and therefore the Black Church needs to be skilled in the art of dispute resolution. They show how the psycho-spiritual effects of disputes can, if handled well, benefit the Church; creating a healthier situation. Smith and Ryan conclude however, that although Christian conflict is not an oxymoron, decisive steps have to be taken to turn a negative into a positive. With Mark Saint in Chapter 6 we get closest to an outsider's view in that of a Black American who has been around long enough to gain an insightful comparison between the Black Church here and in the United States. He argues that until the Black Church, the identity of which he defines by nationality and colonial history, becomes clearer about its identity, it will not be clear about its political agenda. Saint argues that when a pre-eminent Black faith meets untenable social situations, this dynamic mix of the sacred and the secular both demanding correctives will create a long-lasting Black Church political force in Britain.

Chapter 7 prepares the reader for several forays into different social issues, in the chapters that follow. Here Les Isaac positions the Black Church vis á vis the social issues agenda. He argues that for the Black Church to have community relevance its mission must be to scratch where people itch, that is addressing real issues. Les is clear that the church's responsibility is not just to preach the Gospel but to make sure that people can feel the power of the Gospel in the transformation of their lives. He sees the way forward as the urban trinity of government, the police and the church working together in partnership, this however can be undermined by petty rivalry. In Chapter 8, Dionne Gravesande charges the Black Church not to forget its pioneers, its elders, who remained steadfast in the face of myriad difficulties, but whose faith and hope sustained them. The generation whose routes took them away from their roots, and by whose zeal the Black Church has been established in Britain now look to pass the baton to succeeding generations. But, she asks, will new generations keep the faith?

It can rightly be said of Carver Anderson that he has a heart for young people and in Chapter 9 he bares his heart. He makes an impassioned plea for the Black Church and statutory agencies to stop and listen to the real voices of young people: stop criminalising them, stop serving up ready-made solutions and instead respect and involve them in plans for their future. Carver's own story is one of discovering this very truth that young people's 'life on the road' has been shaped, often ruined by the very people who now offer irrelevant solutions to youths well capable of leadership and recovery, and who call for justice. The pressing need is for greater understanding of young people by the Black Church. Chapter 10 stays with the youth theme, although education is not only for young people. Here Cheron Byfield shares the benefit of her PhD research into how

Black boys make it in the education system here in Britain and in the United States. She discovers that the Black Church has played an excellent part in preparing young people for the education system, but need to do much more to scotch the stereotypical 'deficit' view of Black young people as underachievers. Such a view provides an imbalanced picture of Black children. Byfield argues that some Black Churches have a strong culture of education and need to further capitalise on opportunities to operate at national strategic levels, making use of cultural and divine capital.

In Chapter 11, Lincoln Sargeant explores the impact of faith on health. He eschews the received wisdom that the Black community's health must constantly be measured against the White population, instead he argues that any examination of health in Black populations must first attempt to account for patterns of health and disease within these populations without undue reference to other populations. Sargeant exposes the complex nature of health, from mental health to sexual health to aging and argues that the Black Church has an important role in the health education of parents, young people and the wider community. Scoping the health landscape, he proposes that the way to improved health lies in strategic partnerships between the Black Church and health providers like the NHS. In a not unrelated area, given the relationship between economics and health, Christopher Johnson discusses faith economics in Chapter 12. Johnson shows that there is increasing evidence that religious organisations, including Black Churches, are engaged in a variety of economic and social activities. And whilst in Britain the African Churches are ahead of the Caribbean ones in entrepreneurship, wealth creation by faith groups to the benefit of their constituencies and wider community is within the grasp of all. Johnson calls upon the Black Church to mobilise its congregations towards wealth-creation activities and fulfill the Lord's prayer to 'give us this day our daily bread' through faith economics.

Is it possible to be Black and green? Chris Andre-Watson answers this positively 'yes' in Chapter 13. He shows however, that as of yet, the Black Church in Britain is not properly engaged in the climate change debate, yet the areas of the world most likely to suffer first and whose people will suffer worst are precisely the places with Black populations: Africa and the Caribbean. In the face of evidence that global warming is the fault of carbon emissions from the Western industrialised world, Andre-Watson argues that the Black Church cannot stand by in a replay of the 'Me Tarzan, You Jane' scenario whereby the White man controls Black territory for his continued benefit. The climate change debate, he argues, is really about economics and the Black Church needs to prepare its people for the emerging green world which will radically impact their lifestyles. Finally, in Chapter 14, Joe Aldred explores seven key themes as challenges for Black Church leadership in the twenty-first century marked by post-modernity, post-colonialism, post-denominationalism and post-Christendom. Aldred argues that the Black Church must be up to the task of punching its weight in the church and public square. To do so, argues Aldred, the Black Church has to rise to the challenges in the spheres of Black history, theology, ecclesiology, ecumenism, socio-economics and politics, leadership, and missiology. If the Black Church responds well to these challenges it has a ministry not only to the Black community, but to society as a whole.

After all that, what could possibly be missing? As editors we are aware that there are a number of gaps in this anthology. In the first place each topic discussed is worthy of further, more in-depth treatment. Second, one of the topics we are conscious of omitting is gender, most especially a chapter on women, although we would direct the reader to an anthology published earlier on the theme (Aldred 2000). Then we would have liked chapters on inter-faith relations, the media, racial justice and much beside. We trust that others may be encouraged to make up for our lack.

Finally, we wish to thank everyone who has contributed in any way to making this book a reality. To the General Secretaries and staff of Churches Together in England and Churches Together in Britain and Ireland; members of the Reference Group of Minority Ethnic Christian Affairs at Churches Together in England; to members of the Working Group who met on 24 July 2007 in London to follow through the recommendations of the 'Stronger Together – Weaker Apart' national BME Church Leaders Summit, and who insightfully decided this course of action: William Ackah, Sonia Barron, Dulcie Dixon, Rowlando Morgan, Yemisi Onigbinde, Lincoln Sargeant and Katelina Tahaafe-Williams. It is our sincere hope that this anthology will stimulate greater networking, debate, understanding, prayer and action in the Black Church and beyond. May we never forget that as a people and as a world we are 'Stronger together – weaker apart'.

References

Aldred, Joe (ed.) (2000) *Sisters with Power*, London, Continuum

Dixon, Marcia in *Black UK Christian Directory 2008*, Bury St Edmunds, Black UK Publications Limited

Kalilombe, Patrick A. (1999) *Doing Theology at the grassroots: theological essays from Malawi*, Gweru, Mambo Press

Sedmak, Clemens (2007) *Doing Local Theology: a guide for artisans of a new humanity*, Maryknoll, Orbis Books

1   *Theology and the Black Church*

R. David Muir

The Black Church tradition is a rich one, reflecting the history, theology and social reality of a people whose diasporian encounter has shaped the contours of their matrix of consciousness. The diasporian experience of slavery and colonialism in 'New World' Christian civilization has, to a large extent, problematized the nature of black faith in the Diaspora. This is particularly evident in the ways in which we imagine and authenticate this faith and religiosity through the prism of Christianity. I raise this at this early stage not because I intend to resolve it in this short chapter, but rather because it constitutes a fundamental problem in the cultural politics and theology of the Black Church.

Whether one thinks of the formation of the African Methodist Episcopal Church in 1799, the religious awakening of Equiano, the theo-political impact of David Walker's Appeal, the Ethiopian Manifesto of Robert Young, the renaissance of pan-Africanism through the Niagara Movement, or Marcus Garvey; it is through the consciousness of this diasporian reality that we can speak of the 'Black Church' and its theological reflections. And as heirs of this rich tradition the Black Majority Church (BMC) in Britain, and the wider Black Christian movement, cannot isolate itself from the history, theology and politics of this legacy. It is partly this legacy that conditions and informs some of the categories, theologies, ritual and liturgical expressions of what goes on in the religious organizations we traditionally define as 'Black Church', 'Black-led Church', or 'Black Majority Church' in the taxonomy of the Black Church Movement in Britain (Gerloff 1992).

In the literature on Black Church history, tradition, taxonomy and theologies, we find creative and controversial expressions of faith and commitment; we also encounter a joyful, vibrant and celebratory community of believers for whom the immanence (presence) of God is an existential reality and Jesus is 'the same yesterday, today, and forever' (Hebrews 13:8). Recognising that it is not possible to do justice here to the rich theological diversity we encounter in the Black Church, I intend to limit the scope of my discussion to three key areas. Firstly, I want to say a few things about the place of religion – especially Pentecostal/Charismatic expressions of the Black Church – in society and offer some reflections upon the theological challenge to the Pentecostal dogmatic of the *initial evidence* doctrine, referred to by Hollenweger (1972) as a 'tribal mark' differentiating the church from the hostile tribes of the world. Second, I want to comment on what has become something of an important development in Black British theology – the 'Dread thesis' of Robert Beckford. Third, I want to offer some brief reflections on the future of the Black Church and offer an outline of what I call a Theology of Ascent.

The Black Church in society

Sixty years after the *Empire Windrush* it is now fashionable for mainstream church officials, cultural critics and journalists to hold up the Black Majority Churches (BMCs) as a mirror and a metaphor for what is taking place in the 'death of Christian Britain'. The mirror is a reminder of the reality that once formed the centrality of 'faith' in constituting personal and cultural identities for large sections of the community. The metaphor speaks to the notion of the 'empire strikes back', bringing life, vitality and celebratory authenticity to religious signs and symbols that no longer appear credible in post-modern, post-Christendom Britain. So the Black Majority Church finds itself in a strange, challenging and propitious place on the British religious and social landscape. Ian Bradley (2007) puts it well when he argues that 'Black Christianity may well prove to be a key agent in the re-evangelization of Christian Britain'. Where decades of economic decline in our cities have brought in its wake physical decay and social disintegration, we have witnessed spiritual revival and social cohesion as a result of the presence and persistence of Black Majority Churches. However, the growth and development of the Black Church Movement and the place of faith and religion in society should be seen in the context of a wider philosophical and cultural discourse about God, spirituality and the forces of modernity.

Although there are many doctrinal and theological antecedents of the Black Church Movement in the UK, it is the hegemony of the Charismatic and Pentecostal variety that is critical. It is estimated that there are over 500 million Pentecostals in the world. According to McGrath (2004), Pentecostalism has become 'the new Marxism of the third world', displacing its secular rival for the affections and loyalty of the dispossessed. Pentecostalism is a phenomenon of the Spirit, its *locus classicus* is the Lucan narrative in Acts 2:1–4; 10:44–48; 19:1–7. It is more than glossolalia and the experience of 'speaking in tongues'. Black Pentecostalism in Britain can be seen as the accentuation of the Spirit in the lived-experience and spiritual reality of Pentecostals. As a modern 'religious renaissance', Pentecostal spirituality, according to Harvey Cox (1995), has challenged the religious and cultural landscape as well as some of the sociological prognostications of the 'decline' of religion. Cox (1965) showed in his classic work how the seeds and sources of the 'secular city' would produce values of pluralism and tolerance, contributing to an epoch whose ethos would be characterized by 'no religion at all'. In Cox's 'secular metropolis' the 'gods of traditional' religion are dethroned and religion is rendered innocuous; it is reduced to the 'private fetishes' with no role to play in public life.

Three decades later, in the face of the phenomenal growth of Pentecostalism and the wider religious revival, Cox (1995) admits that the 'death of God' pronouncements of theologians and 'the waning of religion that sociologists had extrapolated' did not reach prophetic fulfilment. Pentecostal spirituality, and the religious renaissance in the penultimate quarter of the twentieth century, seemed to have survived both the Marxian theoretical wish-fulfilment for the 'abolition of religion' (Marx 1975, Milbank 1990, Cone 1975, Macintyre 1969, Kee 1990, Clarke and Byrne (eds) 1993), and the Comteian project for a new secular 'religion' (Aron 1965, Becker 1962, 1972), or a new 'sociocracy' as Aron (1965) terms it, precisely because it offers meaning to personal and collective existence, as well as, according to Becker (1972), 'an ideal of strength and of potential for growth'.

Modern day Pentecostalism can be seen as a form of 'religious zeal'; and as Cox (1995) concluded in the closing decade of the twentieth century, has cultural and intellectual affinity with the observations made by Tocqueville writing in the 1830s. 'Eighteenth century philosophers had a very simple explanation for the gradual weakening of beliefs. Religious zeal, they said, was bound to die down as enlightenment and freedom spread. It is tiresome that the facts do not fit this theory at all' (Tocqueville 1968). To a large extent, Pentecostal spirituality and the 'unanticipated resurgence of religion,' as Cox (1995) argues, constitute what Gilles Kepel calls 'the revenge of God'. The phenomenon of Pentecostalism with its understanding of 'experienced' pneumatology and 'charismatic Christianity' is, according to Martin (2002), 'the largest global shift in the religious marketplace over the last forty years'. With estimated annual growth of Pentecostal-Charismatic churches at the rate of 20 million, and with a world wide membership of over 543 million, it is, perhaps, easy to understand Martin's claims of the global shift in the 'religious market place' which is characteristically Pentecostal. For Cox (1995), the Pentecostal phenomenon is a refutation of the 'sobering projection' of the scholars who predicted that the growth in technology and twentieth-century socio-political consciousness would 'increasingly shove religion to the margin'.

Pentecostalism, with its charismatic expression and spirituality, is one of the dominant forms of spirituality in the Black Majority Church. To be a Pentecostal is not merely to assent to a set of 'doctrinal commitments' (Edwards 1992), rather it is the experience of the Spirit in the life, struggles and imagination of believers in a 'charismatic community' (Moltmann 1977). For Pentecostals, belonging to this community and the experience of the Spirit brings life, joy, transformed expectations and power to witness as promised in Acts:

> But ye shall receive power, after that the Holy Ghost is come
> upon you: and ye shall be witnesses unto me both in Jerusalem,
> and in Judaea, and in Samaria, and unto the uttermost part of the
> earth.

> *(Acts 1:8)*

The transformation of this lived-experience and existential reality manifests itself in a number of ways. Often it is seen and experienced in Pentecostal rituals, liturgy, sermons, prayers, enthusiasm and commitment to social change. The 'organised spontaneity' (Edwards 1992, p.68) of Black Pentecostal worship and oral liturgy, referred to by Edwards, is a characteristic feature of what conditions and informs, this community, fuelling the transformation of Pentecostal lived experience and existential reality. Notwithstanding R.M. Anderson's (1979) argument of Pentecostals as 'socially disinherited' people, Pentecostals do not only 'bear witness' to a transformed spirituality, but they also see, in adopting aspects of Weber's 'this–worldly asceticism', a correlation between belonging to their charismatic community and a transformation in their social and economic status.

Initial evidence – glossolalia

While Pentecostal spirituality and its charismatic manifestations inform a large section of the Black Majority Church, its theology is by no means uncontestable. Central to 'classical' Pentecostalism – and what is still a sign of orthodoxy for some denominations – is what is referred to as the doctrine of 'initial evidence', i.e., speaking in tongues (glossolalia) is the sign or initial evidence of Spirit baptism. Theologically, a key question is whether this cherished Pentecostal 'dogmatic' is normative, transitional or cessational in the early church. In his doctoral thesis James Dunn (1970) attempted to refute this Pentecostal hermeneutic. While Dunn's principal aim was to 'introduce scholars, students and ministers to the most distinctive aspects of Pentecostal theology – baptism in the Holy Spirit', he also challenged the sacramentalist understanding and identification of water baptism with Spirit baptism, i.e., the notion that water baptism is synonymous with Spirit baptism. Critical issues are raised by Dunn in his attempt to bring 'clarity of thought' to the discussions.

But does the New Testament mean by baptism in the Holy Spirit what Pentecostals understand the phrase to mean? Is baptism in the Holy Spirit to be separated from conversion-initiation, and is the beginning of the Christian life to be thus divided up into distinctive stages? Is Spirit baptism something essentially different from becoming a Christian, so that even a Christian of many years standing may never have been baptized in the Spirit? What is the place of the gift of the Spirit in the total complex event of becoming a Christian? These are some of the important questions which Pentecostal teaching raises. The Pentecostal doctrine of Spirit baptism makes a new and important contribution to an old debate, and by focusing attention on the gift of the Spirit and separating the gift of the Spirit from conversion-initiation, it both revitalizes the debate and calls into question many of the traditionally accepted views of Christian baptism (Dunn 1970).

The soteriological implications of Dunn's 'conversion-initiation' dynamic become the interrogatory mechanism for refutation and contextualization of the Pentecostal hermeneutic of 'baptism in the Holy Spirit'. According to Dunn, the distinctive Pentecostal view on the baptism of the Holy Spirit is scripturally unsound, theologically untenable and, more importantly, soteriologically defective. It is 'the anointing of the Spirit' says Dunn, 'what makes a man a Christian' (2 Corinthians 1:21), and it is the gift of Spirit which enables one to participate. Similarly, it is the 'baptism in the Spirit' which effects one's incorporation into the body of Christ. For Dunn, this takes place at 'conversion'.

Taking 2 Corinthians 3 as 'a crucial chapter in any attempt to understand Paul's pneumatology', Dunn (1970) argues that the ground is cut away from under the feet of the Pentecostals. In the Corinthians narrative Paul speaks of 'the ministration' of the two covenants, Moses and Christ, the letter and the Spirit respectively. Paul's conclusion is that in Christ, there is no longer any mystification, bondage or death: in Christ 'the veil is done away with'; a new dispensation of 'liberty' is present and by the Spirit believers are 'changed into the same image from glory to glory'. From this chapter, Dunn arrives at the following conclusions:

> there is no thought of a second gift of the Spirit. Indeed there cannot be. The Spirit is so much the essence and all of the new covenant in its application to mean that it is impossible to conceive of the new covenant apart from the Spirit, and impossible to experience the blessings of the new covenant apart from the indwelling of the Spirit ... To become a Christian is to receive the gift of the Spirit,
>
> *(Dunn 1970, pp.136, 137)*

Dunn's challenging thesis, and conclusion, that 'No Christian was without the Spirit, for only these who had (received) the Spirit were ipso facto Christians'; and that one is 'a Christian who has received the gift of the Holy Spirit by committing (her/himself) to the risen Jesus as Lord and who lives accordingly', poses further questions concerning the interpretation of what should be considered 'normative', 'transitional', and 'cessational' in the phenomenon of Pentecost and apostolic pneumatology. Pentecostals and Charismatics maintain that the apostolic experience of Charismatic manifestations are normative; as such they can be experienced by the Church today and should be anticipated by the believer even if these gifts are not directly mediated through the believer.

Dread Theology

I now want to turn to what is, undoubtedly, one of the most exciting and challenging developments in British Black theology – the rise of Robert Beckford and his use of Black expressive cultures, especially his 'Dread' theology. The centrality of Beckford's 'Dread' thesis – a metaphor for the 'uplifting' of black people – provides a number of fecund cultural and political insights, but the symbolism and language of *Jesus is Dread*, as we shall discuss below, present difficulties for Pentecostals. Before we look at Robert Beckford's '*dread* paradigm' and theological construct to 'outline a framework for a Black political theology' (Beckford 1998), a brief consideration will be given to examining the contours and issues explored in this first 'self-conscious attempt to map out a Black Theology for Britain'.

Although a number of Black 'insiders', and 'outsiders', have attempted to sketch what may loosely be called a 'Black British Theology', it is principally in the work of Beckford that we find the fullest expression of such a theology. I will briefly explore the context, content and challenges of what is, decidedly, one of the most exciting Black theological developments to emerge in Britain. Beckford's use of 'Black expressive cultures' (Beckford 1998) as well as the language, imagery, and ideology of Rastafarianism as sources for developing a Black British Pentecostal political theology poses a number of challenging questions for Black Pentecostalism and Black Christians in Britain. There are fundamental issues of psychological dissonance, and theological incongruence, between the 'audience' for whom Beckford writes and the methodology he employs.

In the introduction of *Dread and Pentecostal* Beckford says:

> This book is concerned with developing a political theology for
> the Black Church in Britain and finding viable context for its
> development and expression. The birth of the Black Christian

Civic Forum in the Winter of 1998 reveals a 'wind of change' among second and third generation Black Christians: they are willing to get their hands dirty. This emerging political voice requires a critical theological support. This text, therefore, is also a challenge to the emerging Black Christian body politic. In short, it offers a theological resource for a Black Christian political theology ... a political theology based on 'dread' Pentecostalism.

(Beckford 2000, p.1)

The theoretical and hermeneutical framework adopted by Beckford is culturally and theologically fecund, invoking a rich and nuanced dialectic between the liberational ethos of black religion and political radicalism. Essentially, Beckford's approach utilizes 'cultural theory' methodology to develop a 'political theology' to mobilize and radicalize Black British Pentecostals:

My approach is to develop a black Christian cultural theory as a methodology for interrogating the black Christian experience – in short, to make use of aspects of black culture to radicalise black British Pentecostal church culture and theology. This is not a new phenomenon in black Christian circles. The combination of black expressive culture and the Christian gospel produced gospel music with its radical and political quality. Moreover, in recent times black Christians have *selectively* appropriated aspects of black popular culture in order to enhance and enrich black faith.

(Beckford 2000, p.51)

The ancestral pedigree of Beckford's Dread thesis are partly informed by defining moments in Black diasporian history and experience, especially 'New World' slavery and its creation and perpetuation of the psychology of the 'plantation complex' (Thomas 1998, Curtin 1990, Genovese 1971) and the 'politics of moral orders' (Austin-Broos 1997) informing Caribbean socio-racial hierarchy, morality and religious discourse. The historical relationship between Pentecostalism and Rastafarianism in Jamaica is critically explored by Austin-Broos (p.239–241) who sees Rastafarianism cast as 'the critical religion in the face of Pentecostal hegemony'.

Austin-Broos shows how the 'shared cultural logic' and ritual practice that positions these two religions in Jamaican society are mediated by issues of race, resistance, black exclusivity and transcendence. In the case of the latter, Austin-Broos argues that 'Rastafarian transcendence suggests more of Sartrean existentialism than Christianity as such' (p.240). In the context of Beckford's Dread Theology, and the Pentecostal distinctive of glossolalia, Austin-Broos draws an interesting 'parallel' between the Rastafarian commitment to ganga (marijuana) smoking and Selassie, and Pentecostal ideas of speaking in tongues and commitment to the Holy Ghost and God. Drawing upon the work of Chevannes, Austin-Broos sees these commitments as points at which Rasta and Pentecostal practitioners 'cross the threshold separating the righteous and the saved from the unrighteous and the damned' (Chevannes 1994).

In both *Jesus is Dread* (1998) and *Dread and Pentecostal* (2000), Rastafarian culture is recognised by Beckford as a major phenomenon that affected black youth in Britain and elsewhere. Dennis (2000) and Cashmore (1983) show ways in which this sub-culture/counterculture informed and influenced Black British culture and the 'politics of resistance'. There were also negative images and religious connotations of Rastafarianism in the minds of the older Caribbean people, as Beckford recognizes:

> Whereas for many of my parents' generation, Christianity and
> Black politics were two separate realities, for me they are
> inseparable. Nowhere was the dichotomy between politics and
> religion more apparent for many of my parents' generation than in
> their dislike of Rastafari. Many of my parents' generation
> considered Rasta politics 'anti-Christian' and 'rebellious', and
> Rastas 'dirty'.

> *(Beckford 1998, p.1)*

Ferdinand Dennis (2000) makes a similar point, but places this generational argument in a broader socio-political context as a search for 'blackness':

> Equally disturbing to older West Indians was the conduct of their
> British-born children. Rejected by a Britishness which excluded
> blacks, the first generation of Afro-Britons retreated into a
> blackness which rejected Britain. That blackness was
> Rastafarianism. Back in Jamaica, Rastas were the outcast, the

dregs, the insane of society. To see their children embrace this apparently bizarre cult drove many older West Indians to distraction.

(p.187)

Undoubtedly, part of Beckford's aim is to rehabilitate Rasta ideology and iconography for Black Pentecostals and Black Christians as a theological resource to aid them in their struggles and quest for Black identity. Notwithstanding, the manifold 'difficulties' with this type of theological rehabilitation, Beckford ultimately wants Black Pentecostal churches to turn to Rastafarianism as a focus for politicisation and mobilization. In privileging a Rastafarian 'theo-cultural focus', the essence and logic of Beckford's Dread hermeneutic is disclosed:

> Rastafarianism represents the first attempt to construct a liberation theology in African Caribbean history. For African Caribbean people it is an important resource, because there is no other contemporary African Caribbean religious tradition in Britain that embraces Black identity, politics and struggle. Second, some aspects of Rastafari's theological method resonate with Black Pentecostals ... they both share epistemological roots in the Myal-Obeah complex. Also, a primary resource for both traditions is the Christian scriptures. Hence, there are sufficient grounds for turning to Rastafari to find a theo-cultural focus for politicising African Caribbean Christianity as found in Black Pentecostal Churches ... a critical appropriation of aspects of Rastafari can provide a theo-political catalyst for Black Pentecostals in Britain.

(Beckford 2000, p.160, 161)

The notion that only Rastafarianism embraces 'Black identity, politics and struggle' is a false one, predicated on a rather narrow and arbitrary definition of these concepts and a misreading of what Black religious groups like the Nation of Islam and the African Revivalists are doing in Britain. It also fails to recognize alternative forms of 'politics' and cultural 'struggles' taking place in many Black Pentecostal churches.

The Dread Thesis, and its appropriation of Rastafarian ideology/ theology to politically mobilize the Black Church, constitute both a theological and biblical problematic for Black British Pentecostals, as well as an intellectual one. Pentecostals may argue that the central tenets of Beckford's thesis are theologically and biblically unsound. Intellectually, it could be interpreted as marginal at best, and unbiblical, at worst, in religious communities which are interpretively characterised as 'conservative' and evangelical. The multi-layered hermeneutics and the manifold methodological suggestions, partly, render Beckford's work inaccessible to the purported audience for his theologising, namely, the Black Churches. An analogy of the multi-layered hermeneutics, and the critical theological imagination displayed in Beckford's work, as it relates to the broader Pentecostal constituency, could be made by way of Erasmus' criticisms of the subtleties of 'scholastic argument' of the Ockhamists, Scotists and others:

> Such is the erudition and complexity they all display that I fancy the apostles themselves would need the help of another Holy Spirit if they were obliged to join issue on these topics with our new breed of theologians.

> (*Erasmus 1971, p.156*)

The issues raised, and the methodology employed, in Beckford's thesis have challenging political and theological implications for Black British Pentecostalism; they also have, however, enormous implications for the continued and reconfigured development and expressions of Black British *political* and Pentecostal *theologies*. Among leading Pentecostal theologians, leaders and activists, there is, unfortunately, the danger of dismissing Beckford's theological insights and framework not because he privileges the use of 'Black expressive cultures', but rather because the use of Rastafarianism as the predominant interpretative frame, and medium of cultural expression and appropriation, is seen as alien to Pentecostal ideology and 'holiness' theology. A fundamental aspect of this Pentecostal ideology is the centrality of the scriptures (Gause 1973), and the *use* to which they are put, i.e., the integrity and variety of reading canons and hermeneutical schemes. Most Black Pentecostals are conservative/ fundamentalists in their views on Scripture and its use in doctrinal commitments and political legitimation. For most Pentecostals, the scriptures are *fundamental* (Edwards 2000) to the development of an authentic

'Black theology'; they perform a critical function in the re-construction of Black Christian 'political consciousness'.

One of the fundamental weaknesses in the Dread paradigm for Black Pentecostals is related to the use of the Bible. In Beckford's work, there is a minimalist use of, and engagement with, Scripture. This is perceived as a cardinal flaw in any theological construct destined to inform or influence the political thinking and consciousness of the Black Church, especially the African Christian organizations in Britain. Any Black theology, or liberation theology, which does not privilege Scripture, is doomed to marginality and irrelevance in Black Christian thought and Pentecostal theology. Gerloff (1992) argues that the 'total lack of biblical references both from the Hebrew Bible and the New Testament' in Beckford's paradigm presents a problem for Pentecostal hermeneutics:

> In the Pentecostal context, to forget about the Scriptural foundations can only be counterproductive and does not give due credit to the inspirational Biblical language for freedom from enslaving human beings.
>
> *(Gerloff 1992, p.65)*

The argument is poignantly expressed by Lorna Campbell and Joel Edwards, Black Christian activist and church leader respectively in Pentecostal churches. Campbell (2002) argues:

> Beckford excelled in *Jesus is Dread* in championing Black culture and its strength as a theological resource. Unfortunately, this is problematic in that many Black Christians in Black Majority churches would have difficulty in relating to its content due to the lack of reference to Scripture. Perhaps Beckford should have chosen something with which Black Christians can identify rather than Rastafarianism. As a theological resource it is likely that *Jesus is Dread* would be viewed as unsound and will not resonate with Black Christian thought.

Edwards (2001) views Beckford's theology as striking, on the one hand, but also 'politically incorrect' and disturbing, on the other hand:

> Black Christians like myself who grew up in Jamaica and other Caribbean islands and who dread the idea of Dread should try to

read [Beckford's book] without prejudice. I found his paradigm … evocative. Beckford's point about Dread – the idea of uplifting – as a uniquely Black cultural context for a theology of emancipation is striking if not politically incorrect and emotionally disturbing for most Black preachers! I suspect it will stay within the academy for quite a few years before it finds its way into the average Black convention on a Sunday morning … I fear that the work goes too far in seeking to persuade Pentecostalism – married as it is to a classical, conservative view of salvation – that it should embrace a Dread Cross. 'Christafari' would inevitably carry a Rastafarian doctrine unrecognisable in the New Testament … Dread stands up as a coherent intellectual tool for a Black paradigm but will ring hollow for most Pentecostals. The danger is that the spokesperson would not be recognised by those he seeks to represent.

Campbell's argument about the absence of Scriptures in Beckford's work, and Edwards' assertion concerning Beckford's theo-political construct not being recognizable in Black Churches, means in effect that Black Pentecostals will always find it theologically and intellectually difficult to find 'sufficient grounds' for using the language of Rastafarianism for theological development or political mobilization. Although similar criticisms were levelled at James Cone (Copher 1993) in respect of the use of Scriptures in his theology, there are explicit references in his work to their foundational importance. 'Black Theology', says Cone, 'is kerygmatic theology. That is, it is theology which takes seriously the importance of Scripture in theological discourse' (Cone 1970). Cone later gives a classic statement on his hermeneutical principle for scriptural exegesis; and in this respect, one can understand the difficulties Black Pentecostals would have with Beckford's Rastafarian hermeneutic in light of Cone's view of Scripture. The passage from Cone is quoted at length not only because it illustrates the norms within which Black political/liberation theologians can utilize a variety of sources, especially the Scriptures, to shape and inform their theologies and retain what Cone calls 'a Christian perspective', but also because it discloses the cultural and psychological chasm between Pentecostalism and Rastafarianism. Cone maintains:

The hermeneutical principle for an exegesis of the Scriptures is the revelation of God in Jesus as the liberator of the oppressed from social oppression and to political struggle, wherein the poor recognize that their fight against poverty and injustice is not only consistent with the gospel but is the gospel of Jesus Christ. Jesus Christ the Liberator, the helper and the healer of the wounded, is the point of departure for valid exegesis of the Scriptures from a Christian perspective. Any starting point that ignores God in Christ as the Liberator of the oppressed or that makes salvation as liberation secondary is ipso facto invalid and thus heretical. The test of the validity of this starting point, although dialectically related to black cultural experience, is not found in the particularity of the oppressed alone. It is found in the One who freely granted us freedom when we were doomed to slavery. In God's revelation in Scripture we come to the recognition that the divine liberation of the oppressed is not determined by our perceptions but by the God of the Exodus, the prophets and Jesus Christ who calls the oppressed into a liberated existence ... And if it can be shown that God as witnessed in the Scriptures is not the Liberator of the oppressed, then Black Theology would have either to drop the 'Christian' designation or to choose another starting point.

(*Cone 1975, pp.81–82*)

The richness of Beckford's theology in his first two books and also his controversially titled third book, *God of the Rahtid: Redeeming Rage* (2001) places him at the forefront of Black Theology in Britain. Beyond the contestable truth-claims of Rastafarian in respect of the divinity of His Majesty, Emperor Haile Selassie I, and the image, ideology and language of the Dread thesis, Beckford's theo-cultural metaphors signify important *messages* for Black Pentecostals on a number of levels. On one level, Dread is 'rebellion', signifying 'freedom from oppression' and 'upliftment' and 'empowerment', on another level Dread symbolizes both 'insight' and 'progress', as well as a theological construct of universal dimension:

Dread as progress is concerned with Black thriving, striving and accomplishment. Furthermore, dread is also concerned with the insight gained from engagement with the tragic and grotesque in Black life. Furthermore, while being concerned with Black experience, the word-symbolic focus demands that dread have a universal dimension; I want to suggest that 'dread' as a theological construct, while emerging from Black space, is not confined or limited by it. It also transcends the Black moorings in which I have placed it. In this sense 'dread' is naturally inter-subjective, engaging with other contexts.

(Beckford 2000, p.168)

In Beckford, Black British theology has a formidable and theologically creative 'insider', giving intellectual credence to a Black hermeneutic two decades after Hollenweger raised his concern about the lack of Black students in higher education in general and theological institutions in particular. Additionally, in Beckfordism there is a theo-cultural paradigm which does not lend itself to colonization 'from the other side'.

In the 1980s, Black British Christians were concerned about 'the politics' and status of Black Pentecostal research and discourse, i.e., the way in which the predominant discourse and writings on Pentecostalism, and Black Christian experience, were constructed, 'colonized' and refracted mainly by white 'outsiders'. Beckford's work is a radical departure from the anthropological gaze of the 'outsiders' into Black religious communities. However, the aestheticization of Black 'expressive cultures', principally through Rastafarianism, means that Beckford may have to intellectually resign himself either to what Cornel West (1991:131–146) refers to as the 'self-imposed marginality' of Black intellectuals, or to something akin to the theological isolation and prophetic non-recognition among Pentecostals alluded to in Matthew 13:57: 'A prophet is not without honour, save in his own country, and in his own house'.

Equally important, Beckford's *Dread and Pentecostal*, along with 'dread hermeneutics' in *Jesus is Dread*, will not only force Black Pentecostals to rethink theologically the meaning of the 'insider-outsider' dichotomy and discourse on Pentecostalism and 'Black British' political theologies, but it will also reconfigure the debate about Black religion and Black culture(s), especially the appropriation of the latter to inform a theology which develops within authentic Pentecostal history and traditions. No doubt, we will hear much more from Robert Beckford; and if the Black Church community of scholars and teachers critically engage with his work they will find rich resonances and points of departure in his understanding of Pentecostal pneumatology.

As I draw to a conclusion there are a number of challenging questions. These are questions facing the Black community and the Black Church that need to be answered by church and civic leaders, as well as by theologians. These questions are largely to do with the future of Black Britain and the very nature and function of the Black Church in the twenty-first century. Two decades ago we were asking questions like 'Has Black Theology outlived it usefulness?' and 'When will we no longer need a Black Church?' Needless to say that the first question was not fully understood by the Black Church constituency, for the content of Black Theology was not widely disseminated or discussed in Black congregations. And as far as the second question forced people to look also at the pastoral and spiritual needs of individuals, and the concomitant diversity of church provision that this would require, all talk about 'Whither Black Church?' was just that, talk. The Black Church would remain a permanent and authentic feature of the diversity that is Christian Britain. The legitimate plea, beautifully captured in the title of Joel Edwards' book would be that the Lord would make us one, but not all the same (Edwards 1999).

If the Black Church will fulfil its divine leadership mandate it will not only need a new leadership, but it will also need new theological expressions. The philosophy inherent in the 'Big Move' (i.e., to train, equip, and develop leaders for church and society), as conceived by Bishop Eric Brown, national head of the New Testament Church of God, points to critical aspects of the development of this new leadership; and in the development of a 'Theology of Respect' as advocated by Joe Aldred (2005) we see a number of fecund and creative theological expressions focusing on faith, 'prophetic presence' and self-respect as constituent parts of a dynamic theological mosaic. While both are necessary and will play important roles in this new leadership and theological expression, they are not sufficient. They need a complimentary narrative of advancement which can be owned, recognized and utilized by those inside the Church and Christian community, and those outside it.

We need a narrative that takes into account the experience of diasporian encounter-consciousness and its legacy. I want to call this complimentary narrative a Theology of Ascent. It must speak to, *inter alia*, Black people's social and spiritual development, Black Christian agency, autonomy, and advancement in Christ borne of a spiritual security of divine acceptance and radical equality in the Kingdom of God. In outlining his 'Theology of Respect' Aldred (2005) speaks of the importance of moving away from the 'oppression/liberation dialectic' that is characteristic of Beckford's Black Theology. A Theology of Ascent must establish a new matrix of consciousness, a new celebratory dialectic of personal acceptance and affirmation of radical equality in God. The new matrix of consciousness will help us to define ourselves by the best that's in us, rather than the negativity of our diasporian experience and legacy.

Forty years ago, James Cone created a theological and religious stir when he identified the ethics of Black Power with the gospel of Jesus Christ. Some would argue that the Black Theology that Cone subsequently developed identified too closely the radical politics of Black Power with the Christian faith. A significant part of Black Theology has, undoubtedly, been a response to racism and the legacy of slavery – the fruits of diasporian history and consciousness. We commemorated the Bicentenary of the Abolition of the Slave Trade in 2007 and 2008 in the UK and the US, respectively. Although many are suspicious of the scientific status of what is called 'post-traumatic slave syndrome' (Leary 2005), there can be no doubt about the enduring legacy of slavery on the descendants of slaves. Black theological discourse has constantly tried to find meaning and symbols of redemption in this episode in our history.

The biblical metaphor of the Joseph story (our culpability in our brothers' fortunes/misfortunes), the exodus narrative (from slavery to Promised Land, from oppression to liberation), the Jesus event of intentional sacrifice (the forces of darkness will ultimately be vanquished) are all perennial spiritual and psychological resources from which we draw inspiration. However, it is in Edward Blyden (1887 and 1994) that we find something of a redemptive, though controversial, resolution inherent in the theodicy around some difficult Diaspora questions when he argues that Providence had a part to play in the 'deportation of the Negro to the New World', even though 'wicked hands prosecuted' unspeakable barbarities. Whatever metaphors, narratives or explanations we arrive at, it is recognized that the diasporian history and encounter with slavery and its cadences of desolation continually need reinterpreting and redeeming in light of the Gospel and the reality of the Resurrection. And this is the task of the whole church community, and not just the work of theologians.

Part of this reinterpreting and redeeming is about our use of language and communicative symbols. We need a new grammar of celebration and communication. We need to punctuate our personal and corporate lives differently. We need more exclamation marks of thankfulness – that in spite of the configuration of forces that conspired against us we have overcome, we are victorious. We need to transform, and transcend, one of the dominant themes arising out of diasporian consciousness, racism. We need to see racism, like other forms of 'mind forged manacles', not so much as a *full-stop* foreclosing opportunities but rather as a *comma* to be negotiated. A redemptive belief in one's personal agency which is given by, and authenticated through, the Risen Lord means that we can embrace the future without fear knowing 'in whom we have believed' and that in faith and hope, as Moltmann (1967) argues, we can live 'in the light of the possibilities and promises' of God.

And what about unity in the Black Christian community? We need to invoke the *question mark* less in the suspicion we cast over the theological orthodoxy of those we would work and have fellowship with. The truth is we often have a greater and more profound unity in Christ than we think. Like Aldred (2005), I believe in the 'prophetic presence' of Black Christians in the mainstream and in the Black Majority churches, as well as in the wider society. I believe in the divine ministry of the Black Church in Britain. Over the last sixty years there were manifold opportunities to snuff it out and quench its vitality, but because its formation was more than the mono-causal 'rejectionist' (racism) thesis it still thrives. Thanks be to God. Amen!

References

Aldred, J. D. (2005) *Respect: Understanding Caribbean British Christianity*, Peterborough, Epworth

Anderson, Roberts M. (1979) *Vision of the Disinherited: The Making of American Pentecostalism*, New York, Oxford University Press

Aron, Raymond (1965) *Main Currents in Sociological Thought*, Vol.1, (translated by Richard Howard and Helen Weaver), Harmondsworth, Middlesex, Penguin Books, pp.63–109

Austin-Broos, Diane J. (1997) *Jamaica Genesis: Religion and the Politics of Moral Orders*, Chicago, University of Chicago Press

Becker, Ernest (1962, 1972) *The Birth and Death of Meaning: An Interdisciplinary Perspective on the Problem of Man*, Harmondsworth, Middlesex, Penguin, p.196

Beckford, Robert (1998) *Jesus is Dread: Black Theology and Black Culture in Britain*, London, Darton Longman & Todd, p.2

Beckford, Robert (2000) *Dread and Pentecostal: A Political Theology for the Black Church in Britain*, London, SCM Press

Beckford, Robert (2001) *God of the Rahtid*, London, Darton Longman & Todd, pp. 39–40

Blyden, Edward W., (1887, 1994) *Christianity, Islam and the Negro Race*, Baltimore, Black Classic Press, p.385

Bradley, Ian (2007) *Believing Britain: The Spiritual Identity of 'Britishness'*, London and New York, I.B. Tauris

Buber, Martin (1952) *Eclipse of God: Studies in the Relationship Between Religion and Philosophy*, New York, Harper & Row

Campbell, Lorna (2002) 'An Evaluation of Theological Methodology at Work through a Critical Appraisal of *Jesus is Dread: Black Theology and Black Culture in Britain* by Robert Beckford', unpublished paper

Cashmore, Ernest (1983) *Rastaman: The Rastafarian Movement in England*, London, Unwin Paperbacks

Chevannes, Barry (1994) *Rastafari: Roots and Ideology*, Syracuse, Syracuse University Press, p.219

Clarke, Peter and Byrne, Peter (ed) (1993) *Religion Defined and Explained*, London, Macmillan Press

Cone, James (1970) *A Black Theology of Liberation*, Philadelphia and New York, J.B. Lippincott Company, p.66

Cone, James (1975) *God of the Oppressed*, Minneapolis, The Seabury Press, pp. 39–47, 81–82

Copher, Charles B. (1993) *Black Biblical Studies*, Chicago, Black Light Fellowship, pp.67–77

Cox, Harvey (1965), *The Secular City: Secularization and Urbanization in Theological Perspective*, London, SCM Press

Cox, Harvey (1995) *Fire From Heaven: The Rise of Pentecostal Spirituality and the Reshaping of Religion in the Twenty-First Century*, London, SCM

Curtin, Philip D. (1990) *The Rise and Fall of the Plantation Complex – Essays in Atlantic History*, Cambridge, Cambridge University Press

Davies, Brian (ed) (2000) *Philosophy of Religion: A Guide and Anthology*, Oxford, Oxford University Press

Dennis, Ferdinand (2000) 'Birmingham: Blades of Frustration', in Kwesi Owusu (ed.) *Black British Culture and Society: A Text Reader*, London, Routledge, p.187

Dunn, James (1970) *Baptism in the Holy Spirit: A Re-examination of the New Testament Teaching on the Gift of the Spirit in Relation to Pentecostalism Today*, London, SCM Press, p.5

Edwards, Joel (ed) (1992) 'The Pentecostal Distinctives' in *Let's Praise Him Again: An African-Caribbean Perspective on Worship*, Joel Edwards, Eastbourne, East Sussex, Kingsway Publication, pp.75–83

Edwards, Joel (1999) *Lord Make Us One – But Not All the Same*, London, Hodder & Stoughton

Edwards, Joel (2000) *The Cradle, The Cross and the Empty Tomb: A Faith We Can Be Proud To Proclaim*, London, Hodder & Stoughton

Edwards, Joel (2001) *Review of Dread and Pentecostal* (unpublished paper)

Genovese, Eugene D. (1971) *The World the Slaves Made: Two Essays in Interpretation*, New York, Vintage Books

Erasmus (1971) *Praise of Folly and Letter to Martin Dorp*, (translated by Betty Radice, introduction and notes by A.H.T. Levi), Middlesex, Penguin Books, p.156

Gause H. R. (1973) *Church of God Polity*, Cleveland, Tennessee, Pathway Press, pp.223–224

Gerloff, R. (1992) *A Plea for British Black Theologies – The Black Church Movement in Britain in its transatlantic cultural and theological interaction*, Frankfurt am Main, Peter Lang

Gerloff, R. (1999) 'Response' to Beckford in A. Anderson and W. J. Hollenweger (ed) *Pentecostals After a Century: Global perspectives on a movement in transition, Journal of Pentecostal Theology* supplement, Sheffield Academic Press, p.65

Hollenweger, Walter J. (1972) *The Pentecostals*, London, SCM Press, p.485

hooks, bell and West, Cornel (1991) *Breaking Bread: Insurgent Black Intellectual Life*, Boston, South End Press, pp.131–146

Kee, Alistair (1990) *Marx and the Failure of Liberation Theology*, London and Philadelphia, SCM and Trinity Press International, pp. 3–87

Kee, Alistair (2006) *The Rise and Demise of Black Theology*, Burlington, Vermont and Aldershot, UK: Ashgate

Kolakowski, Leszek (1982) *Religion*, Glasgow, Fontana, pp.9–17, 160–206

Leary, Joy Degruy (2005) *Post Traumatic Syndrome: America's Legacy of Enduring Injury and Healing*, Milwaukie, Oregon, Uptone Press

Martin, David (2002) *Pentecostalism: The World Their Parish*, Oxford, Blackwell Publishers, p.xvii

Marx, Karl (1844, 1975), *Early Writings* (written in 1844, introduced by Lucio Colletti and translated by Rodney Livingstone and George Benton), Harmondsworth, Middlesex, Penguin Books, pp.243–257

McGrath, Alistair (2004) *The Twilight of Atheism: The Rise and Fall of Disbelief in the Modern World*, London and Sydney, Random House, p.197

Macintyre, Alasdair (1969) *Marxism & Christianity*, London, Gerald Duckworth & Co. Ltd

Milbank, John (1990) *Theology and Social Theory: Beyond Secular Reason*, Oxford, Blackwell Publishers, especially chapter 7 'For and Against Marx' pp.177–205

Moltmann, Jürgen (1967) *Theology of Hope*, London, SCM Press, p.31

Moltmann, Jürgen (1977) *The Church in the Power of the Spirit: A Contribution to Messianic Ecclesiology*, London, SCM Press, p.299

Pityana, N. Barney (1989) 'Towards a Black Theology for Britain', in Anthony Harvey (ed.) *Theology in the City: A Theological Response To 'Faith In The City'*, London, SPCK

Reddie, A. and Jagessar, Michael N. (2007) *Black Theology in Britain – A Reader*, London, Equinox Publishing Ltd

Thomas, Hugh (1998) *The Slave Trade: The History of the Atlantic Slave Trade, 1440–1870*, London, Papermac

Tocqueville, Alex de (1968) *Democracy in America*, London, Fontana, p.364

Weber, Max (1930, 1992) *The Protestant Ethic and the Spirit of Capitalism* (translated by Talcott Parsons with an Introduction by Anthony Giddens.) London, Routledge

2   *Ecumenism and the Black Church*

Jonathan Oloyede

'Praise the Lord! Every body ppraaaaise the Lord!' bellowed the preacher from behind the glass pulpit. 'Hallelujah!' replied the congregation in perfect resonance. The year was 1996. It was hot and humid despite the newly installed air-conditioning. I was squeezed amongst 700 other worshippers at the launch of a new church in South London. The minister was immaculately dressed in a tailor-made ash grey suit, shining black shoes with a screaming pink tie and matching pocket-handkerchief. The energy in the place was pulsating and I got caught up with the atmosphere of excitement and pure passion of praise, preaching and prose. Like many other new worship centres, this predominantly West African church was being launched in a converted building, with the support of other leaders and ministers from the UK, USA, the Caribbean, and Africa. This is part of a phenomenon of African churches that erupted on to the British scene in the 1990s as a second wave of Black Christianity. The first wave of African-Caribbean Christian communities emerged in the 1950s. These two new, confident entities are engineering a new kind of ecumenical reality.

In this chapter, I will look at the DNA of Black churches, their ecumenical engagement and their contributions towards the expansion of the kingdom of God. I will look historically, contemporarily and futuristically at Black engagement and contributions towards church unity, worship, music, and the ecumenical movement in Britain. I will take you on my personal journey within the UK Christian landscape, particularly London.

Ancient Echoes

There is a subliminal general impression that Black Christianity in Britain began in the 1950s with the arrival of African Caribbean communities. The facts show that many vibrant Black Christian expressions have been around for a long time. According to both archaeological and printed documents, Africans came to live in the British Isles during the period before 1500 BC. For example, there is historical evidence that there were Black soldiers in Roman legions on Hadrian's Wall (Breeze and Dobson 2000). Two hundred and fifty years ago the cities of London, Liverpool and Bristol had thousands of Black inhabitants. Their most common vocation was manual labour: as servants, artisans, and seamen. By the late eighteenth century, the estimated Black population in Britain had a median of 17,500, which almost equates to the percentage of Black people in the country in 1960. A good number were active Christians in belief and practice.

The abolitionists and former slaves Olaudah Equiano and Ottobah Cugoano, were part of an 'ecumenical' movement of Christians from various denominations rallying together around a common cause (Chike 2007). African Americans William and Ellen Craft and Thomas L. Johnson settled in Britain as missionaries and were part of the Foreign Anti-Slavery Society. They campaigned actively speaking and preaching in Britain and North America. Similarly, John Jea was a popular itinerant Nigerian preacher who apparently filled chapels everywhere he went. There are many more Black men and women who unwittingly contributed to the ecumenical movement through their activities in politics, public life and Christian mission. These include: Harold Moody, Ignatius Sancho, Daniels Ekarte, Samuel Ajayi Crowther, and Celestine Edwards.

The vast majority of Black communities whether from the Caribbean since 1950, or from Africa in the decades post-1970, have been largely protestant. The early Caribbean pioneers, mainly Pentecostal, created independent denominations like Calvary Church of God in Christ, Church of God of Prophecy, and New Testament Church of God (Aldred 2005). Many of the African churches were branches of those already existing in Africa while the vast majority of independent African churches in the 1990s were new offshoots from existing denominations. From the 1970s these new churches started to create links with British historic churches as well as co-ordinate strategic agencies that liaised with local and central governments. In 1979, Olu Abiola helped start the Council of African and African Caribbean Churches, a group of Black ministers started the Afro-United West Indian United Council of Churches, while Phillip Mohabir created the West Indian Evangelical Alliance, that later became the African and Caribbean Evangelical Alliance (ACEA) (Sturge 2005).

While Black immigrants generally found wanting the fellowships, forms and warmth of White Majority Churches, which contributed to their forming new churches, some Black Christians, especially Anglicans, remained within their communion. This produced some Black Majority Anglican churches in towns and cities in England with Black leaders advancing up the hierarchy. This saw people like Wilfred Wood becoming the Bishop of Croydon and latterly John Sentamu becoming Bishop of Birmingham, then Archbishop of York. Other significant developments signalling a deepening of Black involvement in national life include, in 1998, David Muir founding the Black Christian Civic Forum, thereby empowering Black Majority Churches (BMCs) to become active within the political sphere. Joel Edwards from The New Testament Church of God moved via the African and Caribbean Evangelical Alliance (ACEA) to become the General Director of the Evangelical Alliance. In 1996 Joe Aldred became Executive Director of the Centre for Black and White Christian Partnership. Sam King has long been elected the Labour Mayor of Southwark while Paul Boateng, Baroness Patricia Scotland and Baroness Valerie Amos became Labour government ministers. Meanwhile John Taylor has been appointed a Tory Peer in the House of Lords via a failed attempt to become an MP in the Conservative constituency of Cheltenham. The era of being isolated and standing in the shadows was beginning to close. It was clear that a new dawn had begun. But has it?

Where are my brothers?

I was almost in tears. I was angry, depressed, and confused at the same time. It was November 2000 at the Evangelical Alliance Leadership Conference in Cardiff. London Bible College icon, Derek Tidball had just finished the morning Bible reading for the day that was wonderful, but just added to my confusion. Where are all my Black brothers? As I surveyed the approximately 98% white congregation of over 2000 leaders, my thoughts travelled to Brighton four months prior. It was a flagship conference within the Black Christian Community. The theme was Faith in the Future organised by the African and Caribbean Evangelical Alliance.

At that wonderful convention with all its diversity of Black Christian expression and culture, I saw vividly the ominous Black and White divide. I remember questioning my good friend, the former Evangelical Alliance General Director Joel Edwards, 'Why are we all meeting in culture camps?' was my blunt challenge. In his usual amiable and articulate manner his reply was, 'That, Jonathan, is one mountain a conference like this seeks to address and overcome. Our heart as an Alliance is to be a movement for change across the plurality of cultural and ethnic diversity within the church.' I heckled him with more questions about why certain prominent White leaders were absent. Who did the invitations? And a host of barraging questions many of which I can no longer recall.

As I travelled back to London from Cardiff, my mind was made up. I was on the phone to Joel at the earliest opportunity: 'Why is it that …?' – I let out a tirade of questions and protests. He was very patient and set out to calm me down and outline a course of action that began a journey of discovery into the depth and breadth of the chasm between the White and Black Christian Communities in England. I am not insinuating that all is doom and gloom with regards to inter-racial relationships in the Church. I know many wonderful God-inspired ministries seeking to build bridges across ethnic borders. I do not claim to be an authority on race relations or cross-cultural dynamics within the church, but I do speak from personal experience.

I arrived in Britain on an afternoon flight from Lagos Nigeria in the summer of 1991. Fresh from the tyrannical pressure of medical school, I had decided to take a three-month holiday before embarking on my itinerant year at a renowned Baptist Training Hospital in the Islamic enclave of Northern Nigeria. I was a convert from Islam and my intention was to practise as a missionary doctor to Muslims. I am still on my three-month holiday!! Within days of stepping into the British Isles, the Holy Spirit spoke so vividly to my heart: 'Jonathan, you are not here by accident, you are here by divine design. You are here as part of my recruitment to this part of the world in preparation for the coming of my Son Jesus. Drop your agenda therefore and pick up my programme.' It was so clear and scary. So much so that I thought, Jesus was coming back in 1994!

Looking back, I now have a better panoramic view of a divine conspiracy behind the influx of exotic Christians into the UK. Heaven was responding to years of intercession to send help to strengthen flagging British congregations. The Lord Himself was building His Church and Britain was reaping her harvest of centuries of overseas missionary work. Throughout the 1990s on the back streets of Hackney, Leyton, Walthamstow, Lewisham, Brixton, Stratford, Finsbury Park, Islington and many other London inner city districts, I saw churches born. This was the case too in other major urban conurbations across the country. Wherever there was ample space a church was planted; so there were shop-front churches, home churches, warehouse churches, school churches and community centre churches. In old buildings and new ones, in derelict cinemas or showrooms, in old cold and dusty church buildings, on housing estates and even in town halls. African and African Caribbean Christians overlapped in this era of frenzied church planting. Every other week we would get glossy flyer invites to one church opening or new building launch. I thought it was normal and it was much later that I began to find out that historians and sociologists were writing about the phenomenon of the Black Majority Churches (BMCs). I invite you to join me on a whistle-stop journey through Black Church life and relationships.

Definition defying

In his book, *Look What The Lord Has Done*, Sturge (2005) asks, 'What on earth is a Black Majority Church?' He classifies these new worship forms into five broad groups:

- Churches from the African Caribbean Diaspora
- Churches from the African Diaspora
- Black Churches within historic denominations
- Black Churches within white (Pentecostal) denominations
- African and Caribbean spiritual churches

But not everyone is happy with the term. 'I just don't like the terminology Black Majority Church!' vented Bishop Joe Aldred, Secretary of Minority Ethnic Affairs at Churches Together in England and Chair of the Council of Black Led Churches in Birmingham. 'And ... and I would like to go on record stating that certain myths need to be laid to rest! Many if not most of these churches were not birthed out of segregation, marginalisation, or discrimination. Yes, we will not discount totally some of these factors, but the major Caribbean denominations evolved out of denominational expansion and missionary zeal. Many of these churches, like the Calvary Church of God in Christ around 1951, emerged out of house fellowships. They blossomed as outgrowths of established churches in the Caribbean and merely continued here their faith, liturgy, and worship as practised back home.'

According to Sturge (2005), a Black Majority Church (BMC) is one where 51% of its membership is Black. Broadly speaking a BMC is predominantly Caribbean, African or perhaps an intricate combination of both, sprinkled with other nationalities. Definitions can be tricky though, because my good friend Canon John Williams, the English vicar of St Saviour's in East London, has an interesting mix of Caribbean, African and indigenous White Anglicans. Many of his members are Black, but he does not consider his congregation to be a Black Majority Church. Meanwhile the Revd Tade Agbesanwa, an ordained Baptist minister is the Black leader of the Custom House Baptist Church. When he joined 14 years ago, the church was White majority, now it is Black majority. The Revd Roger Grassham is an ordained English minister with the Elim Pentecostal denomination. His congregation has about 45% Black members. He attributes his multicultural Christian community to the values, ethos, and style of the River Church, which was birthed out of a merger between two White Charismatic congregations. These include a focus on prayer, having a vibrant contemporary worship style, a variety of services, a strong pastoral ministry and a welcoming attitude. You therefore cannot place a fixed tag on what a Black Church is or stands for. It all boils down to how the particular church perceives itself and what it calls itself.

The wow factor

I stepped through the doors of the New Wine Church in Greenwich and I could have stepped into the mini-lobby of a five-star hotel. There was turquoise carpet everywhere. The main auditorium looked like a section carved out of The Savoy. The bright and colourful choir were singing on stage, which had electrical moveable sections and glided as they danced! They had just taken over a listed cinema building by the Thames ferry roundabout. That day the Senior Pastor Dr Tayo Adeyemi introduced the guest speaker Dr Creflo Dollar, a charismatic African-American preacher.

Like many emerging African churches, New Wine started in the early 1990s meeting in a South London town hall. Over the years, it has grown in size, influence, and relevance. There was a list of different outreaches from New Wine in one of their recent publications. This included supporting the Greenwich Mayor's Charity, Cystic Fibrosis and Macmillan Cancer Research. Among other ventures, the congregation sent 2,000 shoeboxes with gifts to children in Eastern Europe, raised £25,000 in support of the recent tsunami disaster, and built homes for lepers in India.

The wow factor is evident in a variety of settings. Freedoms Ark, led by the Revd Nims Obunge has been the precursor of the Peace Alliance, a community initiative that works in partnership with the Home Office, the London Mayor's cabinet, the Metropolitan Police and various local councils within and beyond the capital. The Street Pastors outreach was started by the Revd Les Isaacs in Brixton and is now one of the flagship initiatives highlighting the partnership between statutory bodies like the Metropolitan Police and faith communities. The Glory House Football Academy is probably one of the best-kept secrets in East London and has a current White majority membership of 700 East End young boys and their families. Meanwhile Bishop Wilton Powell, who heads up Church of God of Prophecy, based in Birmingham, was awarded an MBE in recognition for his work in the local community, as has Bishop T. A. McCalla from Wolverhampton. The work of BMCs is being increasingly recognised and appreciated by local and national governments.

24/7 Church

BMCs are committed to promoting the prosperity of their members. 'You should get one of these Pastor Jonathan,' said David, a friend, as I sat in his brand new Porsche Cheyenne, with its beige leather seats and walnut dashboard riddled with cockpit-like dials. 'Drive it round the block and feel the power under the hood.' I pressed on the accelerator and was launched backwards. I felt the leather seats press into the small of my back. It was a Black beauty. David and his wife represent the fresh wave of Africans on the block. They had moved from inner-city Hackney to the Chafford Hundred suburb a few years ago. Like a growing number of members of Glory House, they commute three times a week for the services and meetings that take place in church or homes across London.

I consider that the average Black believer has a holistic financial world-view. The language some churches use might be similar to the American prosperity teachers – but there are differences. Also what can seem flamboyant to some White believers is viewed very differently by Black people many of whom came from working-class backgrounds, but aspire to better themselves and their families. Money is regarded not as a master, but is a servant. Many of these churches are built up and sustained by the generous and faithful giving of working-class first- and second-generation migrants! A percentage of these believers are breaking into the middle-classes using their entrepreneurial spirit to set up a wide range of businesses such as nurseries, estate agencies, employment firms and shops.

Black Churches are living, growing organisms in communal cultures where practically everyone is a distant cousin or aunt. BMCs are not just places of religious worship but the hub of the Black community where boy meets girl, business ideas are conceived, mortgages are blessed, children are born, named and nurtured. It is the BMC where life's crises are anaesthetised, friendships and relationships are forged and careers are boosted. The church is open almost every day of the week with different meetings: the grandmothers' club, choir rehearsals, business network seminars, youth prayer clubs, ushers' meetings, the prayer department, cell group leaders' meetings, and the list goes on. The Black Christian faith is integral to life. Theirs is a theology of 'Emmanuel' – God with me, in me and through me. The Holy Spirit's companionship is evident in the speaking in tongues, laying on of hands and miracles in everyday life.

I Wanna Dance!

If you have ever stepped into a Black church, one of its classic hallmarks is the exuberant music, praise, and worship. You are carried along, positively hypnotised by the rhythm and swept away by the sheer mass energy. You sweat with the songs and shout out the choruses. It's enchanting, invigorating, tiring, but exhilarating all at the same time; especially if you're over 50 and expected to move your body like a teenager! It is an experience, period!

Viv Broughton in his modern classic *Black Gospel* (1985) traces the journey of this music genre from the exploits of the Fisk Jubilee Singers in league with Dwight Moody and Ira Sankey in the nineteenth century. On through to the Mississippi based Ultica Jubilee Quartet in the 1920s, to the Mahalia Jackson and Ward Sisters' phenomenon of the 1950s. The arrival of the Caribbean Church community in the 1950s then gave birth to an indigenous gospel expression through choirs, bands, and solo artists (see Broughton 1995, Chapter 2). These included groups like Strings of Prophecy, Heavenly Hope, Harmoniser, and Golden Chords. The 1970s and 1980s saw the emergence of names like Lavine Hudson, the Inspiration choir with John Francis, Kainos with Basil Mead and Joel Edwards, Paradise with Doug Williams and the popular London Community Gospel Choir (LCGC) with Basil Mead.

With raised hands, we sang 'How great thou Art' as the worship leader drew us into song after song. It was a medley of praise, thanksgiving, reflection, and raw worship. Much later as I shook hands with this gifted minstrel, an electric guitar strapped to his back, a turtle neck jumper over worn Levi's, I could not help wondering if Noel Robinson slept with his eyes open. Full of energy and life, Noel and his band Nu-image epitomise the Black Church sound. Other leading music and worship artists in the BMC scene include, Mark Beswick with the Power Praise team, Raymond & Co, and Muyiwa with Riversong. The Black church has always been the incubator for young and raw musical talent, which would later leap unto the secular billboard charts. Music is definitely part of the DNA of the Black Church!

More than numbers

As we discovered earlier, many of the African-Caribbean Churches like the Church of God of Prophecy, New Testament Church of God, New Testament Assembly, and the Wesleyan Holiness Church began to emerge in the UK in the early 1950s (Aldred 2005). Early African fellowships were the *New* Covenant Church, and the Four Square Church denominations. The more recent ones include the Redeemed Christian Church of God, Calvary Charismatic Baptist, Glory House, and Kingsway International Christian Centre among many others. Many urban Black Churches have over 1,000 members, while KICC, Jesus House, Ruach Ministries, Glory House, New Wine, Calvary Baptist and others have between 2,000 and 10,000 members. I don't just want to emphasise numbers, but these figures are an indication of the impact and reach of these inner-city churches.

Peter Brierley of *Christian Research* (2006) estimated that 51% of church attendance within London consisted of Black and Asian Christians. Many of the Black Churches are located within large towns and cities. The growth rate of these Churches has been phenomenal. Mark Sturge (2005) writes: 'For the first time, we encounter "church bombing", where a congregation suddenly appears in an area, either on a Sunday or for a short period, and then disappears. This was because of the saturation of existing premises: for the first time buildings were just not suitable for the needs of rapidly growing congregations.' One exceptional example of this is the Redeemed Christian Church of God.

Follow the leader

'Pastor Jay! Please come, come, come and sit right here beside your beautiful wife!!' Revd Yemi Adeleke called out to me in her rhythmic Nigerian accent, as I entered the hall. As one of the co-leaders of House of Praise within the Redeemed Church of God (RCCG), Pastor Yemi is a bubble of life, giggles, and smiles. The building located close to the Thames in southeast London was converted from industrial to religious use. Tastefully furnished and redecorated, the hub of this parish was teeming with women and men preparing for their ladies' conference, Total Woman, that attracts hundreds of women annually.

As I spoke with her husband, Revd Andrew Adeleke, one of the top leaders in the denomination, I couldn't help thinking that the RCCG network of churches have come a long way. The first set of Redeemed members started within a small house fellowship in 1985. According to the Centre for Studies on New Religions (Killingray and Edwards 2007), RCCG had several tens of thousands of members within London and the Midlands. RCCG represents the new genre of BMCs from Africa and the Caribbean, which do not fit the classic caste. Rather than project a siege mentality, these Christian communities ooze with optimism, confidence, and hope.

From the brow-sweating Bishop John Francis, to the oratory of Celia Collins, to the chic and trendy Ramson-Mumba; and from the authoritative Apostle Alfred Williams, to the pulsating Dr Albert Odulele to the articulate Bishop Wayne Malcolm, the Black leader epitomises the rhythm of church life. She or he is the peacemaker and thermostat, stabilising fibrillations, and regulating the ambience within the pews. An intricate culture of respect for leadership threads delicately through the liturgy, worship, and congregational life. This gradient and medium of honour is one of the distinctive features of the Early Church mirrored by today's

Black Christians. I consider this as one of the key factors in the growth of Black-led churches that allows fluid delegation, team dynamics, and deployment. However, this can be one of its greatest weaknesses when this advantage is abused. Sadly, the failures – where leaders abuse their positions – tend to grab the headlines.

Fresh hope

In the summer of 2007 one of the main Black Christian publications: *Keep the Faith*, published a list of Britain's most influential Black church leaders. This was followed a year later with a list of Britain's most influential Black Christian women. The list though obviously not exhaustive, gives a good snapshot of the Black Christian movement in Great Britain:

Angela Sarkis: the first Woman and Black person to be appointed to the role of National Secretary of the YMCA

Revd Les Isaac: founder of Street Pastors, one of the most successful community initiatives in Britain

Pastor Nims Obunge MBE: the CEO of Peace Alliance – a national crime reduction charity. He is also an adviser to London Crime Stoppers, the Metropolitan Police and various anti-gun crime panels

Revd Kate Coleman: the first Black woman to become President of the Baptist Union of Great Britain

Pastor Matthew Ashimolowo: head of Kingsway International Christian Center, Western Europe's largest church with a regular Sunday attendance of 10,000

Bishop Eric Brown: National Overseer of the New Testament Church of God, one of the most well known Black Church denominations with its network of over 120 churches

Pastor Agu Irukwu: presides over the Redeemed Christian Church of God which has become Britain's largest Black denomination with over 230 congregations

Revd Katie Kirby: the CEO of the African Caribbean Evangelical Alliance, which is at the heart the Black Christian community, Britain's fastest growing church sector

Bishop Wilton Powel: Overseer of the Church of God of Prophecy, one of Britain's oldest Black-led Pentecostal denominations. He received an MBE for pioneering community projects in Birmingham

Right Hon. John Sentamu: Archbishop of York who has become a national prophetic voice for the church and the second most senior cleric in the Church of England.

Apart from those appearing on these lists, a few other leaders in the ecumenical movement worth mentioning include:

Pastor Ade Omooba: leader of the Victory Action Group. He has pioneered many community projects and is a key figure within the Christian lobbyist movement

Dr Jonathan Oloyede: founder of the Global Day of Prayer London. Pioneer of one of London's most diverse ecumenical prayer movements with over 35,000 interdenominational Christians praying together at stadiums and churches in 2007 and 2008

Bishop Dr Joe Aldred: Secretary for Minority Ethnic Christian Affairs for Churches Together in England, Chair of the Council of Black Led Churches, and the former Director of the Centre for Black and White Christian Partnership. He has pioneered various ecumenical and interdenominational partnerships, dialogues, seminars and research

Revd David Shosanya: Regional Minister, London Baptist Asso-
                         ciation, Member of the Council of the Bap-
                         tist Union of Great Britain and Ireland
                         (BUGB). A Managing Trustee of the
                         Ascension Trust (AT) and co-founder of
                         the Street Pastors Initiative (SPI)

Revd Esme Beswick: the first Black woman to hold the position
                         as President of Churches Together in Eng-
                         land

Back to the future

Revd Katie Kirby, the CEO of the African Caribbean Evangelical Alliance believes that there is great hope and potential for the whole church in the UK. 'I want to work myself out of a job,' she says softly but firmly, 'I would rather not see an "us" and "them". It's one body and the Black Church is not "the others" as I heard a devout Christian leader let slip the other day at a large conference. The Black Church is here to stay, not as an isolated distinct entity but an integrated part of the whole body of Christ.' I smiled as I nodded in agreement with her. Katie represents a new vanguard of younger Black leaders ready to engage holistically with the wider church on biblical terms.

The Black Christian community is here in the UK by a divine move of God. They are embedded within the full spectrum of Christianity from Anglicans and Catholics to Evangelical Pentecostalism. Significantly, a sizeable number of Black-led churches are now established members of the main national ecumenical bodies: Churches Together and the Evangelical Alliance. I challenge — myself first, and every member of Christ's body in Great Britain – let us begin to build bridges wherever gaps exist between cultures, churches, classes, or creeds. Let us join forces and unite against a common enemy that is not flesh and blood. Let the death, burial and resurrection of our lord Jesus Christ truly crucify and bury our differences. I pray that the Holy Spirit release the new life that true harmony, synergy and unity brings. However, significant challenges lie ahead.

The Great Wall of Culture

I know many fellow Black Christians, even ministers, who do not believe there are any significant indigenous Christian mission efforts within the

UK. When you ask a Black Christian to name a 'good' White church or ministry within the capital they generally fumble for a name and may come up with Holy Trinity Brompton, Kensington Temple or the Alpha Course. When I asked a Black Pentecostal if she had ever attended Spring Harvest, the response was, 'Spring what?' The reverse is also true. Recently at a leaders' planning meeting with some core Evangelical leaders, I asked if they had heard of the Redeemed Christian Church of God and their prayer nights called Festival of Life. They looked at me blankly and someone asked if I meant to say Festival of Light. I went on to tell them that the meetings are held two to three times a year in London with an average attendance of 15,000–17,000 per night. They really thought I was exaggerating. I was actually being conservative. The current numbers are actually 30,000 per night!

Why do we have such a breakdown in communication across the cultural and ethnic divides? At a National Leaders Conference and then at Spring Harvest, I challenged the many White Evangelical and Charismatic leaders to adopt the spiritual sons that God himself had brought to their shores. Reverend Terry Diggines, one of the founding fathers of the multi-cultural Newham Christian Fellowships (NCF), a central hub for the diversity of churches in East London is a great model. A towering and swaggering man in his sixties, he has such a large heart. With open arms, and a disarming humility of spirit he embraced me and the Glory House family that invaded the urban hamlet of Plaistow where he has lived for decades. 'You have brought fresh oil and fire from Africa. We need you guys here. Thank God you arrived!!' he bellowed one summer afternoon while we had tea at his home. He meant every word and that for me was the real miracle. I sat there looking quizzically at him. I could not help reflecting on whether if I were in his shoes I would be so enthused at a younger (apparently more successful) minister in his prime in the arrival lounge while I was in the departure lounge. Without Terry and Joel Edwards I would not have made it this far in the 'know your White brother' venture from my church nest.

In 2004 I had an experience that pushed me further along in building a bridge across the massive racial canyon. 'Jonathan, this mission will impact London for Jesus!' I looked across the polyester cups strewn all over the wooden table at the man who had just frizzled the core of my bones with a vision larger than life itself. His hair was all over the place dancing in black curls as he spoke animatedly. His shirt was a rainbow of colours and patterns speaking their own language; a bit of a distraction. His eyes were wide and childlike while his smile paradoxically seemed both on the verge of breaking into laughter and a frown at the same time. Yes, Mike Pilavachi leader of the Soul Survivor Movement was an interesting character you didn't forget in a hurry.

The launch of the Soul in the City Mission was just weeks away at St Paul's Cathedral. Bringing 15,000 young people into London from across the United Kingdom and the world caught my imagination. As I arrived at the leaders' reception in the massive crypt of the church, my worst fears were confirmed. I was back in Brighton and Cardiff as I saw a confluence of familiar White faces but no Black leaders in sight. As I jumped and danced with over 2000 White youths singing Tim Hughes' inspired 'Beautiful One', the Holy Spirit came upon me and said 'Strengthen this mission with your gift'. 'How in the world do you expect me to do that?' I retorted. In His familiar unfazed and cool quiet manner, above all the noise and shouting around me, above the ten foot blaring speakers and clanging cymbals, He whispered loud in my heart: 'Get involved Jonathan.'

My involvement in the Soul in the City mission was primarily to see people come to faith in Jesus, and the Church healed of its racial chasms. We were able to achieve 750 projects and 25% Black church participation, a first in British ecumenical history on that scale. Years later as I walked into the Bobby Moore suite at West Ham football stadium, my heart was deeply encouraged. There were around two hundred leaders from all denominations, cultures and streams talking and mingling together. Several hundred more were arriving with their members in coaches outside. The Global Day of Prayer brought together over 500 church leaders to prayer alongside 20,000 Christians! I saw White Anglican vicars teaming up with Black Pentecostal pastors like never before. Long-standing rifts between some church leaders terminated as they came together to pray. Many churches are discovering each other like Mungo Park discovered the river Niger that had always been there. All over London, Anglican, Independent, Methodist, Pentecostal, Baptist, Catholic, and United Reformed churches are linking up with each other. This definitely puts a smile on God's face and gets angels doing the Salsa!! My prayer is that this catches on across the country.

Epilogue

Unity is a very ubiquitous word; on everyone's lips, but very scarce in practice. We all want it but no one seems willing to pay the bill for this costly and crucial element of the gospel. Church unity cannot be about papering over the cracks of injustice to the advantage of church security. It cannot be about constructing alliances against others. It cannot be about flaccid accommodation for the sake of false peace. True unity is about taking gutsy, difficult, discomforting but loving steps towards reconciliation for the sake of reaching out to humanity; the aged, the poor, the rich, the lonely, the sick and the lost.

Real unity is first biblical, forged in the furnace of scriptural admonition to love the foreigner, the poorer, the other as oneself. Within the pressures of family, social, and church bonds, unity struggles to breathe and survive. The fact of the matter is that this utopia is a journey rather than a destination. An elusive El Dorado worth seeking even at great personal cost to all involved. 'I do not pray for these alone, but also for those who will believe in Me through their word; that they all be one, as You, Father, are in Me, and I in You; that they also may be one in Us, that the world may believe that You sent Me. And the glory which You gave Me I have given them, that they may be one as We are one' (John 17:20–22).

I leave you with one little assignment. As a Christian lay person, minister, pastor, or bishop, please make some good friends with those outside your denominational, cultural or ethnic identity. Get to know their homes, the names of their children, eat with them and make them part of your life. Jesus said 'and if you salute your brethren only, what do you more than others?' (Matthew 5:47).

References

Aldred, J. D. (2005) *Respect: Understanding Caribbean British Christianity*, Peterborough, Epworth

Breeze, D.J. and Dobson, B. (2000) *Hadrian's Wall* (fourth edition), London, Penguin Books Limited

Brierley, Peter (ed.) (2003) *UK Christian Handbook*, London, Christian Research

Brierley, Peter (2006) *Pulling out of the Nosedive: A Contemporary Picture of Churchgoing – What the 2005 English Church Census Reveals*, London, Christian Research

Broughton, Viv (1985) *Black Gospel : An illustrated history of the gospel sound*, Poole, Dorset and New York, N.Y, Blandford Press

Chike, Chigor (2007) Voices from Slavery, Milton Keynes, Authorhouse

Killingray, D. and Edwards, Joel (2007) *Black Voices: The Shaping of our Christian Experience*, Nottingham, IVP Press

Sturge, Mark (2005) *Look What the Lord Has Done! An Exploration of Black Christian Faith in Britain*, Bletchley, Scripture Union

3   *The Holy Spirit and the Black Church*

Joe Aldred

The year 2006 marked the centenary of the Azusa Street Revival, the impact of which continues to spread across the world, making Pentecostalism and neo-Pentecostalism the fastest growing sector of contemporary Christianity. This paper focuses upon the understanding of the Holy Spirit within the Black Pentecostal tradition and does so with three key features of contemporary British Christianity in mind, namely: 1) the growth of Black Pentecostalism, 2) the increased presence of Black Pentecostal churches in membership of the Churches Together ecumenical instruments, and 3) the problematic relationship between Black and White Pentecostals in Britain; all of which seem to call for a response. I argue that a better understanding of the pneumatology that is at the heart of Pentecostalism coupled with a willingness to dialogue with those of a different pneumatological persuasion can act as a catalyst for better inter-Christian relationships in this country. This then is a call for deeper understanding leading to 'informed regard' between Pentecostals – Black and White, Trinitarians and non-Trinitarians – and between Pentecostals and non-Pentecostals. Achieving this is not necessarily easy, but it is essential to our Christian witness and mission.

The growth of Black Pentecostalism in England coincides with what appears to be inexorable decline in White-majority mainstream churches. Attendance in Black Pentecostal churches as a percentage of the overall church-going population exceeds by five-fold the Black presence as a percentage of the general population. According to Christian Research, between 1975 and 1989 African Caribbean church attendance remained a steady 5% of combined Free Church attendance (Brierley 1991, p.37). However, by 1998, combined Black church attendance was put at 7.2% of the overall church attendance in England at a time when Black people represented 1.9% of the overall population of the country (Brierley 2000, p.134). By this time also, Black Pentecostals in the country accounted for a third of all of Pentecostal church going.

Table 3.1 Black worshippers in mainstream churches

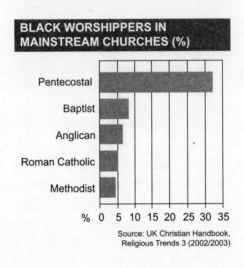

Source: UK Christian Handbook,
Religious Trends 3 (2002/2003)

Source: Religious Trends 3, *UK Christian Handbook* (2002/2003)

Between 1995 and 2005, Black-led churches had increased by half, and represented 10% of the overall church-going population whilst being just 2% of the overall population in England (Brierley 2006). By any measurement this is stupendous growth, and the reasons that occasion it are manifold. This much can be said with some confidence, that anyone who attends Black Pentecostal worship will testify there is at the heart of the Black worship expression an impulse that is driven by dependence upon something other than human reality. There is an interaction with the Holy Spirit that connects the worshipper with a transcendent and immanent God. This understanding of God's immanence is emphasised by such choral refrains as, 'He is here, Holy Spirit, He is here right now'. That Black Pentecostal worship is highly experiential and emotionally charged is indicative of the understanding that the reliance on the Holy Spirit is not just a matter for 'within these walls', but is something that affects the entire life of the person and community.

Table 3.2 UK Church membership

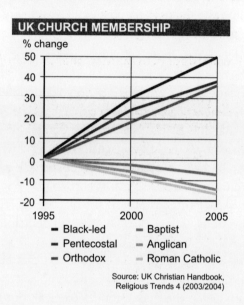

UK CHURCH MEMBERSHIP

% change

- Black-led   - Baptist
- Pentecostal   - Anglican
- Orthodox   - Roman Catholic

Source: UK Christian Handbook,
Religious Trends 4 (2003/2004)

Source: Religious Trends 3, UK Christian Handbook (2003/2004)

Accompanying this numerical growth has been a corresponding increase in the number of Black Pentecostal churches becoming members of the Churches Together ecumenical institutions. This is significant considering a critique offered by Mark Sturge, that ecumenical organisations had failed to engage in a meaningful way with the larger Black Majority Churches (Sturge 2005, p.150). According to Sturge, a key reason for this non-engagement has been the presence in the ecumenical institutions of ultra-liberal historic denominations. I have argued that another reason for the non-engagement of Black churches in the past also has to do with issues of historical-cultural identity and agendas (Aldred 2001b, pp.181–198). Given that the historic churches Sturge refers to remain in membership of Churches Together, what are we to make of this interest in the national ecumenical organisations by these Black Pentecostal churches? Will the Pentecostals lean toward neo-liberalism, or will the historic denominations be cured of their 'ultra-liberalism'?

Whatever the answers to these questions, how unlike the late 1980s when Philip Mohabir (1988, p.190) observed that there were few Black member churches within the ranks of the (then) British Council of Churches and even fewer Black people within its council of management? The ecumenical landscape has changed significantly, especially in recent years, so that in 2008 of the twenty-eight churches and agencies in membership of Churches Together in England, ten can be described as Black-led, of which nine are Pentecostal. And there are other membership applications pending. Black Pentecostals would undoubtedly suggest that as in the case of numerical growth this too is 'a move of God'. But it could also be argued that the Black churches are coming of age, growing in confidence and are now ready to engage and share fellowship with others with whom they do not necessarily agree doctrinally and theologically. Whatever the reasons, this development certainly offers and provides the opportunity for Black Pentecostals and the historic churches to engage in dialogue about various issues, including their understanding of the Holy Spirit.

Another feature of the English church context that comes within our purview is the problematic relationship between Black and White Pentecostals in Britain. Given their common theological root in Azusa Street and the Pentecostalism that has emerged, one might expect there to be a common Pentecostal bonding between these Black and White spiritual siblings, indeed children born of the same Holy Spirit. Philip Mohabir (1988, p.190) once described the relationship between these 'two most dynamic groups of God's people in this country' as one where preferences had become prejudices, which had hardened over the years. This had led, he argued, to them hardly mixing, being largely unaware of the other's existence, and to 'a subtle system of apartheid operating in Great Britain's churches'. Mohabir's statement was made at the end of the 1980s, and it can be argued that the current situation is only marginally different, and may even be one in which White preferences and prejudices are fast becoming the preferences and prejudices of many Blacks also.

However, some things have changed in the relationship between Black and White Pentecostals. For example, in recent years there has been an attempt to initiate a Pentecostal Congress in the United Kingdom, led by Wynn Lewis of the Elim Pentecostal Church, and including some Black Pentecostal denominations. This has not taken root however, and little is observable of a continuing relationship between Black and White Pentecostals at the organisational level. But at the level of the individual and local congregation, there is a noticeable development in recent years. A significant migration of Black Christians from the traditional Black-led Pentecostal churches to White-led Pentecostal churches has been occurring, leading to some of those becoming Black-majority churches. This trend is noticeable for example in various White-led (some former) House Churches, Pentecostal, Charismatic, Evangelical churches such as Kensington Temple in London and Birmingham Christian Centre, to name but two. The reasons for this have not been properly researched as yet, but from conversations between this writer and some individuals who have made the switch it is clear that many of these are Black professionals and socio-economic climbers who whilst embracing the Pentecostal impulse, desire a more structured church and worship life than is the case in some Black-led Pentecostal churches. Indeed, there is now a sharp divide between a sophisticated and professionally run mainly African-led, and working class and orally inclined mainly Caribbean-led Black Pentecostal churches in Britain.

Such migrations do not easily lend themselves to good relationships between Pentecostal leaders, and organisations. Particularly as it can easily be argued that the class difference that may have, at least in part, occasioned the divide between Black and White Pentecostals in the past, is now at work dividing Black Pentecostals between themselves and siphoning off the Black professionals who now feel more at home in a White Pentecostal environment. Interestingly, in White Pentecostal churches these Black professionals are rarely given the leadership prominence they would generally receive in Black Pentecostal ones, yet they appear willing to migrate in growing numbers and pay the price of simply being followers. The need for Black and White Pentecostal leaders to engage is greater than ever, before followership overwhelms leadership with migration patterns that do not foster the unity of the spirit. Jesus' prayer that his church be 'one, that the world may believe' (John 17) requires that the Church in all its diversity actively plays its part in bringing about a true *oikoumene*, i.e. a world reconciled to itself and God as the living habitation or household (*oikos*) of God (Kinnamon 1997, p.1). In this task the church, 'excluded and beaten down by the world', finds its place as the world's salt and light. This working together of those called out by

God, yet rejected by the world, is for the good of the inhabitants of the earth and the glory of God. However, it cannot be done without the reconciliation of the body of Christ to itself in love and respect. Sharing an understanding of the Holy Spirit that powers and empowers the church is a good starting point.

In my book, *Respect – Understanding Caribbean British Christianity*, I proffer a meaning of 'respect' as 'to get to know, to understand' the self and the other (Aldred 2005). I also advance eight means by which respect may be engendered within the church and in society. These are: the provision of quality information, a commitment to relationship, taking people's ethnicity and being seriously, taking people's faith seriously, understanding oneself, understanding the other, basing one's regard or disregard on knowledge, and having a prophetic presence. When these factors are brought together, they engender 'respect', i.e. deeper under-standing of our context. However, it is important to note that the respect process goes beyond observation and understanding. Applying 'respect' to Christian unity through the Holy Spirit requires investigation, a critique of our context in order to shed light on and find common ground between different understandings of the matter that is at the heart of Pentecostal-ism: the Holy Spirit. With such an understanding of the Holy Spirit comes much of what is necessary to act as a united church in a divided world. I contend that as we exchange ignorance for knowledge and pay attention to Pentecostal pneumatology, we observe there a key aspect of the unity we already share, but do not yet fully realise, and the dynamism behind our mission together to the world.

Pentecostalism – The historical root

As Walter J. Hollenweger (1997) points out, the historicity of Pentecos-talism can be located in two key ancestries; one Black and African, the other White and European. The Black and African roots of modern Pentecostalism come to us through the medium of the hideous Atlantic Slave Trade, by which Africans rooted in their traditional religions, them-selves highly spirit-orientated, were transported to the Americas, leading to an identifiable African-American Slave Religion that in turn resulted in the Black Oral Root of Pentecostalism, led by Seymour. James Cone (1989, p.91), the African American theologian disputes the extent of African religious retention, but makes the salutary point that the Black church was born in slavery. Under slavery, the Black person soon learned that s/he could not look to their fellow-human – enslaver or their fellow enslaved – for help, only to the unseen Spirit-God. When, post slavery, the Pentecostal phenomenon emerged in the United States, the descendants of slaves were first in line for their blessings! There are some key reasons for this.

Significantly, after a long period of denial, it is now generally accepted that the modern Pentecostal movement has its roots in the revival that occurred at the Apostolic Faith Mission, Azusa Street, Los Angeles between 1906 and 1909. It is also now generally accepted that, as journalist Frank Bartleman (1980, p.47,57) an eye-witness and participant wrote, 'Brother Seymour was recognised as the national leader in charge'; and again, 'but he (God) chose Brother Seymour, for our Joshua, to lead us over.' What is remarkable about this is that at a time of racial segregation in the United States during which Blacks were viewed by Whites as inferior human beings, if human at all, a one-eyed, semi-illiterate Black man, a descendant of slaves, emerged as the recognised leader of a racially and ethnically mixed local, national and international Pentecostal work. Undoubtedly, the oral tradition of Seymour, rooted in the slave experience, enabled him to function within this new religious setting.

According to Hollenweger (Burgess and McGee (eds) 1993) the White and European ancestral line of modern Pentecostalism emerged from the Wesleyan tradition, itself the result of the influences from Catholicism and the Reformation. Five distinct historical theological developments of this Pentecostal movement have been identified by Burgess and McGee. First, there was the Wesleyan understanding that conversion/justification is followed by a definable (definite) second work of grace, sanctification, in which the 'stranglehold of sin is decisively broken' in the life of the believer, thereby perfecting them. Second, there were the Charles G. Finney group of 'higher-life' teachers, who also emphasised the second experience after conversion, which they understood as the baptism of the Holy Spirit and the endowment of the believer with power for witness and service. A third development was the particularly dispensational brand of nineteenth-century pre-millennialism that emerged from the Plymouth Brethren; including John Nelson Darby and Reuben A. Torrey. A fourth development was the rise of the evangelical faith healing movement, pioneered by Charles Cullis, A. J. Gordon, A. B. Simpson, John

Alexander Dowie, and Maria B. Woodworth-Etter, with its emphasis on miraculous physical healing. The fifth key development consisted of the 'experiential primitivists' and their restorationist longings for a dynamic, spirit-filled, and spirit-led first-century church. These represent influences that are still discernable in modern Pentecostalism.

Burgess and McGee (1993) point out that the development of Pentecostalism as we know it today was at least in part a response to the belief that since the third century, in the West, the concept of a life in the spirit with an exercise of spiritual gifts has been something either loftily ascribed to 'saints' or despairingly ascribed to fringe groups; in both cases it is something outside the normal life of the institutionalised church. In contrast, in the East, emphasis on pneumatology including the life of the Spirit in the believer, resulting in a Charismatic character and expectation, has never ceased. They further suggest that it is the lack of the pneumatic emphasis in the West that rendered the Pentecostal-Charismatic movement of the late 1800s and early 1900s unique since the first century.

Hollenweger (1997) argues that this lack of emphasis upon the life and work of the Holy Spirit in the West has resulted in the emergence of a Pentecostalism that is highly Calvinistic, adhering to a pneumatology that is strictly Christological and which draws its strength from the early church's controversy over the *filioque*, i.e. the doctrine that the Holy Spirit proceeds from the Father and the Son. Thus in the West, the Holy Spirit is understood as a third person, behind a second, the Son, behind a first, the Father (see Figure 3.1) (Pruitt 1981, p.283).

Figure 3.1 Father, Son and Holy Spirit

This, Hollenweger argues, is a corruption of the intended model resulting from the *filioque* controversy that understands the Holy Spirit as emanating from the eternally existing Father and Son (see Figure 3.2):

Figure 3.2 Father and Son, and Holy Spirit

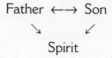

However, in both cases, the Spirit has an identity apart from, and consequential of, the other two. In the first model the Spirit is an expression of the Son who in turns emanates from the Father, while in the second, the Spirit is an expression of Father and Son. Such confusion is absent from the Eastern model of Godhead, which Hollenweger argues, operates with a different pneumatological model in which the Son and the Spirit emanate from the Father (see Figure 3.3):

Figure 3.3 Father, Son and Holy Spirit

In this Eastern model, the Godhead remains Trinitarian and pyramidic, but Son and Spirit are viewed equally in relation to the Father, and as a consequence equal priority is given to Christology as to Pneumatology. Hollenweger therefore posits the argument that it is probable that Pentecostalism's emergence in the West is a direct result of the relegation of the Spirit to an expression of the Son alone, or even of Father and Son. In either case, divine hegemony remains with the Father, and Son and the work and worth of the Holy Spirit is understood in relation to and in consequence of the two-thirds part of the trinity. In this pneumatology the Holy Spirit is located at the bottom of a heavenly pyramid, be that two or three tiered. It could be argued that contemporary Trinitarian Pentecostalism is at least in part, an attempt to restore the Holy Spirit to parity with the Son.

Whatever the historical-theological reasoning, Pentecostalism's emergence in the late 1800s and early 1900s amongst White Westerners had its locus in the concern of some over the spiritless and therefore powerless nature of the church, and a craving for a church that resembled the one they read about in the book of Acts. People no longer believed that the Reformation had delivered this. There were ecclesiastical structures, and intellectual theologising, but as Hollenweger (1997) says, what was being sought was not a new argument for heads but a new experience for hearts. Frank Bartleman (1980) epitomises the early heart-led often anti-intellectual nature of Pentecostalism when he contends that human organisation and human programmes leave very little room for the free spirit of God. 'Against this background of disengaging the intellect, it is not surprising that Pentecostalism has not developed a pneumatology which fits its experience', says Hollenweger (1997). Academic theology has not been its concern. As a consequence, modern Pentecostalism has become strong on experience of the spirit, *pneumapraxis*, but weak on interpretation of these experiences. Nowhere is this truer than among Black Pentecostals in Britain (Aldred and Parris 2001a, pp.50–67). And although this is not to imply the total absence of Pentecostal theologising, much of what there is tends to emerge from academia or White Pentecostalism, exemplified by the *Journal of Pentecostal Theology* (Thomas 2008). A crucial area in which this underdevelopment in Black theological interpretation is evident is that of glossolalia, i.e. 'speaking in tongues'.

Glossolalia

The explicit teaching that glossolalia is the 'initial evidence' of the baptism in the Holy Spirit can be traced to the ministry of Charles F. Parham. It was at Parham's Bethel Bible School in Topeka, Kansas *circa* 1901 that 18-year-old Agnes Ozman spoke in tongues after receiving Parham's teaching on the Holy Spirit. From this, Parham is said to have constructed his thesis that glossolalia was the biblical evidence of being baptized in the Holy Spirit (Synan 1980). In Houston, William J. Seymour, a former Baptist turned Holiness preacher, came under the influence of Parham's teachings on the Holy Spirit, having listened to him from outside the classroom, not being allowed inside due to segregationist Jim Crow laws. Seymour accepted Parham's teachings, and began teaching it himself though he did not initially have the experience of glossolalia. Invited to preach in Los Angeles, Seymour accepted and stayed, becoming the iconic central figure in the ensuing Pentecostal revival that not only impacted Los Angeles, but the world.

Parham's Apostolic Faith held to the five cardinal teachings of justification, sanctification, baptism in the Holy Spirit, divine healing, and the pre-millennial second coming of Christ. These had already been established Holiness teachings; Parham's main contribution was and is the addition of 'initial evidence' of speaking in tongues as proof of Baptism in the Holy Spirit. Although he fell out with Parham, these remained the central tenets of Seymour's Apostolic Faith Mission at Azusa Street as is evident in a collection of Seymour's sermons (Martin 1999). It is clear however, that Seymour did not share Parham's infatuation with tongues, eventually rejecting 'initial evidence' (though not tongues per se) as dogma in favour of a loftier evidence of love ... .

Parhamism means that most US-initiated Pentecostals, including Black Pentecostals in Britain with US roots such as the New Testament Church of God and the Church of God of Prophecy, view tongues as 'the' definitive evidence of Holy Spirit baptism. A review of the 'Statement of Faith' of the two main White-led Pentecostal churches in England is instructive. The US-initiated Assemblies of God is explicit in its teaching embracing 'initial evidence'. But the British-initiated Elim Pentecostal Church, whilst accepting baptism in the Holy Spirit, does not mention 'initial evidence'. Whilst Black British Pentecostals with their mainly US roots tend towards Parhamism in embracing 'initial evidence', it is observable that some newer churches are moving towards the Elim position of non-emphasis on 'initial evidence', though all embrace speaking in tongues. There is soteriological consensus of a sort in that across Black Pentecostalism churches embrace a two-stage (regeneration and Spirit baptism) or three-stage (regeneration, sanctification, and Spirit baptism) process.

A new pneumatology?

From its origins in the twin ancestry of Black and African, and White and European roots, Pentecostalism has developed into three distinct traditions, namely Non-White Indigenous Churches, Classical Pentecostal Churches, and the Charismatic Movement, sometimes referred to as Neo-Pentecostal Churches. All of these emphasise the prominence of the Holy Spirit as central to the life of the church and to the Christian life. We find that as was the case in Acts 2 when there were 'staying in Jerusalem God-fearing Jews from every nation under heaven' (verse 5), so today there is a world-wide co-mingling of all God's children in a new Pentecostal experience. Using a multi-racial/ethnic Azusa Street as a sign, God appears to be inviting us to experience again and permanently what was excitedly proclaimed at Azusa Street; that the 'colour line' has been washed away in the blood (Bartleman 1980, p.54). Indeed this was what caught the imagination of Seymour at Azusa Street: that the baptism in the Holy Spirit empowered people to demolish the walls of racial segregation and in its place built a multi-racial church. A century later and there is still a long way to go and much to do to realise the washing away of the colour line in society and church. But it is clear to this writer that a subtle shift in emphasis, away from Parham's emphasis on 'initial evidence' to Seymour's emphasis on the power to love one another as an irrefutable sign of Holy Spirit empowerment, can lead us to a real pneumatological and ecclesiological breakthrough.

How then might, or should, Pentecostals and non-Pentecostals alike set about constructing an inclusive understanding of the Holy Spirit that can be appropriated by the whole church, and provide the building block for a dynamic and united church in Britain? Like other Trinitarian believing Christians, Pentecostals understand their deity as God expressed in three Persons, Father, Son and Holy Spirit. In this understanding, God expressed as Father is viewed as the 'daddy' of all, Jesus as Son is viewed as having been begotten of the Father, and the Holy Spirit is generally understood as the agent of either Father alone or Father and Son together. The Holy Spirit is said to be at work in the creation of the cosmos, including humanity. Variously referred to in Scripture as breath, wind, power, oil, fire, water and dove. It is the Holy Spirit that is understood to facilitate creation, then and now (Genesis 1:2). Alister McGrath (1994, p.241) reminds us that it is from the Hebrew *ruach* that we derive our theological understanding of wind, breath and spirit. This is the spirit as wind that blew redemptively and parted the Red Sea (Exodus 14:21); this is the spirit as breath that resulted in man becoming a living soul (Genesis 2:7); and this is the spirit as charism that fills and credentialises the person and their ministry (Isaiah 61:1). It is probably worth bearing in mind too that as *ruach* this is the Spirit rendered in scripture as female, not male, which raises the spectre of viewing the Godhead as Father, Mother and Son! This helps us think of the gentler side of God, and brings into focus the understanding that male and female, parent and children are made equally in the image of God.

We cannot consider the British Pentecostal landscape without reference to the presence of a sizable number of Black Oneness Pentecostals (Gerloff 1992) on the one hand, and Black Christians who belong to non-Pentecostal churches on the other. This calls all the more for a pneumatology that can apply to Trinitarians, Non-Trinitarians, Pentecostals and non-Pentecostals alike. This could emerge from a longing for a renewed and revitalised church similar to the mindset of some at the turn of the nineteenth century, in the pre-initial evidence era. A precedent can be applied from an even earlier time than the beginnings of modern Pentecostalism, namely the circumstances of the Old Testament prophet Joel.

With God's judgement against Judah, and under the threat of being overrun by their neighbours, not dissimilar to the church being overrun by scientific secularism, Joel held out a fig leaf of hope. Part of the restoration of Jerusalem and the nation, if Judah repented and turned back to God, was the outpouring of the Spirit upon all people: sons, daughters, young men, servants, the free and enslaved alike (Joel 2:28). The universality of this divine provision is striking – everyone who calls on the Lord will be saved. Striking too are the manifestations of this outpouring, evidenced by prophesy, dreams, visions, wonders in the heavens and on earth; blood, fire and billows of smoke; the sun turning dark and the moon turning the colour of blood. The outpouring of the spirit brought with it spiritual, social and political liberation (Joel 2:32). We see here that the coming of the Spirit is universalistic, liberationist, equalising, and empowering. And it is evidenced by the supernatural and unnatural.

Another well-known Old Testament text that speaks to our situation is Isaiah 61 where the Spirit upon the prophet was for his anointing to preach the Good News of salvation to the poor, bind up the broken hearted, free the captives, release the prisoners, comfort the mourners, provide for the grieving, replace the misery of ashes with the crown of glory, gladness for mourning, the garment of praise for the spirit of despair. The Spirit's anointing of the prophet was also unction to bravely pronounce the Day of God's vengeance, the flipside of the Day of God's favour. The outpouring of the Spirit then is about the ability to preach and act out a message of deliverance to the oppressed and of righteous judgement upon wrongdoing, especially structural oppression by the powerful upon the weak. In the local, national and international contexts there is much that calls for the attention and action of the church to undo heavy burdens, set captives free and hold oppressors to account.

When we look at the seminal text for Pentecostals, Acts 2, we find that Peter aligns this occurrence with that prophesied by Joel. This is that which was prophesied by Joel, he said. However, the reader soon notices a phenomenon that does not appear in Joel, or Isaiah, or in the passages of scripture where Jesus promises the coming of the Holy Spirit (cf Matthew 28 and John 16), or indeed at the time Jesus breathed on the disciples and said, 'receive the Holy Spirit' (John 20:22). A difference with Acts 2:4, as is evidenced also in Acts 8:17–18; 10:44–46; 9:17 and 19:6, is the accompaniment of the outpouring or baptism of the Holy Spirit with speaking in tongues, or languages not known to the speaker. This has become a point of departure for many Christians, as Parhamism and its US Pentecostal offspring have turned experience into dogma. Tantalisingly, rhetorically, the apostle Paul asks, 'do all speak with tongues?' (1 Corinthians 12:30). What is not at issue is the clear acknowledgement that biblically tongues is one of the gifts of the Holy Spirit, however, it is generally agreed that not everybody has every gift.

In view of the historicity of pneumatology, a concern is the appropriateness of insisting that tongues accompany the baptism of the Holy Spirit, when there is no biblical text that mandates this, only examples of it occurring. Indeed, there are more examples of the Holy Spirit being poured out without tongues than with. According to Matthew Ashimolowo (1993), 98% of African Pentecostals speak in tongues, but another estimate I have come across suggests that as little as 35% of Pentecostals worldwide do so. It is recognised also that the exercise of the gift of tongues is not synonymous with a belief in 'initial evidence'. And in this writer's own experience there has always been a sizeable non-tongues-speaking proportion of every Pentecostal congregation known to me, including in one famous instance the leader of a Pentecostal church, that did not have the 'initial experience' of tongues.

As mentioned above, the father of modern Pentecostalism William Seymour who accepted Parham's teaching on initial evidence, preached and taught it well before eventually experiencing it. Was he without the Spirit as he ministered before speaking in tongues? Then, having experienced the character of some tongues-speaking White Christians, who clearly lacked love towards himself and other Blacks, Seymour forbade his members from seeking after tongues, and eventually included in the articles of faith of the Apostolic Faith Mission that, 'no one shall be known as having been baptised in the Holy Spirit simply because they speak in tongues' (*The William Seymour Story, From tragedy to triumph to obscurity.*

A Documentary. (2006)). Seymour became convinced that the real evidence of the baptism in the Holy Spirit was love and unity between those who were so baptised. For Seymour, it was impossible to be baptised in the Holy Spirit and believe, as his early mentor Parham purportedly continued to do, in the superiority of one race over another.

A new pneumatological understanding has also to come to terms with the knowledge that the scriptures make clear that the Holy Spirit has several manifestations. There are the fruit of the Spirit: love, joy, peace, patience, kindness, goodness, faithfulness, gentleness, and self-control (Galatians 5:22) and gifts of the Spirit; among them apostles, prophets, evangelists, pastors and teachers (Ephesians 4:11). A further list of Spirit gifts is provided in 1 Corinthians 12:8–10; the message of wisdom, the message of knowledge, faith, healing, miraculous powers, prophecy, the ability to distinguish between spirits, the ability to speak in different kinds of tongues, interpretation of tongues. Whilst it cannot be assumed that this is an exhaustive list, it could be argued that these among others are as surely evidence of the outpouring of the Holy Spirit as tongues. There is general consensus across denominations, certainly Evangelical and Pentecostal ones, that all the gifts and fruit of the Spirit have legitimacy. This is largely true too of non-Evangelicals and non-Pentecostals. It is my experience that there is a general climate of acceptance and expectation that Christian life and worship needs the infusion of the dynamic dimension that is epitomised by the Pentecostal impulse. Though not a recipe for loudness, cold formalism is desired by very few nowadays.

The challenge seems to be to universalise Pentecostalism as empowerment for the whole church, not just for Pentecostals. The process has began already, but it may be hampered by an insistence, unnecessarily in this writer's view, on initial evidence of tongues instead of an expectation that the Holy Spirit has been given to all along with a series of gifts and fruit, all of which will find expression within the church. Some may be more or less in evidence dependent upon where one is and the emphases or needs of given situations. It helps if Christians understand the Holy Spirit to be their enabler in the liberation of the oppressed, not as an invitation to a linguistic contest. Liberation theologians tend to ask, 'What is the Holy Spirit for?' – and they end up emphasising the liberative dimension of the Holy Spirit. Jose Comblin (1996, pp.146–164) says, Latin American Christians recognise the God of liberation and feel the presence of such a God in their very midst, acting in their own actions and commitments.

The *Dios liberator* is the Holy Spirit – whether known by name or not. Indeed, according to Comblin, the church was born in the Holy Spirit as an instrument of a pragmatic God whose *modus operandi* was and must continue to be the emancipation of human beings from all that oppress. A study of the Holy Spirit therefore has to deal as Paul had to deal with the enthusiasm of a community that had received the Holy Spirit, but proceeded to commute the gifts to an exhibition of the gift of tongues which produces little if any outward fruit even if affording a measure of inward satisfaction. Like Paul, spiritual leaders today must determinedly point people back to the church's charter: 'The spirit of the Lord is upon me, therefore, he has anointed me to bring glad tidings to the poor, to proclaim liberty to captives, recovery of sight to the blind, release to captives and to announce a year of the Lord's favour.' (Luke 4:8–19). The anointing of the Holy Spirit is to break the yoke of bondage and oppression, not merely for the exercise of gifts for their own sake.

Conclusion

I argue therefore that were we to gather around the understanding of a need to engage with a dynamic Holy Spirit in the entire life of every individual Christian, the church and the world, and if Pentecostals can make a needed shift towards a recognition that all of the gifts and fruit of the spirit is evidence of the Spirit's presence and work, then we have a basis for broad-based Christian fellowship. Tongues-speaking Christians would need to accept that there are millions of Christians who are operating in the dynamism of the Holy Spirit, experiencing gifts and fruit of the spirit, yet have not experienced tongues speaking; in the same way that many who have experienced tongues may not have experienced some gifts that others have. Here, those who reject tongues would need to recognise the validity of the experience of millions who have. All this can be achieved without the dogma that glossolalia is *the* defining initial evidence of baptism in the Holy Spirit, or an experience all Christians must have. Such repositioning would bring reconciliation and greater understanding between Christians – Pentecostals and non-Pentecostals.

It surely is the emphasis upon the immanence of God in the dynamism of life in the Holy Spirit that is at the root of the growth of Pentecostalism world-wide and amongst Black Pentecostals in this country. Maybe God is now moving that dynamism into mainstream through membership of Black and White Pentecostal churches in ecumenical agencies like Churches Together and the Evangelical Alliance. Maybe too, a more reasoned Pentecostal pneumatology will bring about a greater understanding between Oneness and Trinitarians, British Black and White Pentecostals and between Pentecostals and non-Pentecostal traditions. I end with some words with which Walter Hollenweger begins his book, *Pentecostalism* (1997): 'It is my hope and prayer that this (volume) will perhaps help Pentecostals and non-Pentecostals to a more genuine understanding of what it means to be a Pentecostal'.

References

Aldred, Joe (2005) *Respect – Understanding Caribbean British Christianity*, Peterborough, Epworth

Aldred, Joe and Parris, Garnet (2001a) 'The Bible and the Black Church' in Rowland, Chris and Vincent, John (eds), *Bible and Practice*, Sheffield, Urban Theology Unit

Aldred, Joe (2001b) 'The Black Church in Britain and Their Relations with the Ecumenical Movement' in, Dahling-Sander, Herausgegeben von Christoph, Funkschmidt, Kai M., and Mielke, Vera (eds) *Pfingstkirchen und Okumene in Bewegung*, Frankfurt am Main, Verlag Otto Lembeck

Ashimolowo, Matthew (1993) *Tongues of Fire*, London, Mattyson Media Publication

Bartleman, Frank (1980) *Azusa Street – Roots of Modern-day Pentecost*, New Jersey, Bridge Publishing

Brierley, Peter (2006) *Pulling Out Of The Nosedive*, London, Christian Research

Brierley, Peter (2000) *The Tide Is Running Out*, London, Christian Research

Brierley, Peter (1991) *Christian England*, London, Marc Europe

Burgess, S. M., McGee, G. B., (eds) (1993) *Dictionary of Pentecostal and Charismatic Movements*, Michigan, Zondervan Publishing House

Comblin, Jose (1996) 'The Holy Spirit' in Sobrino, Jon and Ellacuria, Ignacio (eds) *Systematic Theology: perspectives from Liberation Theology*, London, SCM Press

Cone, James (1989) *Black Theology and Black Power*, San Francisco, Harper & Row

Gerloff, Roswith (1992) *A Plea for British Black Theologies*, Frankfurt am Main, Peter Lang

Hollenweger, Walter J. (1997) *Pentecostalism: Origins, Developments Worldwide*, Peabody, Massachusetts, Hendrickson Publishers

Kinnamon, Michael and Cope, Brian E. (eds) (1997) *The Ecumenical Movement*, Geneva, WCC Publications

Martin, Larry (ed.), (1999) *Azusa Street Sermons: William Seymour*, Missouri, Christian Life Books

McGrath, Alister E. (1994) *Christian Theology*, Oxford, Blackwell Publishers

Mohabir, Philip (1988) *Building Bridges*, London, Hodder and Stoughton

Pruitt, Raymond M. (1981) *Fundamentals of the Faith*, Cleveland, Tennessee, White Wing Publishing House and Press

Seymour, William (2006) *The William Seymour Story. From tragedy to triumph to obscurity. A documentary.* (Dir. Matt Long)

Sturge, Mark (2005) *Look what the Lord has done: An exploration of Black Christian faith*, Bletchley, Scripture Union

Synan, Vinson (1980) *Introduction*, in Bartleman, *Frank Azusa Street – Roots of Modern-day Pentecost*, New Jersey, Bridge Publishing

Thomas, John C., (ed.) (2008) *Journal of Pentecostal Theology 17: 2*, The Netherlands, BRILL

4 *Gospel Music and the Black Church*

Juliet Fletcher

UK Gospel Music ranges from formal classical music and choral singing to the latest grooves in urban music. Arguments persist as to whether the latter can actually be described as 'Gospel Music' as defined, for example, by Viv Broughton (1996). But the use of the phrase 'Urban Gospel Music' remains a description of contemporary religious/Christian music as practised by some from the Black Church. This article examines the relationship between the Black Church and music, highlighting the historical and current state of affairs. It tells the story of Gospel Music more out of, than within, the Black Church – as I believe that is where its greater work lies. Music, arts and media already are an important part of the life of the Black Church and wider community. That being so, why and how should the Black Church care for those who operate on its behalf in these disciplines? The chapter concludes with some theological reflections. Through this article it is hoped that we will see that God has used and will continue to use creative disciplines and tools to advance His purpose through the Black Church movement.

More than any other aspect of Black Church life, music has been its most recognised, replicated, and redeeming feature. Whereas the oratory prowess of church leaders is often accused of lagging behind in relevance and influence; music has maintained the pace, and has given us a consistent public face. As an art form it is admired and coveted, earning its place in socio-political and corporate affairs. But, is the Black Church losing out by undervaluing this powerful, universal tool? Are there any lessons from looking at the past and present state of UK Gospel Music? Could these give the Black Church clear indications of how it could chart a new and more powerfully productive course into the twenty-first century? A course that does not merely seek to survive but to succeed in unprecedented ways for generations to come. An appropriate response to these issues has to come from the entire leadership, artists, promoters and those who stand in the gap between the church and the wider world. There is no telling what new chapters of our history we will write *en route* to reaching our first 100 years as a Black Church movement in Britain, if we respond well. Hopefully, there will be enough in this piece to provoke constructive discussions which could lead to practical and creative developments in the Black Church of the twenty-first century.

From the Caribbean to the UK

The Caribbean, throughout the centuries since the enslavement and transportation of Africans to the region, has seen a true proliferation and entrenchment of Christian denominations – Catholic and Protestant churches alike. By the late 1940s on many of the islands, and in countries regarded as part of the Caribbean, like Guyana, the choice of church included a variety of independent groups led by Black people who were not part of the European church set-up. Africans were establishing their own fellowships and there was no disputing the powerful place worship occupied, and still occupies, in Caribbean life. Nowhere epitomises this more than Jamaica, of which it is popularly said that more churches exist per capita than anywhere else in the world!

A close associate of mine, Flo Ferguson, who grew up in Jamaica before coming to England as a 14-year-old, retains many vivid observations of church life during the 1950s. Her parents were working class, highly respected in the Full Gospel church movement in Kingston. She recalls, 'churches were either well to do or not so well to do and their form of worship was significantly influenced by the social class of the leader. Full Gospel separated themselves from the nominal (European non-Pentecostal) churches by being marginally more informal in worship, but in reality, musically, their conservatism was little different. Across the different churches the spectrum ranged from hymns and organ music and congregational singing (in churches like Church of England and Methodist); to hymns and organ or piano and congregational singing with selective formal choruses (in the Full Gospel and Brethren churches), to hymns and choruses and tambourines and clap hand and jumping and speaking in tongues (in Apostolic Church, New Testament Church of God fellowships).

'One fine example of the difference between some Full Gospel churches and the Apostolic churches is found in this chorus about Jesus and the woman at the well. In my parents' church, the pace was moderate and controlled with the words:

A woman came to fill her water pot, down by the bottom of the well.
But Jesus gave her water that was not down by the bottom of the well.
She went away happy and gay, back to her home never more to roam.
For the Lord God gave her water that was not down by the bottom of
    the well.

(Anon)

'Whereas when I went to the Apostolic church it was fast and up tempo with the lyrics:

Jesus gave of the water that was not in the well,
Jesus gave of the water that was not in the well
And she went away singing and she came back bringing
Others to the water that was not in the well.

(Anon)

'I love both versions, but the latter one is that which everyone knows and loves to sing' (Ferguson 2008).

In a large Caribbean church it was not uncommon to have a full range of choirs; senior, junior, young people, children and Sunday school choirs. Multiple choirs would become a signifier of growth in early Black Churches some 20 to 25 years on in Britain. I imagine none of this was in the minds of those who stood poised between land and sea on the steps of the now famous troopship the *SS Empire Windrush*. In the classic 1948 BBC News media clip, Trinidadian Aldwyn Roberts (a.k.a. Lord Kitchener) hails, in Calypsonian melodic strains, 'London Is The Place For Me', expressing the expectation and hope of both the faithless and faithful as they disembarked in a strange new land. Ironically, our future pastors and bishops yet unknown in the crowds, at that time many just in their teens and early twenties, would be working hard to steer clear of the Calypso, Mento, Ska and Rocksteady rhythms. Although this music signified their 'worldly days' before conversion to Pentecostal Christianity, it would *help* give birth to new songs for the new generations in Britain. Bridging the gap between the church in the Caribbean and the newly created one in England would not be without controversy.

The music of the early British Black Church

It is widely accepted now that cultural differences as well as racial indifference became the foundational justification for the development of the Black Church in Britain. And Gospel Music was to become a defining medium for interpreting and coping with the challenges of the new situation. Regarding racial indifference; the reactions of certain ministers in mainstream churches of the time are cited by Caribbean leaders and laity alike as the source of the divide leading them to create their own denominational home. The late Revd Dr Io Smith attested to this in her ground-breaking book, *An Ebony Cross* (1989). In it she tells a forthright tale of her personal experiences in Britain of the 1950s and 1960s and provides her reflections on the emergence of a recognised Black Church movement. Regarding cultural difference; in hindsight it can be seen that our music – both of hymns and choruses – was and still is a powerful driver for difference and distinction.

Whether among traditions such as Methodists, Baptists or Seventh Day Adventists a particular – or some might say peculiar – way in which we sing, for example a Wesley or Watts hymn 'our way' reveals a deep-seated preference for our exclusive gathering. A real example of this, in my view, is found in the Adventist Church. Arthur Torrington OBE (2008) recalls his early days in Guyana: 'The Adventist Church came out of the Methodist tradition. We had our own (Adventist) hymnal and sang mainly with traditional organ. There were no hand clapping or outward expressions of praise, as you would find in a gathering of Black people of the Pentecostal persuasion. Nonetheless it was warm, friendly and vibrant. But when we came here the situation was different; even though we were singing traditional hymns you had to follow what (or how) the English white brethren were singing, it was just very different. The Caribbean people would sing more lustily, and we did not look forward to it (the White-led church service). A lot of West Indians dropped out.'

This experience supports the evidence of how Gospel Music is said to have developed: enslaved Africans taking the European hymns transforming them – phrasing, rhythm and syncopation – with all the African-ness they possessed, thereby making them uniquely their own. This means that although prejudice and racial discrimination played a key role in assisting the creation of the Black Church it could be argued that it was inevitable a church movement of this culture would form out of the sheer intrinsic need for what is a natural anthropological expression. Torrington (2008) continued to say 'We worship in a Black way. White people cannot worship in a totally Black way which encompasses African, Caribbean or African American worship. It combines the spiritual, emotional and social aspects of our being.' As for the accusation that Black people use singing and dancing as escapism, Torrington responds emphatically 'It is not escapism! What are we escaping from? This accusation is nonsense. Singing and dancing is what we do and is thousands of years old. What our ancestors did is still a major part of our lives.'

As a researcher, historian, co-founder of the Windrush Foundation and the Equiano Society, Arthur is well placed to come to such conclusions. Torrington (2008), citing Olaudah Equiano (1789) the famed freed African slave who contributed to the abolition of the Slave Trade, pointed out that 'Equiano said "We are a nation of poets, dancers and singers", and he was writing in the eighteenth century, one of the earliest records writing about us!'.

A Gospel Music controversy erupted in London at the end of the first decade of the fledgling Black Church Movement in Britain, circa 1958. It began when a young evangelist of that time, Ken McCarthy, took a group of five young men with guitars, drums and amplifiers on the road to support his evangelical campaigns. At the time of writing, Bishop McCarthy (2008) is a very healthy, lively octogenarian, 'still on fire for the Lord', with a lucid memory of what happened. 'I came to England from Jamaica in 1950, and began preaching and teaching. Through the providence of God, my ministry base was in Brixton. We owned our building – which was given to us by a wonderful (White) missionary lady – a former bombsite on Somerleyton Road. The Council charged a peppercorn rent of £1 per annum. Besides owning a tent for outdoor meetings, I held Bible training for Black and White Christians, sending them out as evangelists and missionaries.'

The set of circumstances around McCarthy was unique, and the outcome would dramatically affect the progress of Gospel Music not just in London, or even the United Kingdom, but across Europe. With a high level of astuteness and spirit of enterprise McCarthy took the first touring British gospel group, called the Soul Seekers, on the road. The group consisted of Tony Mossop – (who would later leave Gospel, change his name to Tony Tribe and have a 1970s hit with 'Red Red Wine') – brothers Denver and Carl Grant, Ray Powell, 'and the drummer whom we only ever called "Doc", recalls McCarthy. The group began to impact young people of all cultures and languages, travelling through Sweden, Finland, Austria, Holland and Norway. McCarthy recalls how the group signed a record deal with Norwegian Philips International, the biggest record company at that time, and produced a double-sided single with the tracks, 'Across The Bridge' and 'I'll Fly Away Home', both well known melodies. A treasured vinyl recording still exists today. The doors also opened for McCarthy to take the group onto the airwaves, probably the first contemporary Gospel Group so to do, with a weekly radio gospel show on the controversial but pioneering floating ship that hosted Radio Caroline.

Bishop Noel Dyer (2008), of Ministry Of Restoration was a teenager at the time and remembers well the impact of the Soul Seekers. 'They were fantastic. They sounded like the Shadows in many ways, and looked good too – sharp and well dressed. For us they became the benchmark everyone wanted to reach'. Noel himself became a member of a Gospel group The Persuaders, set up by his older brother George Dyer. 'We didn't travel into Europe but we sang all over the UK, often in White churches, in coffee clubs and church events. Most Black Church leaders were against us playing the sounds. Reggae rhythms were an absolute no-no, even just a "light feel". I remember we were playing at a fellow musician's wedding. The elders present told him to tell us to "stop play that reggae feel". We said to him "It is your wedding and this is what you asked us here for. If they make us stop we will pack up and leave." He went back to talk to the elders, but the pressure was too much for him, and very amicably with him we packed up and left. That's what it was like!'

The irony here is that most forms of popular music derive their influence and draw on the idioms, idiosyncrasies and other musical and performing fundamentals of Gospel Music. Secondly, the development of popular music, from the mid-1950s through to the 1960s and on, drew heavily on

Black Music, rhythm 'n blues in particular. In the UK, white groups were busy obtaining and practising songs written by Black performers to jump-start their musical careers. So in real ways the Gospel bands had a right to creatively use the pop music that has its roots firmly in the influence of Gospel. The struggle to give birth to British Gospel was not only in London. There were similar developments happening in other major British conurbations like Birmingham, Bristol, Nottingham and Manchester.

The challenges internal to the UK were joined by a significant external one; the influence of US social politics and Gospel Music. It started from the mid-1960s when my peers and I became more conscious of many things happening around us. I was brought up in the Calvary Church of God in Christ, COGIC, as it is known; a church which has, on both sides of the Atlantic, one of the richest legacies in Gospel Music. COGIC and the wider British Gospel Music were infused with Caribbean, Country and British pop rhythms as performers like the Soul Seekers, the Singing Stewarts and others led the way. However, these British artistes took a back seat when the American Gospel recordings, particularly on the Savoy Gospel label took centre stage. Like a camera lens defocusing everything around and pinpointing the central object, we began to see and hear nothing else.

Our parents were struggling socially and financially, and we were experiencing discrimination, prejudice, injustice, and unemployment. We could feel an atmosphere of imposed inferiority. Yet few Black voices of church leaders or artistes dared to articulate these problems. Black social activists were springing up all over the place, mirroring developments in the US, but they did not speak for us in the church. Between ourselves as young people we whispered disgruntedly, but mostly we bottled up our passion inside us. At the same time the image and sound of Black art and oratory were coming through to us in the pictures and sounds of Mahalia Jackson accompanying Martin Luther King. We saw him walking on the streets of America, standing on the steps of the Lincoln Memorial in Washington DC, and in finality slain on the balcony of the Lorraine Motel in Memphis. We also witnessed on TV screens Tommie Smith and Carlos Jones performing the Power to the People 'black glove' salute and listened to Enoch Powell's 'rhetoric of hate'. We were not neutral observers, but we had no means of communicating our feelings. It seemed we only had Martin Luther King doing this for us, from afar.

Then, at last, there was a surge of British Gospel choirs, which was timely because their emergence gelled with the songs of freedom we had in our hearts and heard coming out of the US. Suddenly all that we saw on our television screens of Black America in the midst of civil unrest, we could empathise with in a real way; we had a right to sing 'We shall overcome'. We could tie our faith into the context of our life experiences. Singing in church had a whole new meaning. God had given us His Spirit to rise above all that would hold us down. At this juncture many of our churches were denominationally connected to the US, and the music of their churches. There were large choirs and groups in concerts that became our strongest meeting point, regardless of denomination.

We might have felt 'stranded on an island' but now we were involved in the 'bigger picture' of the Black Diaspora. We had the perception that our music was leading the way. It was this vision in my own heart that spurred me as a 17-year-old when an almost audible voice said 'I want you to devote yourself to this music, it's going to mean something in Britain in time to come.' He, God, would use this music to speak peace, truth and life to everyone regardless of race, age, culture and status. I set about telling people, anyone who would listen that there was a new wave of music coming that people in Britain hadn't heard. Somehow I ended up on radio interviews, making a film about it and meeting many behind the scenes of Christian music.

By the end of the 1970s there were hundreds of groups, choirs, soloists and musicians, staging concerts in various churches such as the New Testament Assembly, Church of God in Christ, and Bibleway Church of God. There was a unity amongst us young people, we were on one platform and sharing a vision that we had, music that we could proudly sing to the world, and with it change the world. A big spin-off was that young people had a real social life! So by 1978 and 1979 when Andrae Crouch came to the UK to record Live at Hammersmith Odeon, UK Gospel was on the boil! And from the 1980s to the present day we have had continual explosions of music and arts: independent album releases and compilations, theatre productions; mini films, full length DVDs, and today we are still pushing the boundaries. We have just got on with creating and making music, and many of our musicians and singers, producers, vocal trainers and technicians, journalists and specialist consultants are now recognised as 'world class' and 'professionals'. All this happened outside the 'church circuit' and without the Black Church's caring involvement.

The Black Church that began, under the providential guidance of God, with the commitment of a few Caribbean men and women has now expanded. Now we know better, we can officially reclaim our Caribbean church music roots with all the richness we have now: we are joined by the fresh new fire of our African brothers and sisters, and with them comes a new dimension in music. The growth of this aspect of the Black Church has taken place during a massive increase in knowledge, property acquisition and confidence in technology, media and music in Christendom. And some, particularly African church leaders, have grasped it! There has also been a dynamic growth in Gospel art forms in the Black Church over the past forty years. This movement now involves hundreds, if not thousands of people who have been and are seeking to speak to their generation in brand 'new expressions' that even a generation ago we did not anticipate. This is not something desirable, it is crucial.

During the past decade, before this horrendous rise in gun and knife crime amongst young people, there was a 'posse' of young Christians, who struggled and wrestled with communicating the gospel through reggae, hip-hop, and ragga. Those young people who have inspired many from destructive lifestyles by 'rhyming a lyric' about Jesus to a set of beats have my support. Gospel Ragga artist 'Witness' from Birmingham is officially recognised as a social artist, and 'Watchman' from London runs a government-sponsored mentoring programme in Brixton Prison where he was once an inmate. The youth on the streets were not listening to the pastors, but they did listen and respond to their peers ministering to them in the language they recognised. This is the power of the gospel within music created by artists under-resourced in, but adding value to, the Black Church movement. Now there are those whose unmoveable opinion is that Gospel Music is a particular sound and musical form. Others, without knowledge of musicology, argue that Gospel Music and its gospel message only relates to the lyrics. My personal view is as follows: in the midst of this controversy there is a danger that if the Black Church does not take ownership of the legacy and heritage of its music, as each generation reinterprets the sound, its rich historical legacy will dissipate. US Gospel has shown it is possible to maintain both contemporary and traditional genres – each feeding off the other; and there are great lessons to learn from this.

The future is bright but for who?

What will the Britain of the future be like? God only knows, and that's a fact. Instead of resisting, the church must respond. And in a world that is hearing many voices, if we create music in our churches that only speaks to us and God, we are missing both a huge opportunity *and* the reason why we are still here in this world! We may also alienate ourselves from the next generation. To get a personal perspective from someone of the now generation, I spoke to Jake Isaac (2008), less than half my age and a worship leader in Christian Life, Greenwich. Jake also works for Street Pastors, co-founded by his father Les Isaac. Using Psalm 145:3–5 as a point of reference, Jake said,

> There's a big difference between one generation taking on a culture and tradition and that same generation taking on the gospel and interpreting it for their generation. We can't live off the blessing of another generation … In the church, music is a key and core element of our relationship with Jesus Christ and beyond the church everything is interpreted via music. It is about writing songs about a generation … who don't only sing but dance, and rap before the Lord as worship … they want songs they can sing out of the church on the college campus. If the older generations want to see the legacy of Gospel Music passed on then it is in their interest to get involved.
>
> (*Isaac 2008*)

Jake articulated a very clear vision of worship for his generation. It was inclusive, relevant and powerful. But will he and others like him be released to achieve this for the future Black Church?

The past twenty years has seen the development of a UK Gospel Music industry, full of worship leaders, writers, singers, wordsmiths, poets, musicians, producers, technical engineers, filmmakers, promoters, radio DJs and presenters, managers, expert consultants, public relations specialists, event organisers, online website operators, music teachers and educators, music mentors and motivators. We have got some access to broadcast music videos, documentaries and programmes on specialist radio and television mediums: on terrestrial and satellite as well the Internet. You are more likely to hear a Gospel Music track, see a performance or read a write-up in the mainstream press than you would with any other type of Christian or religious music. So what's the problem?

From my knowledge and experience, having built this industry, most Gospel Music sector individuals are often alienated and not given sufficient regard by the church for their achievements which are largely on behalf of the churches 'mission' cause. Could their efforts be rewarded with the support of the spiritual and financial resources of the Black Church movement?

We need to rise to the challenge and get a dialogue going with our Black Church leaders on the strategic ways in which we can engage with the world of the arts – both in our churches and in the wider world. Then we can cement conclusive ideas in published prose that will become a living legacy of a spiritual and practical approach to that involvement.

We have a unique art form that is multi-dimensional in application. We can see how our 'cousins from across the pond' have used it. There, individuals, record companies and the churches have benefited. But to purely emulate them could mean we become infected with some of the ills which currently plague their industry; we will need to do things differently. Can we pull all the bits together, and work at creating a robust infrastructure on which the creative life of the church can run, with music at the centre? Is it possible that a series of cross-denominational initiatives in association with leaders and Gospel Music practitioners could result in a transformed gospel industry – and Church? Is there a win-win strategy that could please all? Maybe if there is a follow-up edition of this book we will publish the sure answer.

I further propose there are greater issues and tasks to be achieved by and through the Black Church: I advance an argument that we are identified as a Black Church movement of African and Caribbean churches 'distinct yet the same' whose mission is to help bring to full bloom the diversity of Christianity in Britain. Music is a major tool in bringing this about, through the language of worship for example. We have had worship leaders and music directors, like Steve Thompson, Steve McGregor, Noel Robinson, Nicky Brown, Mark Beswick, Muyiwa Olarewaju and Ken Burton who share platforms across the Christian spectrum. However, their works as songwriters and composers, both classical and contemporary, are yet to appear in the songbooks of the wider Christian world. But we cannot ask of others what we do not practice ourselves, for in the years of our presence in Britain, with music at the heart of our churches, we have not produced a recognised songbook reflecting the music of our own churches. But watch this space!

In God's kingdom we are meant to be distinctive enough to be recognised, yet similar enough for it to be known that we belong to Christ (Revelation 7:9; 2 Peter 1:1–3). I believe the two-fold purpose of the Gospel Music of the Black Church is first, to worship God, and second, to bear witness in the world. Holding our distinctiveness and purpose in tandem our leaders can do three key things that will begin to make necessary changes within the Black Church regarding its music:

1. Recognise, empower and release individuals from within the Black Church that have demonstrated spiritual virtue, professional commitment and expertise to manage resources and direct effective strategies.
2. Allow systems and structures within and across the Black Church that support education, training, investment and resourcing at all levels.
3. Engage in dialogue and constructive discussion above denominational boundaries and agendas with an on-going commitment to deliver the Black Church's part in the 'bigger picture' that God has for this nation.

Conclusion

The Holy Spirit is never wrong and cannot be moved from the three points of His revealed work as spoken by Jesus in St John 16:5–11: The Comforter has come to convict the world of sin, righteousness, and judgement. The Holy Spirit did not come to give us a sense of God in the atmosphere, as many of our churches strive to experience in our services. Of course it is good when spiritual atmospheric changes happen, but the real revelation of God at work tends to happen in the world beyond the four walls of the church service. It is in the world where the Holy Spirit seeks to fulfil His tasks (His Harvest). Throughout the rest of John 16 and 17 Jesus says that the Holy Spirit will speak to us, i.e. 'show us how'. This 'how' will be in relation to the original stated purpose 'to convict the world of sin, righteousness and judgement'.

Since the Holy Spirit will work with whomever He chooses to make an impact on the world, we must also be willing to use whatever tools we can to communicative His truths. Looking at our musical trends over the last sixty years, it is plain that the Holy Spirit has been pushing us and our music out into the world, on centre stage. But I observe that when we have ventured out, we have limited ourselves. Why? Because we are afraid? Perhaps we don't feel as though we are in control 'out there' as we are in the safe havens of our churches. In this age there are methods beyond preaching that capture the minds and hearts of people in every nation. Like the Apostle Peter – even after the wonderful work of the Holy Spirit with Cornelius the Gentile – we prefer to play safe – instead of being a risk taker like the Apostle Paul who acted fully on the revelation that 'in Christ Jesus shall all the nations of the earth be blessed'.

At least the Apostle Peter and the others in Jerusalem made up for it by releasing Paul. Peter also said of Paul that there were matters in his writing 'in which are some things hard to be understood' (2 Peter 3:14–16), yet he embraced Paul, calling him beloved. Those of us in the creative world of music, arts, and media need to be both embraced and released by our churches. We need to be trusted to create and innovate work that holds the gospel message in unusual, non-traditional, ways. Scaremongering statements like 'the world is coming into the church' do not help. We need to be mature enough to realise that our weaknesses, propensity to failure, and sheer self-righteousness have never hindered the Lord using us. It can be clearly proven that when churches have trusted creative individuals and upgraded their approach; where creativity and innovation is joined with a focussed vision – people respond. And isn't that the whole point? People = God's treasure, God's passion, God's heart.

The Black Church of the twenty-first century and beyond, if it wishes to maintain a distinctive and reputable identity needs to be the church that operates comfortably and effectively within and without the church walls or buildings. However, I add this caveat: I believe the physical presence of buildings that are consecrated ground as spiritual, social and (with a small 'p') political safe havens must be retained. We must secure our landmark buildings and spaces dedicated to the worship of God and specialist activities. The place of gathering is still a crucial 'place of power – in agreed and united fellowship'. It is still the place where the creators and innovators of Gospel Music must receive and give their greatest inspiration – offering up the first fruit of their works to God before taking it out to distribute to the world. This for me is an essential biblical principle of our accountability and responsibility to God as creators of music and other artistic endeavours.

This is what will make us powerful, potent and credible in music, arts and media. It is this approach that will make us leaders and not followers as we go into the world geographically, systematically, politically, socially, culturally and every other way. By so doing we build upon the vision and sacrifice of the early trailblazers and give hope and support to contemporary artistes.

Key achievements in UK Gospel Music:

- Autumn 1986: Channel 4 broadcasts the first British Black Gospel television series called 'People Get Ready', from an idea by producer and broadcaster Andrew Barr. The production team is uniquely made up from the Gospel community, TVS Production Company and TVS staff. The show included many of our leading singers and musicians and was presented by John Francis and Juliet Coley. The series was also produced by Roy Francis.
- October 2003: the inaugural annual Gospel Grand Summit, the music industry event for bringing together everyone involved in Gospel. The 2008 theme 'Cultural Leadership and Influencing Change' attracted representation from the London 2012 Cultural Olympiad.
- November 2003: Revd Dr Tani Omideyi leads the opening of Liverpool Lighthouse, a £2 million refurbished former cinema, as the UK and Europe's first dedicated urban gospel arts centre.
- 2007–2008: *From Hymns to Hip-Hop*: the showing of first theatre production on the story of British Gospel. Created by the Millennium Action Group (South London), performing to sell-out audiences at the Albany Theatre, Deptford, and the Shaw Theatre, London. There was a special performance before Boris Johnson, Mayor of London at the London Citizens Assembly Hall.
- November 2008: Tyndale Thomas receives an MBE from the Queen for services to African Caribbean Gospel Music in the community in the North.

Key remarks by UK Gospel Music leaders:

UK Gospel could have been better served by church leaders being at the fore of the 1970s–1990s surge. The burden of bringing about this reality (UK Gospel) has been left to those whose artistry and creativity has led them to be independently resourceful in taking their music ministry outside of the church walls ... in the main, artists of the present and the future, are hoping for more than a blessing from their churches in support of their ministry.

(Audrey Lawrence-Mattis, Music Consultant/Gospel Music Specialist)

UK Gospel Music has grown up almost like a child without its parent. It has managed so far, but it wants to find its place 'at home' in its own right. The onus is on the Black Church, 'the parent' to make that happen.

(Roy Francis, Specialist Media Consultant)

Gospel Music (whether as congregational worship or outreach performance) has been central to the growth of Britain's Black-led churches. We can be certain that one would not have evolved in the same way or to the same extent without the other.

(Viv Broughton, Gospel Music Author and Historian)

It would be great if the Church could show more appreciation for its creative talent by supporting and rewarding them more consistently so that they can afford to be sustained within the circuit of church as well as outside of it.

(Revd Bazil Meade, Founder/Director, London Community Gospel Choir)

The future of Black Gospel is firmly rooted in the support infrastructure of the Church. Any community that functions or thrives, the power comes from the root.

(Nicky Brown, Independent Record Producer and Music Minister)

References

Publications
Broughton, Viv (1996) *Too Close To Heaven: The Illustrated History of Gospel Music*, London, Midnight Books
Equiano, Olaudah (1789) *The Interesting Narrative of the Life of Olaudah Equiano, Or Gustavus Vassa, The African*, London

Smith, Io, with Green, Wendy (1989) *An Ebony Cross: Being Black in Britain Today*, London, Harper Collins/STL

Interviews
Torrington, Arthur, telephone interview, 14 August 2008, London
Lawrence-Mattis, Audrey, series of telephone interviews, August to November 2008
Meade, Bazil, telephone interview, 10 November 2008
McCarthy, Bishop Ken, face-to-face interviews, conducted between August and November 2008
Dyer, Bishop Noel, telephone interview, 2 December 2008
Ferguson, Flo, face-to-face interview, 30 November 2008, London
Isaac, Jake, telephone interview, 2 December 2008
Brown, Nicky, telephone interview, 10 November 2008
Francis, Roy, series of telephone interviews, August to November 2008
Broughton, Viv, email, 10 November 2008

Internet
www.bbc.co.uk/1xtra/bhm05/features/video.shtml
https://www.strategicnetwork.org/index *and*
    www.jamaicatripper.com/jamaica/religion.html
Witness – www.facebook.com/l/af8ca;myspace.com/ywitness
Watchman – www.rapmentors.org
Street Pastors – www.streetpastors.co.uk

5   *Conflict Resolution and the Black Church*

Julia Smith and Carl J Ryan

The focus of this chapter is to examine the need for conflict resolution strategies within Black Churches. This is imperative, because 'the church', though an organisational structure, is principally a relational organisation. More so, it is a spiritual organisation which Christians continue to believe is guided by God, in spite of its perceived and actual human inefficiencies and frailties.

It is not uncommon in Black Churches throughout the United Kingdom, following Saturday, Sunday, or week-day worship, to find congregants in small huddles in discussion about an unresolved problem that, at least from their perspective, is developing into a conflict. At one local church, a problem which had begun as a difference of opinion about the leadership style of the pastor and lay leaders, which had remained unresolved over several months, had escalated into what was perceived by many to be a power war between an influential new member and the established 'leadership' who were probably less experienced and skilled in leadership and church administration matters. What on the face of it could and should have been addressed through consultation and open dialogue was in the end permitted to spill over into an open church forum, resulting in greater and unforeseen spiritual and emotional harm to congregants, especially the young people and new members to the church.

While certain specific problems are somewhat unique to a local Black congregation, the basic elements of conflict and the way in which it is managed is irrespective of denomination, polity, size, and colour. The sources of conflict and the means for resolving conflict are universal. In an article 'Conflict in the Black Church' by Robert T. Newbold, Jr (1980), the author acknowledges the historic influence of the church as one of the strongest institutions in the Black community. However, he also observed its failure to manage internal conflict creatively. This is often because of the tendency to believe (a) that conflict is wrong and (b) that a situation involving conflict is sinful. As a result of this perception, the individual who generates a conflict is often viewed as an agent of the devil. In his book *Managing Change in the Church*, Douglas W. Johnson (1974) observed that one of the reasons the Black Church has not managed conflict well is because Church leaders often feel guilty when conflict is generated or becomes a major part of the decision-making process. This guilt arises from the belief that conflict is abnormal.

Alternative Dispute Resolution consultant and lawyer Deborah Mendez-Bowen (2006) defines conflict as varied perspectives, belief systems and interests. Conflict arises, when one or more participants view the current system as not working. At least one part is sufficiently dissatisfied with the status quo that they are willing to own the conflict and speak up with the hope of being able to influence the situation to arrive at an improved condition. Every form of social conflict, and by extension, church conflict, she suggests, implies there is a perception of divergent interests, whether or not they are divergent in reality. It is often the perception of divergence based on the belief that conflict is abnormal and 'un-Christian' that prevents the Black, White, ethnically and culturally diverse churches from viewing conflict as an opportunity to do things differently, redefine relationships and positions, and as a positive experience that the church can learn from and grow.

The scale of conflict in churches

A national survey of 14,301 church congregations in the USA (FACT 2000) found that over 75% reported some level of conflict in the five years preceding the survey and over 25% reported they had had a serious conflict in the three years preceding the survey. A different survey by *Christianity Today* (2004) that interviewed pastors to examine the sources of conflict found that the biggest source of conflict was 'control issues' (85%) and 'vision and direction issues' (64%). The same survey found that less than 25% of pastors reported conflict on core theological issues, indicating perhaps, that whilst churches are relatively secure and in unity on matters of theology, the more complex human issues such as diversity, management style and interpersonal issues are the ones that continue to vex churches and church leaders.

Recent works by Boyd-MacMillan and Savage (2008) focused on gathering data from a conflict transformation training programme they designed for 29 senior church leaders from the Anglican, Baptist, Church of Scotland, Methodist, Roman Catholic and United Reform Churches. The project was commissioned by the Foundation for Church Leadership. The training programme focused on the special challenges confronted by senior church leaders covering physiology, inner conflict, interpersonal difference, group dynamics, thinking patterns, difficult people and the help and hindrances characteristic of faith communities. The researchers found that in one classroom activity the participants were unable to resolve situations; which gave rise to tensions, conflict becoming personal, deterioration in trust and communication with each group representative out to win the conflict in a way that makes the other side a loser. The goal of showing up each other led each side to assert the superiority of its own view in a way that belittled the other side. It was found that the senior leaders were quick to recognise these behaviours in their opponents, but not in themselves. These findings highlight the complexity of conflict and its resolution processes within churches and underlie a particular challenge for conflict resolution which appears to be inherent to church communities.

The Christian and conflict

The reality of the existence of conflict is also in stark contrast with the Biblical aspiration of 'brethren dwelling together in unity' (Psalm 133) and being in Christ (John 17). This unity is one of the critical factors for effective church ministry and when conflict threatens, pastors and lay leaders often react either by ignoring the conflict, in the hope that it will go away, or by treating the conflict as a hostile or even satanic element. Ken Newberger (2006), a Christian Conflict Resolution expert in the US, observed that too often, for a church to acknowledge conflict in its midst when it is supposed to demonstrate love, is to acknowledge failure. That's why, he suggests, church leaders and pastors under-report the amount of discord in their churches since its acknowledgement is inconsistent with their highest ideals.

Donald E. Bossart (1990), Associate Professor of Interpersonal Ministries at The Iliff School of Theology in Denver, Colorado, suggests that the expectation that the church should be without conflict 'is incongruent with Biblical theology', since the church has to remember that the purpose of Jesus Christ's life can best be seen against the backdrop of our destructive patterns that typically result in conflict-producing behaviour. The Son of God came into the world to die for human sin so that a person, through faith in Christ, can experience God's forgiveness. Conflict existed among God's people throughout the Old and New Testaments, for example, Genesis 3:14–16, Matthew 5:23–24, Matthew 20:24, John 8:44, Galatians 1:10 and Galatians 2:11, to list a few. Furthermore, the book of Acts (e.g. 15:36–40) is graphic in its account of the conflict which existed in the emerging Christian church. There we are given insight into three types of conflicts; leadership and administration, theological beliefs, and personal or personality conflicts that existed among the early church community and which are just as evident and presents the same challenges for the church communities today (Newberger 2006).

Becoming reconciled with God, Newberger (2006) suggests, does not change our underlying human nature. The well-known phrase 'sinners saved by grace' recognises the fact that we are still sinners. Very few imagine that a person's new commitment to God eradicates self-centred, conflict-producing thoughts and behaviour. Jesus made it clear that we would experience conflict even as Christians (Luke 17:1). Scripture lays out the proper way to handle one-to-one differences with a brother or sister in Matthew 18, however, since the presenting issue in the conflict is seldom a simple matter of differences one-dimensional in nature, and since, as Christians each one is tempted to believe that she or he is being guided by the Holy Spirit in the positions each has taken, the application of Matthew 18 in affecting early resolution in personal matters is difficult. Where the situation is more complex, or concerns less personally directed, such as those related to 'leadership direction' or 'the administrative effectiveness' of the church; the misapplication of Matthew 18, the lack of a willingness to address the conflict, or a lack of understanding of the issues being highlighted often underlie an unwillingness to learn how to manage conflicts in a way that will be beneficial to the kingdom of God.

The physiological and practical nature of conflict

There are two sets of conflicts that preoccupy our human form. First, there are internal conflicts which occur between such emotional states as hate, anger, hostility, arrogance, bias, intolerance and revenge on the one hand and humility, kindness, empathy, compassion, generosity, love, tolerance, understanding and forgiveness on the other. These are usually strong, extreme elements that cause internal turmoil when choice, compromise and decision-making have to be applied to problem solving. Sometimes solutions are more forthcoming when spiritual intervention through wisdom and faith are applied. However our strong human desires sometimes seem to override other helpful interventions, by thinking that our self-centred solution is best. A second set of conflict is external conflict and refers to situations that we are confronted with from external sources including the actions of our counterparts and other societal factors.

Because of human diversity, conflict is inevitable. Generally, conflict is positive and valuable for human growth and development. Approximately 95% of conflict situations are resolved through peaceful communication. Usually a small portion perceived as negative and destructive threatens the solution process. Conflict is mostly perceived as negative and destructive when the involved parties persistently insist on their self-centred right of way without recognising the rights and views of the opposing party to exist. Though this often goes unrecognised, the church community is highly diverse in its values and organisation and ensuing conflicts create huge demands on the leaders' ability to maintain appropriate resolution strategies. The church as an institution generally makes positive and significant contributions towards human development through its various resources. However, these can be over-estimated in some cases where there might be significant inequalities among church members in their abilities to engage with each other.

In the quest towards dealing with the negative impact and resolution strategies of church conflict we cannot ignore some of the resulting physiological and practical consequences. Some of those might be compounded by incapacities surrounding mental health issues such as depression and personality disorder traits. In extreme cases there might be violent abuse and litigation. There might also be other internal factors such as:

- Muscular tension
- Indigestion and loss of appetite
- Headache
- Coronary failures
- Hyperventilation
- Characteristics of post traumatic stress syndrome
- Breakdown in relationships
- Skin eruptions
- Dysfunction of some body systems
- Sense of helplessness and doubt
- Panic or anxiety attacks
- Random emotional outburst
- Guilt

The physiological effects are likely to subside after the conflict has been resolved. However if the impact is severe it might require interventions such as psychotherapy or other medical interventions.

A perception of church conflict

Church conflict might be perceived as unique, but in general it is hardly different from any other organisation. Early work by Bridgebuilders (2006) into conflict in some Christian churches indicated that churches are voluntary institutions whose structures and processes may permit and even promote the indiscriminate unaccountable use of power and authority. Also, because the church is in some ways a natural sanctuary for people with various extreme needs, it is inevitably consumed by higher levels of anxiety and emotional demands.

There was also the notion that Christians somehow learn to avoid confrontation so they are reluctant to challenge behaviour that disrupts fellowship, resulting in periodic explosions amongst those trying to cope. The church suffers from a lack of capacity to deal with diverse personalities and challenges among members' differing leadership styles within the church, along with unresolved emotional pressure. By its very nature the Christian Gospel invites social and personal changes to individuals who then find problems of combining church life with community life (Bridge-builders 2006). Then there are other notions of perceived conflicts. For instance, some churches might be perceived as being driven by a particularly strong tension between head and heart, or between elders and congregation, or amongst the congregation. Unaware of the physiological and social effects of anger and injustice, some church members may radically seek theological explanation and justification for other members' behaviour.

The unrealistic expectations and unmet Christian needs along with a lack of clarity and processes might affect church decision making. However when we collaborate and share our Christian needs and values we are required to demonstrate truth, justice, transparency, leadership, accountability, repentance and humility. This can restore our faith.

The reality of church conflict

Though some congregational disputes produce damaging scars, most conflicts are far from fatal. In the *Christianity Today* survey (2006), almost all of the pastors reported positive results (94%) from the congregational conflict resolution they experienced. The most common finding was that pastors felt stronger (60%) following the conflict resolution and about one-third reported being thankful and hopeful for the future of their congregation. Few mentioned the negative outcomes. This helps us to see that the fear of addressing conflict is far greater than actually doing so and that the outcome can be far better for the church and God's work.

The nature of conflict and its resolution processes in Black Churches are yet to be empirically investigated. Research into conflict in the Black Church in the UK is still in the early stages of development. There appears to be a paucity of good empirical data on the issue which the Dispute Resolution Centre for Faith Communities (DRCFC) in partnership with University of Kent plans to progress over the coming months. Preliminary work carried out by the authors during the summer of 2008 found that with the exception of the London Baptist Association and the New Wine church, few church organisations and fewer still independent churches had taken any proactive steps to address conflict as a leadership issue, or indeed to inform and educate the membership about conflict and effective ways of resolving these when they arise.

At an organisational level, it was concerning that whilst the established traditional churches such as the Catholic and Anglican churches had taken steps to at least develop resource materials that could be accessed by their church leaders, even in these churches organisational developments were still relatively new. At the time of writing, very few Black Church leaders have to date been involved in the work being developed by the Southwark Dioceses to develop conflict resolution skills in their senior church leaders. The early work by DRCFC and University of Kent has found that, of the church organisations contacted, few had given any meaningful considera-tion to the need for a strategic and policy response to conflict resolution. There is currently little meaningful work being undertaken to understand the extent to which the independent churches in the UK deal with conflict and their policy decision to actively train their church leaders in conflict resolution skills. There is, however, a high level of interest in the issue of conflict from all the organisations contacted, all recognised that this was an issue that required early attention.

Negative impact of conflict on the church

Dobson *et al.* (1992) suggest that as societal ties become more fragile church members place even greater significance on their church commu-nity for the security that is lacking in other aspects of their lives. This can lead to stronger personal and emotional investment in the church commu-nity. When conflict arises, members may experience it as a betrayal and destruction of the spiritual and emotional security that they had 'bought into'. As a consequence, there is a greater tendency to avoid conflict or to feel the impact greater when it is managed poorly. This insight is particu-larly significant for the Black Church, where for many members, the church is a substitute for the extended family that are absent. Also, for others, the church might represent a sanctuary from the societal problems that they are fleeing. The church then becomes more than a place of worship; it is a place where the leadership and membership need to be made aware of ways in which they can provide holistic care for each other. This makes the work of the Black Church leader one which is particularly challenging, but the more worthwhile because of the importance that the church places in the lives of current and future members.

There is also a financial impact on churches that either ignore or manage conflict ineffectively. Over 39% of churches were financially affected as a direct result of the conflict, in the FACT 2005 survey. Almost 70% of those churches reported a loss in membership following conflict, with a quarter of the congregation resigning, retiring, being fired, or otherwise disengaged with the work of the church. In the *Christianity Today* survey, almost 70% of the pastors reported damaged relationships as the highest collateral damage following a church dispute. For any church, such an admission is a woeful symbol of failure of its very mission and purpose. Although there is a tendency to avoid dealing with conflict when it arises, the cost of not doing so far outweighs the risk of resolution intervention.

Approaches to dealing with conflict

Since conflict is a natural part of the world system (Luke 17:1), it should be viewed as an opportunity to grow or to bless someone else in the process, rather than dwelling on the negative aspects of conflict in the church such as divisiveness, power plays, and control issues. The church should begin to recognise conflict as an opportunity to turn a negative into a positive. A careful review of the vast amount of writings by Christian conflict resolution professionals demonstrates a consistency in their understanding of the positive outcome of well managed conflict and disputes in the church. Indeed, some like Donald E. Bossart (1990) believe that conflict is not just inevitable but also indispensable; a uniquely valuable component of our personal and organisational lives without which we lose our ability to hear new ideas and work together toward creative solutions. Bossart suggests that without conflict, no change or growth ever occurs.

Alternative Dispute Resolution

Alternative Dispute Resolution processes can be used to assist those church members who propose to resolve disputes other than by the traditional process of litigation. These processes include negotiation, conciliation, use of an ombudsman, arbitration and mediation. Of these, mediation is particularly suited to the church community. It is a structured but informal process conducted by a 'neutral third party' who intervenes in a conflict, with the consent of the involved parties, to facilitate private and joint meetings with the parties to formulate a mutually acceptable resolution.

Mediation is a powerful process that is premised on problem solving. It is practical, and addresses the emotional and personal needs of the participants and therefore is both immediately functional and therapeutic. It focuses on strengthening relationships and teaching skills that will equip people to manage, or even avoid, future conflicts. The skill and application of mediation is particularly suited to the church community since it helps to reconcile relationships whilst at the same time achieving resolution to the problem. Unlike the litigation process, which is rights-based, mediation allows the parties to address deep-seated concerns, it is culturally sensitive and the process is respectful of the theological and biblical perspectives that parties may bring to the mediation.

Benefits of mediation

The benefits to using mediation are extensive when compared to the traditional litigation process outlined in Table 5.1:

Table 5.1 Comparing mediation and litigation

Mediation	Litigation (court)
Confidential	Precedent set
Binding if there is an agreement	Usually binding
Informal	Formal
Decision not based only on law	Decision based primarily on law
Timely and fast	Time consuming
Usually win-win	Usually win-lose
Greater compliance with decision	Less compliance with decision
Relationships maintained	Relationships destroyed
Greater flexibility	Little flexibility

(*Source:* Deborah Mendez-Bowen, Institute for Dispute Resolution Limited (2006)

Preparing for conflict transformation

By April 2009 all employing organisations, including church organisations were expected to have processes in place for mediating conflicts and disputes that arise in the workplace as part of the UK statutory grievance process. This is already a voluntary option in the UK civil procedure rules and the courts already make recommendations for parties to seek a mediated outcome to resolve matters. Bossart (1990) suggests that the church has much to gain from the effective use of conflict. The conflict will be there, the question is, how will we choose to handle it? Conflict can alienate and block effective work or it can clarify and broaden the understanding of important issues, thereby becoming a source of motivation and a release of new energy since the more 'conflict-competent' the congregation, the more likely that love will be sustained to the glory of God.

In order to achieve this, an ongoing programme which teaches members that conflict can arise when there is a natural outgrowth of the human desire to be self-centred, has to be put in place. This accords well with the Scripture that teaches: 'there is not a just man upon earth, that doeth good, and sinneth not' (Ecclesiastes 7:20).

The leadership role in resolving church conflict

Church leaders have a key role to play in the mediation process. Leaders need to adopt a position that views conflict as an opportunity for church members' growth and discipleship. They need to support members to take a positive and practical perspective towards conflicts that will arise. There must be a commitment to resolve conflict within Biblical principles underpinned by skills in dispute resolution. Leaders also need to provide adequate resources for training, and since many conflicts result from miscommunication, it is imperative that the church's mission be clearly communicated to the congregation as well as to those who serve in a managerial capacity.

A Conflict Resolution Committee (CRC) is essential. One of the keys to selecting an effective CRC is the capacity of the members to be good peacemakers. Committee members should be well trained and possess the ability to develop good conflict resolution and mediation skills including for example, being confidential and empathic with excellent listening skills and being objective rather than judgmental while maintaining equality and neutrality. Christian dispute resolution organisations such as the Dispute Resolution Centre for Faith Communities (DRCFC), RTEQ Training Institute, Bridgebuilders and the Transitions Agency are able to assist in developing and delivering bespoke programmes for churches to ensure that their denominational needs are factored into the training.

For the CRC's work to be successful, the congregation must be able to understand the nature of conflict and the discipleship function of the church to seek resolution within as well as outside its walls. There are a range of reasons why some conflicts may not be able to be resolved internally. When this happens, the church should be able to seek the expertise of a Christian dispute resolution organisation, or Christian solicitors that specialise in dispute resolution. These experts will provide the church with a resource to help reconcile relationships and resolve conflicts that may not be resolvable using internal procedures.

Conflict resolution and the Black Church in the UK

The Foundation for Church Leadership (2008) recently published an excellent manual for church leaders on managing conflict, arising from a research development programme in which it was identified that over 70% of senior Anglican Church leaders who took part in the programme cited their inability to manage conflict effectively as one of the greatest challenges to their leadership.

There is an emerging body of knowledge and available expertise in conflict and dispute resolution in the professional and legal community and within the Christian church in the UK. Bridgebuilders, the conflict resolution and mediation programme run by the London Mennonite Centre, is one of the few established training programmes for church leaders. One Black Church leader who attended the programme has voiced concerns about the Eurocentric nature of the programme. There is therefore an identified need to look at a programme that will address the cultural dynamics of the Black Church in the UK. The DRCFC is currently working with the University of Kent and Black Church leaders to research this area in more detail and to develop a recognised accredited conflict resolution programme which will be able to produce trained and accredited Christian conflict and dispute resolution specialists, and accredited mediators who will have the skill and biblical insights to be able to help churches resolve conflicts and disputes in ways that focus on the positive benefit that conflicts can contribute to the growth and progress of the church.

Conclusion

As mentioned above, one option, proposed by Bryan H. Sanders (2008), is the formation of a Conflict Resolution Committee (CRC) with individuals trained in conflict resolution and mediation skills to help church members resolve their disputes in compliance with the standard of scripture and the principles of dispute resolution. Such a committee, he suggests, would need to have the same status as the most important committees of the church, but not be under the direct supervision of the senior minister since it will need to be perceived by the church members as objective, impartial, transparent and confidential. A committee of this nature could take many forms, but should include extensive training in order to constructively and effectively resolve conflicts.

Some commonalities of a CRC for constructively resolving conflicts should be considered. It should:

- Commit to resolving conflict scripturally
- Establish the committee's mission in writing
- Select committee members who possess skills in confidentiality, listening and objectivity
- Train committee and church members in conflict resolution and mediation skills
- Teach the congregation to understand the nature of conflict and the discipleship function of the church
- Be willing to seek assistance outside the church

Becoming skilled at conflict resolution requires professional training and years of experience. But there are some basic principles and techniques which can help Black Church leaders and their church to understand and utilise conflict when it occurs. A well trained internal Conflict Resolution Committee can be of great help, but sometimes a neutral third-party, outside of the congregation and sometimes outside of the organisation, may be required. These suggestions are based on the idea that change takes place in people not in the problem, and that conflicts are but the raw material for stronger relationships.

References

Bossart, Donald E. (1980) *Creative Conflict in Religious Education and Church Administration*, Birmingham, Alabama, Religious Education Press

Bossart, Donald E (1990) *Growing through Conflict. Reflect: A Series of Faculty Reflections on Contemporary Issues*, Denver, Colorado, Iliff School of Theology

Boyd-MacMillan, Eolene and Savage, Sara (2008) *Transforming conflict*, University of Cambridge

Bridgebuilders (2006) London Mennonite Centre, London

Dobson, Edward G, Leas, Speed B and Marshall, Shelly (1992) 'Masterminding Conflict and Controversy' *Christianity Today International*

Christianity Today (2004) Survey, *Christianity Today International*

Dudley, Carl S, Zingery, Theresa, Breeden, David (2000) *Insights into Congregational Conflicts*, Faith Communities Today

FACT 2000, 2005, Faith Communities Today, http://fact.hartsem.edu/

Goodman, Denise W. (2000) *Congregational Fitness: Healthy Practices for Layfolk*, Herndon, Virginia, Alban Institute publication

Halverstadt, Hugh F. (1991) *Managing Church Conflict*, Louisville, Kentucky, Westminster John Knox Press

Johnson, Douglas W. (1974) *Managing Change in the Church*, New York, Friendship Press

Mendez-Bowen, Deborah (2006) *Mediation Skills Workshop*, Institute for Dispute Resolution Limited

Newbold Jr., Robert T. (1980) *Conflict in the Black Church*, Christian Library.com http://ctlibrary.com/le/1980/spring/8012099.html

Newberger, Ken (2006) 'Conflict in my church' www.resolvechurchconflict.com http://www.resolvechurchconflict.com

Sanders, Bryan H. (2008) *Conflict Management Series*, Enrichment Journal, Pentecostal Ministry

Scazzero, Peter (2003) *The Emotionally Healthy Church*, Grand Rapids, Michigan, Zondervan Publishing Co.

Scottdale, P. (1983) *When Caring Is Not Enough: Resolving Conflicts through Fair Fighting*, Herald Press

http://ctlibrary.com/le/1980/spring/8012099.html

The Teal Trust: Understanding Conflict Bible Study

www.teal.org/www.christiandisputeresolution.com

http://www.christiandisputeresolution.com

Transforming Conflict (2008) York, Foundation for Church Leadership

6   *Politics and the Black Church*
Mark Richard Shelton Saint

Take My Hand, Precious Lord: **Thomas Dorsey**

As we witness a prepubescent but rapidly maturing twenty-first century, we find the Black Church in the UK in a powerful position, yet in a strange state of mind. Like a conscious amnesiac or an unconscious dreamer it searches for identity and purpose, and such inquiry viscerally cries out for critical reflection. What, or who, is the Black Church in the UK? What, if any, engagement should it have with politics? Is the church spiritually and politically impotent, or does it have the capacity to sow seeds of love, life, and transformation for the body politic? The theologian Tertullian posed a question in the 3rd century and wielded it like a weapon when he asked, 'What does Athens have to do with Jerusalem?' In laymen's terms, what does the church have to do with politics or contemporary culture?

In finding itself, in either regaining its memory or reflecting upon itself the Black Church in the UK will find out if it is spiritually relevant and what, if anything, it has to do with the greater society. Is it pimp or prophet? Whore or holy? Player or pastor? Colonizer or liberator? Bench player or 'big baller, shot caller?' As we engage with these questions of ontology (being) and praxis (doing), what emerges will determine the church's capacity to help protect, shape and positively transform society in this burgeoning new century. As in all things, let us begin at the beginning. Who is the Black Church?

In a world of lies, truth is revolutionary – and it is never more so than when standing beneath the unflinching gaze of the *Logon Eschaton*, the gaze of the Lord. In like manner, the Socratic dictum of 'Know Thyself' and the Pauline instruction to 'examine yourself to see if you be in the faith' (2 Corinthians 13:5) point with an impatient persistence to the need of all genuine critique to begin as ontological introspection. In such an effort, the concept of the 'Black Church', which is a ubiquitous classification, must be gently moved from the universal to the particular to be apprehended, comprehended, and summarily appreciated. Careful examination reflects and reveals subtle to stark differences in nationality, Christology and soteriology while concurrently sharing a common phenotype, ecclesiology and eschatology.

Differences aside, the Black Church is a multi-hued garment held together with a musicality born of suffering and joy, isolation and mutuality. Birthed out of necessity and in direct response to structural racism and cultural imperialism, the church emerged from a womb of genuine faith and an existential theological inconsistency. In laymen's terms, the Black Church emerged essentially because the established church 'talked the talk, but didn't walk the walk.' Like its counterpart in the US, African and African Caribbean believers faced a Christian experience that did not reflect the text from which it received its name. In light of the need for them to protect their biblical hermeneutic from a theological situation akin to the 'law of diminishing returns', Black Christians congregated and became a church unto themselves.

The revelation of this segregation is best demonstrated in the birth of the Black Church in America. In 1790, the Bethel African Methodist Episcopal Church was organized and founded in Philadelphia. One of the first official Black Churches in America and the founding church of the African Methodist Episcopal denomination, it was born from a church split in St George's Methodist Church. A growing and *soi-disant* 'refined' church, its members were accustomed to an ethos of status, and that status was also afforded to its members of African descent. Things seemed to be going well as the Blacks took on the social mores and cultural trappings of the majority White race, not recognizing of course that they were still social and spiritual parvenus in a Republic redefining itself. This illusion of social equality remained unchallenged in the church until the membership began to swell, as Albert Raboteau (1999, p.23) explains:

> One Sunday morning in the early 1790s, the Black members of St. George's learned to their surprise that they could not sit in the

benches they normally used. Instead, they were ordered to sit upstairs in a balcony that had recently been added at the rear of church. Although the situation was unfair – like the Whites, they had contributed to the remodelling of the church – they obeyed the order. As the opening prayer began, one of the White ushers told Absalom Jones, a respected Black parishioner, to get up and move from the front to the back of the balcony. Jones, a dignified man in his late forties, asked the usher to wait until the prayer ended, but the White man insisted he move immediately and motioned for another usher to help him lift Jones from his knees. As soon as the prayer was over, Jones and the rest of the Black worshipers stood and walked out of the church in a body.

In this record of witness, Raboteau captures a reality that resonates profoundly with many in the Black Church in the UK. With shifting populations from a massive migrant influx from Jamaica and other isles in the Caribbean in the 1950s, African Caribbeans found themselves looking for acceptance from their fellow Christians in established churches across the land, mostly to no avail. In 1955, the New Testament Church of God (NTCG) was formed in response to the aforementioned racial marginalization and cultural rejection by the Church of England. Eschewing the delimiting community that rejected them, they sojourned to communities of acceptance, namely creating their own denominations. Ira Brooks, the author of *Where Do We Go From Here?* (1982, p.13) unveils the social conditions that fostered the establishment of the NTCG:

> The new (Jamaican) immigrants with their different colour were seen by the indigenous community as a threat and especially the working class whose minds were still fresh with the deprivations of the recent World War II. As a result, misunderstanding and suspicion fermented into intolerance in the indigenous population and they were totally unprepared for any social or cultural adjustment. This unfortunate situation set off a chain reaction to which the immigrants themselves adopted a heightened sensitivity. Even those who had entrusted themselves into the fellowship of the established religious institutions of the country began to sense an environment of growing coldness. With the natural human desire for fellowship and acceptance, most of the

immigrants discarded their old religious differences, and in their need for consolation accepted the Pentecostal gospel message.

Meeting for worship in each other's homes, this disaffected community began to create an indigenous community deeply saturated in the Pentecostal tradition. Like the planting of churches in the first century they gathered, prayed, read the 'good book', listened to gospel preaching and broke bread together. Eventually, the congregations started approaching local established churches for the use of their buildings, and the rest is history.

Blessed Assurance, Jesus is Mine: **Fanny J. Crosby**

Although the Black Church in the US and the UK were birthed out of similar social and spiritual conditions, there are elements that are dissimilar primarily connected to historical political engagement and the dissidence between the African and African Caribbean paradigm. In the former, the US has a heralded story of political participation – both direct and indirect – while the Black Church in the UK does not boast such a chronicled history. In the latter, the tension between the African ideological ethos and the African Caribbean post-enslavement ethos is most virulent and defined in the UK and does not have a huge counterpart in the Black churches across the pond. Because of this latter reality, when attempting to appropriate just what the Black Church is, dissidence raises its head and a multiplicity of definitions rise to the fore with none claiming the right of prominence. A microcosmic example is the paper presented in 1999 at the Churches Community Work Alliance conference that raised the question, 'What do we mean by "Black Majority Church?"' The paper presented the following as suggested definitions:

> A church which belongs to one of the larger denominations identified as originating in the Black community e.g. New Testament Church of God.
>
> An independent church originating in the Black community (with a leadership and membership/congregation largely of Black people).
>
> Any church which has a leadership largely or completely of Black people.

Any church in which the majority of the members/congregation is Black (including Anglican, Roman Catholic, Methodist, Baptist, URC, etc.).

Each of these suggested definitions are uncertain, accept 'schism' as a normative state, and says to the world 'We are legion' when asked the singular question 'What is your name?'

The problem lies in the orientation of the hearer of the question. An occidental orientation will lean toward a definition that is static and rooted in a *temporal now*. An oriental orientation, on the other hand, seeks a dynamic answer that is rooted in the commonalities of 'now' and the possibilities of what can be. In other words, the same orientation that was used to keep colonized people colonized and enslaved persons enslaved is the orientation that keeps the potential power of the Black Church fragmented, politically impotent, and fighting battles that can only produce pyrrhic victories. There is a definition of what the Black Church is in the UK, but it is not limited to or subjugated by the limitations of the aformentioned discourse. Let's walk through what is and what can be and come to not only an answer of what the Black Church is, but also of what its engagement with politics has been and could be.

The Black Church in the UK represents shades of identity defined by nationality and colonial history. Lumped together beneath a single banner, the African church and the African Caribbean church stand in marked contrast to one another and yet are connected in bonds of mutuality. Most congregations that are considered a part of the 'Black Church' are organized via these two national origins. I have used two mega churches in the UK as examples, to highlight these contrasts.

Arguably the largest church in the UK, Kingsway International Christian Church (KICC) has over 10,000 members, the vast majority of which are Nigerian. Ruach Ministries, another Black Majority Church in the UK with over 6,000 worshipping members, is mostly African Caribbean. Despite both churches broadcasting across the globe and claiming an international following, nationality still constitutes their core membership. This relationship to their core constituency speaks to complex structures that are beyond the remit of this chapter, nevertheless it is noteworthy to mention the base constructs on which these differences revolve: Scriptural hermeneutic (holiness, prosperity gospel, evangelical), Reformed or Armenian theology, polity, Pentecostal vs. Charismatic ethos, national origin, missional or insular theological trajectory. While these churches have many differences, they and the branches of the Black Church that they represent have key things in common: ecclesiology, Christology, eschatology, and most importantly, faith.

One of the core similarities and intrinsic connections between the disparate elements in the Black Church is its ecclesiology. The tribal history and the familial connections create a mutual commonality that is an essential element of the Black Church at its best. It generates a kind of *hermeneutic of hospitality* and a *hermeneutic of inclusion* that inherently creates *koinonia* (community). J. Deotis Roberts (1974, p.177) engages in this as he delves into family systems from a biblical basis.

> A family membership is assumed and anticipated when there is a conversion of any member. In a similar manner a Jewish rabbi may reckon his membership in terms of families. This is, in essence, the model which the new Black church style must follow. While we take our cue from the practice of 'familyhood' rooted in our African heritage, it will provide in the Black church that reality of community which will make of it at once a family of God and a household of power.

Rooted solidly in scripture while also bearing witness to a shared origin, this ecclesiology creates the bonding necessary to unify and become what Dr Martin Luther King Jr. called, 'the Beloved Community'. Roberts (1975, pp.36, 40) sheds light on this in another one of his works on the Black Church.

> There is a need for (a) careful theological statement on the Black Church. The purpose of this theological enterprise will be to discern clearly the nature of the Black Church in order to understand more adequately its mission. The very nature of the Black Church is in the mission of liberation ... The Black theologian has a great opportunity to make constructive use of 'the family' as the people of God expressed through the Black Church. Thus we speak of the Beloved Community, the Black Church as the Family of God.

When Roberts posits that ecclesiology within the Black Church can be used as a model of what it is to be the 'family of God', he strikes what is transformational and essential in the ontological exegesis of the term. Anytime one embarks on a quest for definition – a question of *being* more than a question of *doing* – they immediately run into terms of ultimate meaning. Inherent in the ecclesiology of the *Black Church* is the ontological proof that such a classification exists in the first place.

Ecclesiology, as a lived and organic experience, must be centered upon a charismatic ideal or a subject greater than itself. The radius and circumference of the Black Church as a dynamic community is shaped by Jesus of Nazareth. Although the view of Jesus varies within the Black Church community, there is a distinct unity in the ontology of Jesus the Christ and his programmatic empathy for and mission to those Franz Fanon (1965) called the 'Wretched of the Earth'. Black Church biblical conservatism on the belief in the literal virgin birth, the life, crucifixion, death and physical resurrection is amazingly unified. They are also strangely unified on Jesus' missional connection to the poor, irrespective of what words are used to define the term 'gospel' (prosperity, evangelical, etc.), and the expectation of the '*parousia*' *of the Christ* and his eschatological role. These distinctives separate themselves from the non-essential and solidly define a *fatidic* community of faith. A community that by nature is consistent, dynamic, delineated from other aspects of Christendom, and yet firmly a part of the Christian faith and is, in power and ethos, the 'Kingdom of God.' Hence, the definition of the Black Church is greater than phenotype or national origin (although it stands as a distinctive), but is one that is constituted by a high Christology, an oriental ethos, a dynamic ecclesiology, and a missional predilection for social justice and liberation beginning with the 'least of these' (Matthew 25).

Great is Thy Faithfulness: Thomas O. Chisholm

The Black Church in the UK, by its inherent nature, peculiar history, and strategic placement has the spiritual obligation and biblical mandate to minister to the world, and to do so will require an active engagement in the political arena. As previously mentioned, in relation to its American church counterparts there is not a great-chronicled history, but there has been a concerted effort for political engagement in the UK. Over the years, there have been many attempts to engage in the political process with limited success. Let's take a look at a few of those attempts and their results.

One cannot begin to engage in a conversation about the Black Church and political participation without mentioning Bishop Eric A. Brown. The Administrative Bishop of the New Testament Church of God at the turn of the twenty-first century did much in the previous decade to engage in prophetic witness, and has continued that tradition. Paradigmatic of this is his work in 1996. Working together with Neil Jameson, they founded the Citizens Organising Foundation, initially called the East London Communities Organisation. A group comprised of organizations joining together to fight for social justice – represented in its current 'living wage' and 'Strangers to Citizens' campaigns – it is marked by the absence of Black Church participation beyond a few congregations in the denomination.

Similarly, we can cite the work of Reverend Nims Obunge, the Pastor and founder of Freedom's Ark Church, which he launched in 1993. A successful minister, he was challenged by Bishop Eric Brown of the NTCG to become more involved in the political process to better represent his community and to bring about change. Reverend Nims answered that challenge and founded The Peace Alliance, a national crime reduction charity working on a local basis in partnership with faith community and voluntary organisations, the police and local councils and other statutory agencies. An active member of many boards in advisory and other practical capacities, he is currently engaged in the political process and his organization stands as an example of one of the ways the Black Church can engage with politics, both in the UK and abroad.

Another attempt at a prophetic political connection was the Black Christian Civic Forum. Organized by David Muir in 1999, it aimed to increase the political involvement and social action of Black Christians nationally. Muir made a valiant effort to bring together the disparate elements in Black church leadership to establish a powerful voice for justice, but that sound was ultimately stifled by the lack of cohesion and discord of the occidental orientation.

As this cannot be an in-depth study of this subject, I will not list the many start-ups and tyronic overtures of the Black Church into the political sphere, and all the people involved, but I would be remiss not to mention as a matter of record the advocacy of people like the Revd Joel Edwards, Councillors Betty Evans-Jacas and Lorna Campbell, the recent connection and involvement of Bishop John Francis and Ruach Ministries into the city-wide and national political conversation, Bishop Wayne Brown and London Citizens, the Revd Katie Kirby and the African Caribbean Evangelical Alliance, the Revd Julia Smith from the Seventh Day Adventists, the Revd Claudette Douglas's seminal work at Churches Together in Britain and Ireland, David Shosanya and Wale Hudson-Roberts from the Baptist Union, and Bishop Joe Aldred and his colleague Richard Reddie and Set All Free at Churches Together in England.

Despite the great work of the aforementioned, and many more who deserve more credit for their work, there has not been a marked, sustained political movement by the Black Church in the UK. When placed beside the political engagement in the US, the Black Church here looks almost stagnant – but as always, looks can be deceiving. Throughout history, political engagement and spiritual movements have always been prompted by social conditions. The sacred and the secular both demand correctives when untenable situations become normative and create an environment with no social homeostasis. Local communities and even nations at times become so unbalanced as to have a need for deliverance. The soteriology of the Black Church has at its core a power to deal with spiritual deliverance, 'sozo' and with physical deliverance, 'rhyomai', terms that are both translated in English as 'salvation'. History proves that when this imbalance becomes intolerable, a saviour or deliverer will rise. I believe that the many entrees into the political sphere by the Black Church in the UK have not been failures at all, but stand on the one hand as planted seeds waiting for seasonal conditions to change, and on the other hand as catalysts: 'Prepare ye the way of the Lord' (Isaiah 40:3).

What will mobilize the Black Church in the twenty-first century and make it more active politically is the social pressure it is currently under. Many churches are entering into the political process out of necessity in order to acquire land, planning permission, and/or funding for building projects, and are running into difficulty. The Charity Commission has displayed ignorance at best or antagonism at worse towards some of the larger Black churches. Kingsway International Christian Centre (KICC) was investigated for over two years, which the church claims cost them over £10 million, and concluded that the church was innocent of any wilful wrongdoing. This signalled to many 'seeds' that their time had come. The recent investigations and demonization of popular churches by the media have also caused some forward thinking.

At the grassroots, church members are furious because parents have been denied places for their children at 'good' schools because they are not a part of the Church of England or Churches Together in Britain and Ireland (CTBI); and the mixture of local youth crime and reported police corruption, racism, and structural mendacity have made the atmosphere so volatile that it has caused some politically silent leaders in the Black Church to feel like they have 'fire shut up in their bones'. The season is changing and it will be the Black Church peacefully, but prophetically leading the way. A foreshadowing of this has been the shifting of alliances within the Anglican family as members follow the leadership of the Black Church in Africa in regard to the homosexual issue.

We've Come This Far by Faith: **Albert A. Goodson**

The Black Church in the UK stands as the most capable of all organizations and social forces to create positive change for the country. It is the fastest growing organization in the country, and its capacity to impact on the political process is unprecedented. A bastion of socio-political power with literally hundreds of thousands within its body politic, the Black Church stands as the *sine qua non* of prophetic activity and social justice in the UK. Its organizational skills and ability to mobilize have been fine-tuned; its leadership has been well schooled, and through resistance it has developed the strength to overcome and endure.

The tie that binds everything else together in the Black Church is faith. Through the many toils and snares it has encountered in the UK, faith is the source of its fiery passion and the guide of all the necessary elements that make the Black Church what it is. The ontology of faith is defined by the writer of Hebrews as the 'substance of things hoped for and the evidence of things not seen' (11:1), but the praxis of faith is best defined by the pre-eminent theologian of the twentieth century, Paul Tillich, who defines faith as that of 'ultimate concern'.

> Faith is the state of being ultimately concerned: the dynamics of
> faith are the dynamics of man's ultimate concern. Man, like every
> living being, is concerned about many things, above all about
> those which condition his very existence, such as food and shelter.
> But man, in contrast to other living beings, has spiritual concerns
> – cognitive, aesthetic, social, political … If it claims ultimacy it

demands total surrender of the will of him who accepts this claim, and it promises total fulfilment even if all other claims have to be subjected to it or rejected in its name

(1957, p.1)

In the Black Church faith in God is pre-eminent. It infiltrates every aspect of governance and saturates every one of its parts to make it whole. By faith, the Black Church not only will but must engage in the political power structure; for if government is 'for the people by the people' then to bring salvation to the people it must inherently connect to them. By faith then, the Black Church will bring the power to save and deliver, and by obedience in faith it will be able to reach the secular world.

Finally, in community organizing parlance, power is *organized people and organized money*. In biblical tradition, the Holy Spirit gives power and faith and becomes the vehicle in which that power is shared. Interestingly enough, when the Holy Spirit came in Acts 2, the resultant effect was organized people, 'three thousand were added that day' (verse 41) and organized money 'they all gave to those who had need' (verse 45). For illustrative purposes, it took eight years of George Bush's policies and more than ten years of Barack Obama's community organizing, fuelled by an enduring faith in God, to make him the President of the United States of America. In that vein, the power of the New Testament Church of God, the Church of God of Prophecy, the Church of God in Christ, the Redeemed Christian Church of God, the Mountain of Fire and Miracle Ministries, the Black Baptists, Pentecostal Independents, and other Black Church groups combined strategically, will be an active, long-lasting force in the UK in the years ahead.

References

Brooks, Ira V. (1982) *Where do we go from here?: A History of 25 Years of the New Testament Church in the UK 1955–1980*, Great Britain, Charles Raper

Churches Workers Alliance: http://www.ccwa-i.org.uk/index.php/news_articles

Fanon, Franz (1965) *The Wretched of the Earth*, Macgibbon and Kee

Peace Alliance, www.peacealliance.org.uk

Raboteau, Albert J. (1999) *Canaan Land: A Religious History of African Americans*, Oxford University Press

Roberts, J. Deotis, (1974) *A Black Political Theology*, Westminster Press

Roberts, J. Deotis, *A Black Ecclesiology of Involvement*, *Journal of Religious Thought 32*, (Spring-Summer 1975)

Tillich, Paul (1957) *Dynamics of Faith*, Harper and Row Publishers

7   *Social Issues and the Black Church*

Les Isaac

Early reflections

In the 1970s when I first began to reflect on what I saw of the Black Church Movement in the UK, I recall observing an introverted institution made up of organisations that were 'holding the fort until Christ come again'. Black churches' activities were aimed at those already inside, and there was a massive gulf between those that were Christians inside the church and those that were non-Christians, or at least non-church-going, outside it. I wanted to spend the majority of my time outside the four walls of the church, to demonstrate the gospel in practical ways by making sure it was expressed right where people were facing real socio-economic and political issues. I said, 'If you are a drug user, then the message of Jesus for you is bound up with how Jesus can help you out of your addiction', or, 'If you are a gunman, the gospel begins for you with getting the gun out of your hand'. The message of Jesus has to have a contextualised, tangible out-working for the jobless, homeless, under-educated, disadvantaged and excluded.

In the 1970s, mission evangelism did not appear to be on the church's agenda as it is today. The church was lacking a heart, a mind and a strategy for outreach to its wider community. My vision was to see the gospel, in its holistic concern for the whole person, shared in places and among people that the church as a whole was not touching, or where it was not effective. I could see the need for Christians to get into places where there were social problems, violence and crime. I wanted to make my Christianity fit right into that social context; go into those areas of life and bring Jesus to them. This task, however, was bigger than me because mission evangelism, far from just being one person's gift, is a ministry for the whole church. Mission evangelism is actually the key to challenging and reviving the church, and a mean by which Christians behave as 'salt and light' (Matthew 5:13) in the world.

Community relevance

In the early 1980s, when I was in my twenties, I was called to pastor a small congregation in South London. I became a pastor with a heart for mission evangelism that I wanted to infect my members with! Together we were going to impact our community for God. Every congregation needs to think about how it can serve its community spiritually, socially and practically. I very much wanted our church to be locally focused so that it could put its community first, and be the focal point of that community. As a leader, I found I had a lot to do to change people's thinking, so as part of our preparation for growth and readiness to receive new people, I instigated seminars and training on the social, historical and religious issues that gave our community its identity.

Churches need to be focused in their outreach, so I asked myself, 'What are the needs of this community?' I firmly believe that if you want to serve the place where you live and minister, you need to know it; you need to get out there, walk around on a Saturday night, Sunday afternoon, on weekdays, to see what is going on. I spent time at the town hall and the library researching the community we wanted to serve. It is difficult to pray effectively and intelligently, and plan strategically for the needs of a community, unless we study and pray over such information. That is what we did. My aim was to 'scratch where it itched'. After a few years my congregation had grown significantly and we were faced with the challenge of finding larger accommodation. We chose to rebuild and enlarge the existing premises; which was consistent with our ethos of community outreach and relevance. We needed to build something we could use to cater for the whole person.

We organised a survey of the borough in which the church was situated. To my amazement, I discovered that our locality had the highest rate of single-parent families in the borough, as well as one of the highest educational drop-out rates. It was after that that I began to realise that if we wanted to reach our community, we ought to think about providing nursery facilities and educational facilities in the church building. I drafted a feasibility study for the church's proposals in this area. I didn't want a church that would close its doors from one Sunday to the next, maybe opening again for its midweek Bible study. I believe a church building should be open to the community, and be for the community, as well as being a place of worship. It is not the building that is the most important thing; it is there to serve the people. I had no problem with the idea that we use the church during the week as a gym, or a youth club, because it was serving the community.

We decided that we would have a nursery for forty children as well as run a Saturday school and a homework club. I was already working closely with local schools, and as a church we wanted to develop this. I would occasionally get called in to help resolve problems in the nearby school, and had also been on weekends away with teachers and children. As I saw it, there should be bridges from the church into the community, and from the community into the church, and I wanted people to be constantly crossing those bridges. In this regard I once led a group of students onto the streets in Birmingham, and the remit I gave them was not to make converts but to walk the area around their church with a questionnaire. I gave them two questions to present to their community: 1) 'Do you know our Church?' and 2) 'What do you think our church should be doing for the community?' Lastly, they were to take the opportunity to tell members of the public what the church was doing and give details of its various programmes and meetings.

They discovered that although their church was on a main road and very prominent, few people really were aware of it. Most interestingly, the conversations they had with people opened up a huge catalogue of social needs and areas in which local people wanted the church to be involved. The students that day heard how bored young people were, how there was nowhere for them to go which would be safe and free from drugs. Others told them that there were many people in the neighbourhood with mental health needs. They were asked, 'What is your church doing about mental health?' All these are real and big issues! A church must get the right people in place to deal with them, and have the finance to make a difference. This particular group of students came back overwhelmed by the needs they had heard people talking about, and many of them asked

'Where do we start?' Simply, they had to get back to the church's need to have a burden and a vision for its community. Out of that came prayer, listening to God, analysing their strengths and weaknesses; and slowly building up from the things they knew they could do, and growing into the areas that were more challenging.

Our responsibility is not just to preach the gospel but to make sure that people can feel the power of the gospel. This might mean going to a family where a child has just dropped out of school; talking and praying with them and encouraging the child to go to school. Demonstrating the power of the gospel may mean dealing with the teenager who has got pregnant and being able to offer a nursery place for her baby so that the mother's education can continue. These are the things that make us genuine and credible, and they are the fulfilment of the gospel in us.

It is very important that each church looks carefully at what it is trying to do in the community. Are you just seeking a nice building for Sunday morning worship, or are you going to establish something that reflects the kingdom of God and the holistic gospel that Christians believed in? I feel very strongly that any new building has to reflect the social, spiritual and educational needs of the community. My heart is for each church property to be a place that caters for the whole person; a place of worship, education and care, and a place where people can come for leisure activities. One of the biggest challenges for the church as we move further into the twenty-first century is to be relevant to the whole person. We will struggle to exist legitimately if we do not reflect the needs of our community in our preaching, in our social action, even in the design and use of the buildings that we have. Our ultimate challenge is to engage, with what to some will be a new paradigm.

The Urban Trinity

Partnership happens when people and organisations come together, recognising that goals are achieved best through cooperation and teamwork, using the strengths and abilities of all parties. Working in partnership for me has the ultimate goal of benefiting the community. I partnered more, in the early years, with local schools and community organisations. As years have gone by, I have come to perceive that other partners are important to achieve effective and lasting change, such as other churches, local authorities, the police and non-Christian groups.

As the saying goes, 'There's nothing new under the sun.' Some fourteen years ago, whilst reading *The Urban Christian* by American theologian Dr Raymond Bakke (1987), I was struck by his analysis of the city of Chicago. He looked at what different cultures and groups of people brought to the city. He highlighted the Irish community and made three key observations about them. First, the Irish in Chicago recognised the concept of government and the power of it to create and implement far-reaching policies. Consequently, over the years, in that city, the Irish sought to produce politicians. Second, they noted the power and authority of the police in the city – this was a position or institution of great importance, therefore they encouraged their people to become police officers. Third, the Irish understood the power and influence of the priest in the community upon individual lives. Notably, the priest was more influential where Irish personnel had moved into the police force, or local government and still submitted themselves to the ritual and leadership of the religious institution they had allegiance to. Like Bakke, I regard this 'Urban Trinity' consisting of the church, the police and local government, as the three biggest 'gangs' in the city, due to their influence, resources and leadership.

Black Churches in Britain, over the past fifty years or so, have developed, consolidated and are now at the stage where we can establish partnerships on a basis of equality with the other two components of the 'Urban Trinity'. Each element of the Urban Trinity brings to the partnership in Britain's cities its own distinctiveness to achieve more than they can independently. The police have power, influence and resources. In differing ways local government has power, influence and resources – but the church has Holy Spirit-led vision, passion, influence and resources, which differ from the other two. Power is the ability to make or hinder happenings. Influence is the ability to convince others to do what you want them to do. Resources are in essence revenue, capital and personnel. As the church, our vision comes from God, and we are passionate about what He has commissioned us to do. Black Churches in the city form one of the largest, most influential and cohesive community groups. They therefore have a significant contribution and role to play as part of the Urban Trinity. The church brings to the table some of what the police and local government do not, and both of them bring elements of what the church lacks. We need one another in the struggle to redeem our community.

I recall a meeting just over a year ago with a Police Superintendent at which we discussed the matter of community safety. As I was leaving the station, I observed police officers and vans coming and going, and I suddenly remembered my sentiments thirty years prior. In those days, when I saw a police station, I would shout, '*bun* Babylon!' My attitude was born out of my experience and a history of antagonism between the police and the Black community; consequently, I saw as desirable the demise of what I saw as principalities and powers. Whatever our past experience of the police, central or local government, we must engage and partner with them for future effectiveness and change.

Working together on social issues

The Black Majority Church has come a long way since the 1950s. Having worked in it and with it, I have seen many developments and changes. I saw our elders plant churches, set up Saturday and Sunday schools and luncheon clubs. Some congregations developed their local ministry, and some, local social action programmes. Many such churches were very effective. However, there were significant shortcomings that hindered progress. For example, programmes were set up for local and immediate needs with little regard for the long term and strategic planning. Some ministries and small projects were birthed out of personal vision and tenacity and would have benefited from shared resourcing and support from other Black churches. I recall a mentality that can be summed up in the words of the old song, 'You in your small corner and I in mine.' Many leaders said they were working for Jesus in their 'vineyard', when in fact the reality was that fragmented efforts were confined to 'allotments' because of lack of partnership. The 'politics' of partnership got in the way; and I dare to state explicitly that partisan political factors rendered some pastors incapable of taking the 'bull by the horns' when making conscious decisions about working together for the sake of our communities and the gospel. 'Mistrust' was the overarching issue, and under this heading, I have identified three factors which have fuelled this problem and hindered the Black Church's potential to identify and tackle the many social issues that are prevalent in our communities.

Rivalry

Since the 1950s, there have always been church leaders who are articulate, strong, charismatic and dynamic. God has used these qualities to develop great ministries, sound leaders and social action programmes. They had a vision for their day. However, many felt threatened by these strong personalities, as their ministries and influence grew. Liaison and open dialogue were hampered by insecurities, superiority complexes and a sense of competition.

Sheep-stealing

There was a general expectation that once you joined a congregation or worked on a local initiative with a church, you would never leave or help elsewhere. To do so was seen as a form of disloyalty. This attitude still exists to some degree and is fed by a misguided sense of 'ownership', a fear that if members go and get involved in 'kingdom business' elsewhere, they will be lured away and will not come back.

Splits

In the early days, Black Church congregations experienced a lot of 'splits', i.e. individuals or groups within churches 'falling out' and leaving to form another church. The advantage of this was that it spread the work and took some people into different areas with the gospel and social action. Out of people's bad experience of 'splits', however, came a wariness of partnerships on a deeper level. Under the surface, in many quarters, this mistrust still exists and continues to enforce barriers to partnership, wider progress and greater effectiveness in dealing with current social issues.

The benefits of partnership

Twenty-first century Christian ministry has to be holistic because the social challenges we face are big, complex and far-reaching. This can only be achieved through partnerships. Take for instance, prison ministries. Many African and Caribbean churches have a prisons outreach ministry, which is very good. These ministries have tended to focus on visiting inmates, holding services and offering pastoral care. I have seen first hand some excellent initiatives as I have visited prisons around the country. However there are two fundamental areas that are not being emphasised enough.

Firstly, preventative work. Black Churches need to consider what ministry should be developed in local communities to prevent, particularly, young men and boys ending up in prison. We know that there is a link between the high levels of school exclusions in their adolescent years and the high level of incarceration of Black men (Blair 2001). We know that children of single parents, coupled with a number of other social factors are more likely to end up in trouble with the law. What ministry do we have in place to cater for these great challenges? Working together Black Churches stand a better chance of dealing with these issues.

Second, rehabilitative care ministry. We know that many young ex-offenders struggle to stay out of prison (Social Exclusion Unit Report 2002). Therefore there needs to be a stronger focus on how we help people from becoming prolific re-offenders. Ministries which tap into local services and develop their own in the areas of training, employment and housing can help young people successfully exit a life of crime and anti-social behaviour.

These ways of working cannot be the sole effort of an individual congregation or member. This ministry has to be a part of a church's wider agenda locally and nationally. And if there is to be any major in-road or sustained impact upon this problem, African and Caribbean churches must develop strategic partnerships to realise their local and national vision for change. Partnership means bringing together expertise, finance, personnel and capital. It means the shared ownership of and response to issues by churches alone as well as by working within the Urban Trinity. Social challenges in the African and Caribbean communities are increasing in scale. Indicators do not show signs of abatement, therefore the church community must be proactive in developing an infrastructure and appropriate system of resource allocation to make a valid contribution and response to these challenges.

The church must aim to accommodate, facilitate and support individuals within their congregation who have a strong vision for responding to particular social needs. Churches should create the infrastructure to develop initiatives, support and accountability. The challenge for us as Black Church leaders is to be more proactive at senior leadership level, to anticipate the social challenges and therefore create a structure and put resources in place to address them.

A practical example: Street Pastors

In 1995, Ascension Trust – the organisation of which I am the Director – studied the challenges that faced our urban communities. We saw a need to challenge the church in terms of its urban mission, in particular, how it relates to local communities. We made several observations:

1. Whenever the church went out, it was always telling the world how bad it is.
2. There was a lack of consistency and continuity in terms of engaging people outside the church.
3. We tended to spend a lot of money on materials with very little results.
4. There were some local 'no go areas' – groups or localities – where church people never ventured.

What we discovered from our analysis, on the street, was that people wanted friendship, relationship and a show of caring. From 2001 to 2002, we continued our process of investigation by holding community meetings, where we gave local people opportunities to articulate their concerns and respond to the question, 'What could the church do to help?' Out of this dialogue, a number of themes became evident. Firstly, communities believe that the church has a vital role to play in restoring and helping those who feel excluded and marginalised. Second, the church holds important values that underpin good community ethics and its role is to relate and encourage those values wherever possible. Third, the church is a historic institution that the majority identify with as a place of good grounding, social values and experience of positive spirituality.

One of the community forum events that year was held in a church building where 90% of those gathered were non-Christians. During the course of the heated and heartfelt discussion, a number of Christians walked in. This sudden influx encouraged me momentarily as I thought they had come to add their voices and thoughts to this very important debate. Unfortunately my excitement was short-lived as I observed them walk in and skirt around the edges of the meeting hall to gather in the adjacent room – for choir practice! The juxtaposition of these two events was both stark and grave. Whilst we, in one hall, were discussing the problem of guns, drugs and gangs and how best to engage the issues, the activity of the Christians in the next hall was choir, i.e. 'business as usual' and disengaged from their local community's issues. I found this disturbing and challenging. It also highlighted the challenges that we face as the Black Church in Britain. We cannot afford to continue our Christianity as if it were 'business as usual' in the face of so many social ills.

At the end of our tour, a number of recommendations and action points were agreed, which were based on a commonality of values shared by the church and the wider community. The five core values were:

1. The sacredness and sanctity of human life.
2. Valuing and honouring the community.
3. Being a person of integrity.
4. Taking personal responsibility.
5. The growth and development of the individual to their fullest potential.

The essence of the churches' response, it was agreed, should be practical – caring, listening and helping, in the following ways:

1. Caring was to be demonstrated by being available there in the context in which the community lives and moves, i.e. the streets, clubs, etc.
2. Listening was to be demonstrated in a willingness to hear and acknowledge what people wanted to say first and to respond to that.
3. Helping was to be demonstrated in supporting the individual and making links with them to agencies that could address their particular needs.

The Street Pastors Initiative was birthed following this consultation period with churches and non-church communities. As training began for volunteers there was some media attention which focused on the initiative, but also polled members of the public about its likely reception on local streets. Responses on the whole were at best guarded and at worst, extremely sceptical. Individuals wrote in about the prospect of Street Pastors being 'judgmental', 'spoiling their fun' and 'preaching at them about their lifestyle'. However, as teams started to walk the streets of Lambeth, people were inquisitive to know who we were, what we were doing and why. People were actually stopping us – not the other way around! They noticed our practical help and sensitive interactions and ultimately commended our presence on the streets.

On one occasion, as I was speaking to four white young men, one of them asked, 'Why has it taken so long for the church to do this?' He concluded by saying, 'You guys are good guys,' and gave me a hug! This was 2:30 a.m. on the streets of London. On another occasion, a drug dealer came to me on Atlantic Road in Brixton as we were engaging with young people standing outside of a club. He whispered to me, 'Pastor, you're doing a good job – don't get discouraged, keep up the good work!' Today the Street Pastors Initiative is spreading across the country and abroad and symbolises what is possible when the church gets involved in the social affairs of our community.

References

Bakke, Dr Raymond (1987) *The Urban Christian*, Nottingham, InterVarsity Press

Blair, Maud (2001) *Why Pick On Me – School Exclusion and Black Youth*, London, Trenthan Books

Social Exclusion Unit Report (2002), *Reducing Re-offending by Ex-prisoners*, London, Crown Copyright

8   *Elders and the Black Church*

Dionne Gravesande

Myrtle Octavia Liburd was born on 29 July 1923 in a small village named
Cole Hill, in the parish of St John on the island of Nevis in the Leeward
Islands in the West Indies. Myrtle's early life comprised of working alongside her family to maintain house and home, this included looking after
siblings and picking cotton on the family owned land. Access to school and
further education was severely limited and career options as we know
them today just did not exist. The education Myrtle received was supplemented by an enthusiastic Sunday School teacher. Christian education
was an area of church life which Myrtle enjoyed and thrived on. The
principles and values of the Christian Gospel gave her a framework and
outlook on which she built and maintained her adult life. Hope, vision,
belief and determination became the outworking of Myrtle's faith. Aged
37, Myrtle left the distant shores of Nevis and travelled to London,
England. No doubt she was filled with the excitement of a new vision of a
life for herself and her family. Armed with little more than her dreams,
hopes and faith, the vision was that life in England would present the
opportunities in which Myrtle would flourish economically, socially and
spiritually. She would serve her God alongside new found brothers and
sisters in the motherland. What could go wrong?

Myrtle's experience once reaching the shores of England was not what
she expected. The dream which kept her saving the hundreds of dollars for
several years to meet the costs of the 'passage' slowly drained away.
Where were the streets paved with gold? Where was the fellowship of the
communion which welcomed the stranger with love and affection, and

where was the sun? Myrtle spent the next decade or so trying to make sense of this new experience and during this time her tolerance and response to the raw and ugly face of racism was quite remarkable. Throughout Myrtle's 46 years in England, she built a strong prayer life and joined with other migrants from the Caribbean to pray through the troubles and strife of being in a strange land. These early prayer communities became an important part of her life and Myrtle often spoke of her absolute belief that God would intervene in her situation and bring about deliverance, healing and prosperity. Their solidarity of experience, culture and faith created deep roots and a lifetime of fellowship. Myrtle demonstrated and lived out two Christian teachings throughout her life; one, to love the Lord God truthfully and faithfully and, two, to love her neighbour as Jesus had loved her. It is these two principles above all else Myrtle taught me and although at times I grapple with the latter more than the former, her gentle words remind me God is able to do immeasurably more than all we ask or imagine (Ephesians 3:20).

Myrtle Liburd was my grandmother and was the first member of my family to travel and settle in England. Her story could so easily fit the story of many of the hundreds and thousands of Caribbean migrants who came to Britain between 1948 and 1972 to make a better life for themselves and their families. Like many, her plan was to stay five years and then return 'home', but four decades later, in retrospect, could it be that there was a bigger plan in the making? This was the beginning of an influx that was to change the Christian landscape of Britain.

Roots and routes

The Revd S. E. Arnold (1992) recalls, for those who had never travelled beyond the confines of their village communities, the challenges of the voyage across the Atlantic. The uncomfortable train journey across Italy, Switzerland and France to Calais, and across the English Channel to Dover were traumatic experiences that many have never forgotten. Some travelled other routes or by air, whilst a minority came on the famous banana boats. The *Windrush* testimonies bear witness to the major contribution African Caribbean people made to British Society in all aspects of its life, culture and wealth. The memory of these experiences is a source of tension between African Caribbean people (including their descendants) and (indigenous) British people. These experiences are the main factors that have developed the roots (beginnings) and routes (journeys) of African Caribbean Christianity in Britain today.

African Caribbean people are primarily the descendants of West Africans captured or obtained in trade from African procurers. They were then shipped by European slave traders to British, French, Dutch, Spanish, and Portuguese colonies founded from the sixteenth century. On arrival, the majority of Africans were set to work on the vast Caribbean sugar plantations for the benefit of the colonial powers. Migration from the Caribbean to Britain was rare before the Second World War, and little is known about the experiences of those who made the move. There are records of small communities in the ports of Cardiff, Liverpool and South Shields dating back to the mid-nineteenth century. These communities were formed by freed slaves following the abolition of slavery. Typical occupations of the early migrants were footmen or coachmen, though a growing Caribbean presence in the British military led to approximately 15,000 migrants arriving in the north-west of England around the time of the First World War to work in munitions factories (Reddie 2002).

Since the Second World War many African Caribbean people migrated to North America and Europe, especially to the United States, Canada, the UK, France, and the Netherlands. As a result of the losses during the war, the British government began to encourage mass immigration from the countries of the British Empire and Commonwealth to fill shortages in the labour market. The 1948 British Nationality Act gave British citizenship to all people living in Commonwealth countries, and full rights of entry and settlement in Britain. Many West Indians were attracted by better prospects in what was often referred to as the 'mother country'. At this point is it worth noting African Christians have a different history and experience and their routes have a variety of implications for African Christianity in the Britain today. That said it is also important to recognise there is no single experience of being African or Caribbean, but many.

The majority of Black elders are profoundly religious people and these people are the largest component of the Black Church attendees, in what is a rapidly growing social and religious phenomenon in Britain and Ireland (Reddie 2002). It is well documented both literally and by testimonies that many of the Black Churches well known today were established by groups of families for the sake of prayer, fellowship and support. In addition they found themselves being able to express worship through their culture.

These kinship networks were used to recruit new members and issues of struggle, marginality and diversity often identified the membership of these groups. Black Christians belong to a rich variety of denominations of different histories, traditions, theologies and cultures. Today, many belong to traditional mainstream churches, others to national 'Black-led' or 'Black-majority' Churches (BMCs) as well as to independent fellowships. And as Anthony Reddie (2002) argues, these individuals are uniquely placed to undertake the role as guardians and heirs of a tradition that straddles the world of yesteryear – in this case a world that was situated in a pre- and post-colonial era in the Caribbean and Africa – and the world of today.

In researching material for this chapter I undertook a number of informal interviews with Black elders. These were predominantly people of West Indian descent and worshipping in the New Testament Church of God. In those conversations, it was clear that the experiences of the elder genera-tion are ones of deep and at times unquestionable commitment to con-servative Christian beliefs and values. Their oral tradition speaks to the experience and rich spirituality of a people who are still on a journey with their God. The testimonies of many state how time and time again God was on their side, ever present and literally delivering them out of the hands of the enemy. One elder, a man in his seventies stated 'If God did not save me as a young man in Jamaica I don't know what would have happened to me in England, I truly believe I would have died within and lost all hope.' Another faithful elder I interviewed simply sang this chorus:

> He never failed me yet
> He never failed me yet
> Jesus Christ never failed me yet
> Everywhere I go, I want the world to know
> Jesus Christ has never failed me yet

(Anon)

I received many similar comments, reactions and reflections during my conversations with the elders. It became clear to me that they have developed a language which in part is coded; it speaks to pain, isolation and exclusion, but never actually names the 'evil' activities which keep them feeling as the 'other'. It became clear to me as I listened to the many stories that the elders had developed a collective and bi-lateral dialogue with the host community and each other. As is well known today, many of the early settlers had no intentions of remaining in Britain for more than the notorious 'five years', especially those who faced hostility and severe hardship in finding adequate housing. Often, as they searched for accommodation to rent, they came across signs in shop windows which read, 'NO IRISH, NO BLACKS, NO DOGS'.

Many elders spoke about the choruses and hymns which kept them anchored in the faith day by day and week by week: 'Amazing grace', 'Great is thy faithfulness', 'Nobody but Jesus' and 'Stand the storm' are just a few they mentioned. For this early generation these were not just songs for singing, but narratives for overcoming the harsh realities of living and surviving in Britain. Some of the elders that I spoke with remembered the late Revd Dr Oliver A. Lyseight (the founding father and first national overseer of the New Testament Church of God in the UK), and are able to recall the early days of the church. Bishop Dr Selwyn Arnold, a former national overseer of the New Testament Church of God records their story:

> The emergence of the New Testament Church of God (NTCG) in Britain was a direct result of the large number of NTCG members who were among the migrants who came to Britain. Among the émigrés were pastors who for the first time were exposed to the harsh expression of riotous and licentious living on boats, and so they made no delay in registering their evangelistic concerns for the souls of their shipmates. Many preached and prayed for them that they should not forget God in their search for riches and pleasure. On arrival in Britain some Christians were shocked by the attitude of the indigenous population to worship and church attendance, and sensing a need within the growing Black community for fellowship and spiritual guidance away from home, and realizing that many of their friends were falling prey to the spiritual inertia that was 'rampant everywhere', Rev Dr O. A. Lyseight, Mrs Lyseight, and other colleagues embarked upon a plan to establish a fellowship to preserve their spiritual life until they could return to the Caribbean.

> The first public service by the Wolverhampton group was held in the YMCA Hall in Waterloo Road, in September 1953. Under the

direction of O. A. Lyseight and H. D. Brown. When the Church was later organized with twenty-five members, three White British families were included. About the same time, G. A. Johnson, Enos Gordon and other believers began a fellowship in Handsworth, Birmingham. Contact was made between the Wolverhampton group and the Handsworth group, and O. A. Lyseight often visited Handsworth to minister to that group. Both O. A. Lyseight and J. A. Johnson were ministers of the New Testament Church of God in Jamaica before coming to England. In time general leaders of the Church of God officially recognized the groups in Wolverhampton and Handsworth, and Dr O. A. Lyseight was set as the National Overseer, a position he held for twenty-four years.

(Arnold 1992)

One of the questions asked during my informal interviews was 'What was it about your faith that helped you survive the early years in Britain?' The response from a church mother said 'I trusted God to bring me through however much the storm raged; God would not forsake us.' Another said, 'Well, after travelling six weeks by boat I believed God would not bring me this far to leave me, it was hard, I rented a room in a shared house and decided I would just do my best.' The final answer I recorded was very moving, the story of a 75-year-old church father spoke of his life back home serving in the army; he arrived in Britain in 1960 and was met by an uncle. He travelled from London to Birmingham and during the journey did not speak once; the trauma of the journey and the sights and experience in a strange land caused him to weep uncontrollably. He said 'That was the darkest day of my life, I was 22 and felt so alone. I sat on my bed and asked God: "Why did you bring me to this bitter place?" After a while I felt a calm presence in the room with me, and from the darkness I felt a sense of peace, I felt I heard God say "Hold on – a better day is coming."'

Although life may have been grim at times, it is important to note that the birth of the Black-led churches is not the sole cause of rejection by the White churches. Indeed the Revd Joel Edwards states, 'Black Churches were not brought into being solely as a result of racism. This would make them entirely a community by default. Black Churches came into being to fulfil spiritual, social and cultural needs which would otherwise have gone unmet' (Edwards 1993, p.103).

Passing on the baton

The faith of the early generation was strong, these people firmly held a belief in a risen Christ that was real. They believed the heart of God could be touched and moved, that God was concerned with the condition of his people. That generation learnt to serve God on their knees; they prayed and cried out to God daily. Many of the pastors, such as Dr Lyseight were driven by the 'Great Commission' of Jesus: 'Go ye into all the world, and preach the gospel to every creature. He that believeth and is baptized shall be saved; but he that believeth not shall be damned' (Mark 16:15–18). This teaching was a key motivating force for early Black-led church activities in Britain. The mobilisation of a movement was in the making and the pastors and bishops held fast to the vision of evangelising the good news message no matter the cost. For some the cost of the vision was great, many of the early church pastors sacrificed time with their families and personal ambitions to plant churches across the land. Recently a bishop shared with me the fact that pastors in the 1960s would travel from the Midlands to plant and nurture churches as far away as Southampton. These journeys were not easy ones to make, the roads were rough, no direct routes were available and vehicles were uncomfortable rides. Regardless of these hindrances, the call of God on the lives of these men and women was great and above all they would see through a vision of a world in which Jesus' name would be praised and all people would draw nearer to God. So it is off the backs of this persistent and steadfast spirit that the early Black-led churches in Britain began.

In 2002, the Christian Research Association cited the Black-led churches as the fastest growing part of the Christian Church in England. Today, it is fair to say we are experiencing the fruits of that unwavering and faithful generation. They endured and established their own presence in a plethora of African Caribbean Pentecostalism, Apostolic, Holiness, African Charismatic and African Indigenous churches within the Britain isles. In acknowledging church leaders' major role within Black communities today *Keep the Faith* magazine, (one of Britain's leading publications on Black faith) produced their Top Ten Black Church Leaders list. According to *Keep the Faith* (*KTF*) 'when church leaders talk, people listen, when they give directives people follow'.

'The Top Ten Black Church Leaders in 2007', according to *KTF* were:

- Pastor Matthew Ashimowolo, senior pastor, Kingsway International Christian Centre. He leads Britain's largest Black Majority Church, based in Hackney, east London which has a regular Sunday attendance of approximately 10,000.
- Bishop Eric Brown, Administrative Bishop, New Testament Church of God. One of the most well-known and largest Black Church denominations with a network of over 120 churches serving 30,000 followers.
- Revd Joel Edwards, Former General Director, Evangelical Alliance. He made history when he was appointed the first Black General Director of the Evangelical Alliance (EA). The EA represents over 1 million evangelical Christians and plays a key role in lobbying government on behalf of the Christian community and uniting churches to work together on common goals.
- Bishop John Francis, senior pastor, Ruach Ministries. He is the founder of one of the largest Black Churches in the UK, with an average Sunday attendance of 5000 people.
- Revd Agu Irukwu, National Overseer, Redeemed Christian Church of God, Britain's fastest growing Black Pentecostal denomination. In just 10 years it has grown to over 230 congregations situated across the UK, serving in excess of 30,000 people.
- Revd Les Isaac, Director, Ascension Trust, an organisation which provides evangelism training. He also runs Street Pastors, one of the most successful community initiatives to rise out of Britain's Black Christian community.
- Revd Ermal Kirby is one of the highest ranking Black Methodist ministers and is Lead Chair of the Methodist London district, an area containing over 250 churches, serving 22,000 members.
- Pastor Nims Obunge, CEO, The Peace Alliance, a national crime reduction charity.
- Bishop Wilton Powell, National Overseer of The Church of God of Prophecy, one of the Britain's oldest Black-led Pentecostal denominations. Founded in 1953, it has over 88 churches dotted throughout the UK, and 25,000 attendees.
- The Most Revd and Rt Hon. Dr John Sentamu, Archbishop of York. Upon his appointment as Archbishop of York in 2005, Dr John

Sentamu became the second most senior clergyman in the Church of England.

(*Keep the Faith* magazine 2008)

These leaders are amongst those who have received the baton passed on from the early Black Church generation. It is noted that this list produced by a magazine it is not the result of any scientific poll or analysis, however it is generally accepted that these leaders are among those who bring the influence of the church to bear upon the wider community. They are building upon the work of previous generations of leaders. Another point of note is that these leaders are all men. This is an interesting fact since it is well known that approximately two-thirds of the Black Church is female. Part of the lack of female leadership at the highest level is related to the female ordination debate, whilst another factor has to do with the wider interpretation of the role of women in the church. That said, of the many great women who kept the faith with passion and tenacity, one is the late Revd Dr Io Smith, a minister in the New Testament Assembly, one of the UK's best known Black Majority Churches, in which she served as pastor and international representative. Dr Smith was a key figure in establishing Black Christianity in the UK, ensuring Black Christians, particularly women, had a voice in Britain's ecumenical forums. Arriving in London in 1957, as a Baptist, she responded to the rejection and unfriendliness she experienced by joining a Black Pentecostal Church. This paved the way to leadership roles in the church and wider community.

Keep the Faith (2007) states that women comprise approximately 65% of Britain's Black Christian population and so in May 2008, *KTF* published its first ever list of Britain's foremost Black Christian women. This included:

- Angela Sarkis, the first woman and Black person to be appointed to the role of National Secretary of the YMCA.
- Revd Kate Coleman, who made history when she became the first Black woman president of the Baptist Union of Great Britain.
- Pastor Dionne Lamont, leader of Bethesa Ministries, the largest church in her denomination, the Church of God of Prophecy.
- Revd Rose Hudson-Wilkin, an Anglican minister who was recently appointed chaplain to Her Majesty the Queen, and who also serves as chair of the Committee for Minority Ethnic Anglican Concerns.

Some of the foregoing men and women leaders are from the first generation of Black Church leaders, others are second-generation who, according to Mark Sturge, former General Director of the African and Caribbean Evangelical Alliance, are those, unlike the first generation, insisting on their right to be treated equally, and for their culture to be valued, affirmed and respected. They see participation in society as essential, but with mutual respect and on equal terms (Sturge 2005, p.95). This inevitably leads to internal and external tensions. For example, the journey of the original elders and the church between 1975 and 1990 was at times a fretful one. Sturge (2005) describes these years as restless, integrated and diverse, noting that many of the first evangelists were now pastors working in an unreliable salary structure and the pioneers were tired and in need of a fresh 'touch' themselves. However the restlessness was proving fruitful in other ways as some churches were beginning to respond to the social needs of their communities by offering educational and work related training schemes. The churches at this time had to rethink their work and strategy with young people if it was to survive and be relevant to the next generation.

Black Church elders were mindful too of organised action and ecumenical relations. So, along with other agencies, The Afro West Indian United Council of Churches (AWUCOC) was established in 1977 to bring a collaborative Black British voice to the faith, social and political agenda. This organisation was able to gain support from central government and became a partner in delivering education for Black children, securing families to work with the foster and care system and contributed to mental health thinking and service delivery. Since the creation of the AWUCOC many other organisations have developed to give authentic voices to Black Christian life, the best known is the African and Caribbean Evangelical Alliance. Started by Philip Mohabir, the vision was to connect Black and White Christians.

In my interviews with the elders from the New Testament Church of God, I asked 'What is it specifically that attracted you to the faith and what keeps you going?' Nine out of ten echoed the reply, 'This is what I believe!' and each one spoke passionately of the Church's statement of faith, which each absolutely believes and embraces. The faith of the elders is deeply embedded in customs and traditions, but most especially in biblical authority, depicted by the NTCG Statement of Faith that includes this: 'The NTCG believes the whole Bible to be completely and equally inspired and that it is the written Word of God'. It is no surprise to me to hear how precious and important the rituals of the faith are to the elders of the church.

Many spoke of the loving fellowship brought by the communion and the washing of feet. One church mother laughed as she recalled past events and describes them as 'sweet', but her expression changed as she explained that washing of feet does not happen very much these days. For this generation, holding on to the fundamentals of the faith is crucial, for this is the faith which they brought with them and passed onto their children with the hope their children would pass it on. Sadly some of the elders' children were not holding on to the faith, but that does not stop them dutifully praying and calling on God to intervene, as one church father said, 'the children must be saved'.

Holding the dream

The 2001 Census revealed that the UK today is more culturally diverse than ever before. It states that over one-third of the population, 20 million people, living in Britain today are aged 50 and over. The fastest growing age group in the population are those aged 80 years and over, they currently constitute 4.5% (2,749,507) of the total population. This age group has increased by over 1.1 million between 1981 and 2007 (1,572,160 to 2,749,507), from 2.8% to 4.5%. This is mainly a result of improvements in mortality rates at older ages over the second half of the twentieth century. From these total figures *Social Trends* (2006) reports that amongst the Minority Ethnic population in the United Kingdom in 2001, 11% of Black-Caribbean people were aged over 65, and 2% of were aged over 85. The picture and landscape of Britain is changing, its cities are ethically and culturally diverse both in its population and social lifestyle. The elders have made Britain their home and the faith of the early generations has been fundamental to understanding the world day by day both in a local and global context.

My interviews revealed that faith for many of these men and women brought two things together. One, moral and ethical beliefs and, two, a Christian framework. These two things inspired people to do something for their new found community and that was to offer hope, justice and love all as expressed in the gospel of Jesus Christ. Today the fourth and emerging fifth generation of Black African and Caribbean families who were raised in the Christian faith have a responsibility to live out the dreams and aspirations of our great grandfathers and grandmothers who themselves dared to dream. I count myself amongst those whom I am speaking of. We must do what we can to harness and activate the power of spirituality to bring development or material, political, spiritual and social blessings to all, especially to those living in the underbelly of society. The ability to hope and to dream is a tool for us to use creatively based on a faith that is real.

In the last four decades, and as a sign of hope, the elders' generation has witnessed occasions of history in the making where people acted on faith and dared to believe a new earth was possible where freedom and liberty would reign. 'For we walk by faith and not by sight' (2 Corinthians 5:7) speaks to the ability to see beyond the immediate circumstances to what is possible despite the obstacles and challenges and in spite of structural hindrances. It may be that the events of history gave them the ability to hold on a little longer. Such events include the victory of the Civil Rights Movement led by Revd Dr Martin Luther King, mobilised by the famous 'I have a dream' speech delivered in 1963 to more than 200,000 civil-rights marchers at the Lincoln Memorial in Washington, DC.

Another example of hope fulfilled was the eventual release of Nelson Mandela on 11 February 1990. Nelson Mandela was freed from prison in South Africa after 27 years. He did not lose sight of the dream, hope or vision of a better future. Mandela epitomised the historic will of African people to pursue freedom and justice at any cost. Many African Caribbean elders prayed and travailed on behalf of their Africa brothers and sisters for many of their early years in Britain, before some of these changes materialised. A recent example of hope realised is the recent win of Senator Barack Hussein Obama who built his campaign on the ideas of hope and change. Like Dr Martin Luther King and Nelson Mandela, Obama engineered a movement of people committed to hope as a result of which he has been elected as the forty-fourth President of the United States of America. One of the poignant phone texts that did the rounds and which hit my inbox several times throughout the day after the 2008 US elections read, 'Rosa sat so Martin could walk, Martin walked so Obama could run, Obama ran so our children can fly.' (Anon).

For our church elders who have endured the bleak winter of their experience in Britain and indeed in the wider world, this is a welcome spring for the children to fly, to take the baton that our elders won with their prayers and determination and run like the wind, achieving and surpassing the goals and ambitions of those who ran before us. The sacred text tells us the race is not for the swift but for those who endure till the end. Our fore parents did not always run with speed, neither did they get it right all of the time, but they did endure; they did not give up. The hope and dream of leaving those distant shores of the Caribbean and Africa was to find a better life, and with God's help seek to embrace education and new knowledge; to live in peace and harmony with their neighbour and to bless others so that a blessing would be received in return.

I end this chapter by returning to Myrtle's life, with which I started. For me, Myrtle demonstrated it is not only possible to transcend what is immediately seen and felt, she also demonstrated that a lifetime's journey with God can transform the mind to see beyond the 'now' and to hold fast to a vision of a new and better day. Indeed, one day I hope that, like Myrtle, I will achieve eldership having contributed to the dawn of a new earth.

References

Arnold, S. E. (1992) *From Scepticism to Hope*, Nottingham, Grove Books Ltd

Edwards, Joel (1993) 'The British Afro-Caribbean Community', in Martyn Eden (ed.) *Britain on the Brink*, London, Crossway Books

McGreal, Shirley (2008) *Keep the Faith* magazine

National Statistics (2006), table 1.5 (Population: by ethnic group and age, 2001) Great Britain, Crown Copyright

Reddie, Anthony (ed.) (2002) 'Singing the Lord's song in a strange land', in *Black Theology in Britain: An International Journal*, London, Continuum Publishing

Sturge, Mark (2005) *Look What the Lord Has Done: The development, role and contribution of Black Majority Churches*, Milton Keynes, Scripture Union

9   *Youth and the Black Church*

Carver Anderson

Engaging young people – the Obama factor

The world stood still to witness one of the greatest election outcomes of this century, if not in the history of political elections. The election of Barack Obama as President of the United States not only brought hope to the masses, but a sense that anything is possible if the right strategies and processes are in place. The *Daily Telegraph* (Wednesday 5 November 2008) cited one Mr Johnson, a senior who was interviewed following the election, who said 'I never thought I would live to see this day. I don't know if you believe in God but I believe God has a plan for people same as he had for the Children of Israel.' For Mr Johnson, President Obama is the manifestation of divine providence. I do indeed concur with Mr Johnson that God has a plan and in the context of this article, the plan is for the empowerment of our youths. It is important to note that the voices and votes of young people were crucial in the process of electing Mr Obama as President.

Referring to the US elections, Telegraph.co.uk News (7 November 2008) stated, 'Youth voter initiatives say young people are energised by issues such as healthcare, education and the war in Iraq. And they praise the way both candidates have reached out to young voters via websites and television.' 'It has really been extraordinary', said Miss Young, 'This is the first time that candidates have really fought hard for the youth vote, and that makes young people feel wanted and important and inspired and really care about the election because they feel like they matter.' It is clear that young people can be engaged, empowered and will respond at defining moments, especially if their welfare and wellbeing are on the agenda.

The election of President Obama, through divine providence and human strategy, demonstrates how churches should respond to the serious and often fatal issues facing our youths in the UK. How do leaders and churches manage to live, work and worship disengaged from individuals, families and communities that are captivated by poverty and violence, many of whom live in oppressive state of minds and emotions? The manifestation of divine providence and the search for appropriate and effective intervention strategies should be the aim and focus of our leaders and churches in relation to our communities' youths. Without negating the needs of the 'saints' within our churches, we must never forget the mandate placed on us to be the good news within our respective contexts. Joel Edward's book *An Agenda for Change* (2008), highlights four key things we must do if we want to transform our society: i) pray for revival, ii) actively engage, iii) be actively involved and iv) act strategically. We cannot expect a redeemed, transformed and empowered community with productive young lives, if the key principles mentioned here are not seriously deployed. Are our churches and leadership resistant or reluctant to sacrifice time and resources (human and financial) in order to emerge as a relevant and prophetic voice of the twenty-first century for young people?

A personal story

In seeking to address the above question let me start with a testimony. It's the story of a young man convicted of murder at the age of 18 years. Having attended Sunday School from an early age, the influence of church diminished as he grew up. He lived in a community that challenged his race, masculinity and morals and where violence, anger, revenge and survival were daily expressions of life for him and many of his friends. I first came across him during a conference regarding youth empowerment. He came to give his testimony, having been allowed day release from an open prison, which greatly impacted those of us present. Following a discussion with him, we agreed to consider some joint work around youth transformation and reformation issues. He explained that his life changed in prison, following a discussion with a prison chaplain who challenged him about his anger and attitude regarding his conviction.

My communication and relationship with this young man developed and in February 2008 we jointly presented a seminar on the theme, 'Youth of Destiny'. He explained to those present,

> I had grown up in an environment of guns, drugs, knives and gangs but did not see myself as a gang member. I did not know my dad, so had no real father figure or good male role models around me. My mom could not cope with me, so she sent me to live with my grandmother (her mom). My grandma was not fully aware of the pressurised environment that was surrounding me. In fact I would pretend I was all right. This of course was not the case. Because I was known for my temper and a youth not to mess with. During my time 'on road' I was involved in many challenges. But the day came when I got caught up in a serious fight and a knife was pulled on me. I was handed a baseball bat by one of my mates, which I used in the fight. This resulted in the death of my peer.
>
> The next day I was arrested and charged with murder. However, just before my trial one of the chaplains from the prison spoke to me, challenging me about lifestyle and attitude. During the following days I was in turmoil as I thought through my life, and how I had ended up in prison now awaiting trial. After a couple of weeks I was found guilty and sentenced to life. Following this, I remember, one evening whilst sitting on my bed I again 'looked' at myself and what I had done; the words of the chaplain came back to me and I decided there and then to change. So that night in the cell I said to God 'If you are real and able to change me and people like me, then do it!' I recall feeling a deep sense of conviction, which brought me to tears. It was from that point I knew I had changed. It was due to my conscious change and practice as a Christian that I conducted myself well in prison, becoming a 'model prisoner'. This resulted in me being granted parole after fourteen years.

Now aged 34, released on licence and, back in the community, he agrees that he deserved the sentence he received. And he notes that the young man he killed deserved life, not death. As a result of his life journey he is on a mission to be an example and support for those youngsters involved, or are at risk of involvement, in activities and behaviours that can lead to brokenness, hopelessness and death. This is an example of the kind of person the Black church needs to engage, mobilise and support.

Supporting young people

The vital question that I want to look at is, what do our young people and children deserve? And can our churches develop a contextually impacting message that is able to engage, inform and sustain young people at either end of the developmental spectrum? In other words, the Black Church must meet them at their point of need; at transition into and in adulthood, whether they be those with minimum challenges or the ones classed as 'hard core' and seriously disaffected. According to Josh McDowell (1994), research and statistics tell horror stories in many towns and cities of how youths are affected by lifestyles and activities that can lead to death. Have we not heard and read that without a relevant church our communities will continue to diminish into places of hopelessness?

Paul Grant and Raj Patel in their anthologies, *A Time to Speak* (1990) and *A Time to Act* (1992), challenged the churches' relevance. Their anthologies are must reads for church leaders and members who seek to be 'salt' and 'light' (Matthew 5) in a society that is asking what the church is doing for young people, particularly those who do not fit into a traditional Pentecostal or Evangelical frame. Over the past five years we have seen many Pentecostal and independent Black and White majority churches planted and existing in some of this country's most deprived communities. However, their presence begs the question, what impact do these churches have on the lives of the young people and children around them? The over representation of African Caribbean young men in the criminal justice system signifies a serious challenge for those with responsibility regarding ethical, moral and social factors. This concern should also be evident in our churches that are located in these communities.

The *Just Justice* study, undertaken by the Children's Society (Wilson and Rees 2006) into Black young people's experience of the youth justice system argues that, 'The over representation of Black young people in the youth justice system is well documented, yet relatively little is known about how young Black people experience and perceive the youth justice system'. The study continues to say that the Children's Society believes that 'only by listening to young people can we fully understand their experience and seek more effective solutions to the challenges they face'. It is also interesting to see similarities with a US project which aims to raise the profile of young people. The Black Youth Project Chicago states,

> When one looks at a wide array of some of the most controversial and important issues facing the country, African American young people are often at the center of these debates and policies. Whether the issue is mass incarceration, affirmative action, the increased use of high-stakes school testing, HIV and AIDS, sex education in schools, or welfare reform, most of these initiatives and controversies disproportionately impact young, often vulnerable, African Americans. However, in contrast to the centrality of African American youth to the politics and policies of the country, their perspectives and voices generally have been absent from not only public policy debates, but also academic research.

Whether in the US or here in the UK, these young people need support and the church may be their best hope.

It is within this very concerning context that I wish to pose a few more questions to those of us who believe the Bible to be truth and our guide and compass for impacting lives. How can we worship and praise in churches that are in communities that are broken and not have relevance and impact? How do we live and be an example? Luke 4:18 'God's Spirit is on me; he's chosen me to preach the Message of good news to the poor, sent me to announce pardon to prisoners and recovery of sight to the blind, to set the burdened and battered free, to announce, This is God's year to act.' (*The Message: New Testament* 1994).

The social challenge

Over the past 50 years generations have grown up seeing their parents and grandparents experience disaffection and hopelessness due to the consistent failure of public authorities in education, health, police, prisons, social care, health and employment on top of a lack of community responsibility. Social exclusion as a consequence of the foregoing, has led to at least two, and in some cases three generations sharing this experience of isolation, lack of trust and public confidence. Concurrently, thousands of young people do attend church each week, expressing their faith in worship and praise sessions. They work hard in Sunday Schools, youth groups and Bible studies; they are considered 'salt and light' in their communities because they are not caught up in lifestyles of criminality or anti-social behaviour. However, many more thousands of young people, who look just like the ones attending church, view the church as a contradiction or an irrelevance, especially in their times of difficulty. What does church have to say when they are beaten at school, or their grandparents go to so many hospital appointments but still suffer, or the council does shoddy repairs and their homes are damp, or their mothers are forced to work at three jobs to make ends meet? What do they deserve?

The irony is that many people, organisations, communities and groups are struggling to be 'relevant' to the young even whilst examples of their hopelessness seem to multiply. In the face of corporate impotency, scarcely a weekend passes without a young person dying pointlessly. 'Post code' fear and intimidation seem to shape entire communities. From Glasgow to Newcastle, Liverpool to London and Manchester to Birmingham, we hear of gangs, murders, guns, anti-social behaviour and thug culture. For the most part, the media portrays young people as violent and uncaring. They are presented as predators, packs of, or lone, 'wolves', without sensitivity, morals or responsibility. Before our own eyes, our children and young people are made into, as it were, animals. Are you shocked when I say 'our children and young people'? They are ours, our sisters, brothers, friends, sons and daughters. If we have one Father, then these youngsters belong to us just as much as the ones who attend church and fellowships; including the ones whose lives are made invisible – unless they are the victims of a tragic accident or some senseless act. The media renders the nurturing and caring young person invisible; their success at school rubbished, their roles in keeping families together forgotten, their struggles to make sense of the world dismissed. Do they deserve this?

The call for change from the streets, the pews and the academy is becoming louder. Dr Robert Beckford (2006) challenges especially Black Church leadership, to develop a spirituality that resists and counters oppression. In other words, churches must represent the presence and power of the work of God that has impact in young people's everyday struggles. However, the churches' internal fragmentation hinders appropriate response, against which the Revd Joel Edwards (2008) argues for a radical rethink of how the church represents the gospel (the Good News) within the communities they are part of. He suggests that we must aim to move our ideas from the 'page to the streets', and he asserts that Evangelicals must begin by joining the conversation on how to unite to present Christ credibly as good news to society. It is from a position of unity and strength, he argues, that the church will have earned the right to speak in the public square. United, we will be able to re-imagine how we might transform society. Only together can we move forward to implement long-term strategic change for the benefit of our youths. As yet, I am afraid to say, we are some way off.

New life from death

Please do not read what follows as a cheap shot across the bow of the establishment, government, church or other structures. I am wholly committed to the church's mission to young people and communities. However, I need to explain about the spiritual and psychological 'place' I now inhabit and the tough journey that has taken me many years. I was a Sunday school teacher, scout leader young men's group coordinator, youth leader, and local pastor. Becoming The National Director of Youth and Christian Education for The New Testament Church of God enabled me to consider very seriously issues facing young people in and out of church. I travelled the world from Europe, to Africa, to north and south America, encouraging the development of ministries for young people. I had a vision for Christian youth to be a force for shalom, i.e. wholeness, peace and redemption in church and community.

However, in 2003, the direction of my work changed. I realised that I was jetting here, there and everywhere, but lost my sense of peace. My spirit was restless and I knew something was changing. I felt this in my core being. Then a local gang killed two teenage girls, Charlene Ellis and Letisha Shakespeare, outside a New Year's party in Aston, Birmingham. The whole community was in shock and the country stopped for a moment to think about the killing of two Black girls. I involved myself in dealing with some of the aftermath of the murders and learnt so much about the lives of young people 'on road'.

I understood that if my ministry was to have real meaning, it had to make sense in this context of the premature loss of young Black lives. My soul burned and I commenced work to raise awareness and help my denomination to see the importance of the urban mission field. I wanted people to come to Christ and realised that as the body of Christ the church had to go to them. Dr Joe Aldred (2005) in his book *Respect* suggests that one of the key principles of respect is relationship building, he argues that 'to get to know others, we must get close enough to form a relationship'. My response to this position was clear, I stepped down from my national role with its focus on 'churched' young people and instead committed myself to work with young people 'on road'. I felt they deserved more and I said I would overcome any difficulty to make Jesus' words, as recorded in Luke 4:18–19, a reality for them. The death of Latisha and Charlene brought new life and purpose to my life and ministry.

Life on the road – the context

I did not anticipate that one of my first difficulties would be me. I am an ex-bad boy, pastor, social worker and social scientist and I thought I already knew what young people deserved and needed. I could only wonder why the problems still existed alongside so much information about young people. I concluded that young people needed listening to, careful and compassionate guidance, a chance to escape and God's love. Since the death of Charlene and Latisha, I've seen the mistakes that I previously made and have unlearnt so much. My religious mindset had to be deconstructed; in other words, I had to go through pain to try and see the community and its people as Christ would do. In relating to young people, I could not base my thinking on a denominational paradigm, which limits one's freedom to creatively engage with community and the un-churched. That's not to say that I was wrong previously about what was needed. I simply did not understand the context and complexities in trying to find solutions.

I would like to share some of the things I had to get to grips with during the early years of being on the road. Perhaps one of the most important things was that young people, just like anyone else, dislike nothing more than being given a promise that is then not delivered. The Commission for Racial Equality (CRE) says that Black and other minority communities are pushed to the side of society. They are often denied good education and training, proper health care, decent employment prospects and quality housing. Home Office research shows that Caribbean and Asian young men are over-represented in school exclusions, unemployment figures, the mental health system and the criminal justice system (*House Of Commons Home Affairs Committee* 2007). The arguments that these trends are the results of personal choices, family structures or culture are simply untenable. Instead, for me, they signify the need for an overhaul of a system which so clearly puts discrimination and criminal justice before social justice and inclusion on the pathway to adulthood.

I have discovered that as confirmed by the Children's Society (Wilson and Rees, Just Justice Report 2006), we really do not know the impact of racism on our young people's lives. As long as young people have to 'come forward' to make a complaint, we will never find out 'what is really happening'. We should seek out their views. Academics agree that the voices of young people are clearly absent from policy and research that concerns them. This is often to the detriment of those young people and their communities. *The Barrow Cadbury Report* (Parston 2005) says that it is in all our interests 'to have as many young adults as possible mature as fully and as early as they can with as little damage to themselves and others as possible along the way'. However, much of what we do, for example in the area of criminal justice policies, can be argued to do the opposite of what we hope for. They do 'unnecessary damage' to the life chances of young adult offenders and make it harder for them to lead crime-free lives. Again I ask the crucial question, what are our churches doing to empower, challenge and represent the good news of the gospel of Jesus Christ in these circumstances?

The Howard League (Neilson 2008) reports that nine of the ten most violent prisons in England and Wales are young offenders' institutions. The League's Director, Frances Crook, says that 'children come out of custody hardened and brutalized, with reconviction rates within a year of almost 70%'. Clearly, our society criminalises, even brutalises, our children. Our institutions damage the young people placed in their care. Arguments based on numbers: e.g. 'it is only a few who get damaged'; financial practicality: e.g. 'it is simply too costly to provide the services'; or morality: e.g. 'it is stupid to help "bad children" when the good ones get nothing', all share the language of hell. Whose children are expendable? Which young people do we condemn to broken lives and social exclusion? What youths are 'beyond redemption'? These are important questions, but we have to be very careful how we handle them.

Week after week in our churches we hear songs and sermons about how great God is and that there is power in the name of Jesus. Young people challenge that greatness and power to become relevant and impacting upon their situations. Can the church meet this challenge? For me, it started with the acknowledgement that I was not fully applying the words that I sung and read. For example, how could I say, 'the Lord is my light and my salvation, whom shall I fear, the Lord is the strength of my life' (Psalm 27: 1–2) and then back off from engaging with a young man labelled 'hard core' knowing that he needs someone to show him love? This certainly is a contradiction, and one which I have sought to address as the relevance of my kingdom journey to real life has emerged and impacted me. It is vital that if the Black Majority Church, or any other, is willing to engage and impact the lives of urban youngsters then we must be prepared to be in relationship with them and hear their stories, no matter how pained.

US theologian James Cone (1986, p.113) develops the perspective of Black liberation. He points to a God who fully associates with the oppressed and marginalised. He quotes a poem entitled 'Listen Christians' that was circulated at a poor people's rally in Albuquerque, New Mexico. Evidently, churches may see this as a critical challenge; however, I suggest that we use it as a tool for self and church assessment:

> I was hungry
> And you formed a humanities club
> And you discussed my hunger
> Thank you.
> I was imprisoned
> And you crept off quietly
> To your chapel in the cellar
> And prayed for my release.
> I was naked
> And in your mind
> You debated the morality of my appearance.
> I was sick
> And you knelt and thanked God for your health.
> I was homeless
> And you preached to me
> Of the spiritual shelter of the love of God.
> I was lonely

> And you left me alone
> To pray for me.
> You seem so holy
> So close to God
> But I 'm still hungry
> and lonely
> and cold.
> So where have your prayers gone?
> What have they done?
> What does it profit a man
> To page through his book of prayers
> When the rest of the world is crying for his help?

This poem challenged me to seriously consider how valid my prayers and expressions are if they are not also validated by practical activities. Am I listening to the people for whom I pray?

Life on the road – the experiences

Recently, I researched how young people think and feel. I went around the country to listen to individual young people and focus groups talking about their own lives. The young people were very kind and very forgiving of an old man asking 'foolish' questions. They shared honestly and I was much moved and provoked by what they said. Below are some of their words:

> I find it hard to express how I feel to my parents, they don't know the street.

> The older people can't deal with us, they just cuss us down.

> Police see us as always wanting to cause trouble.

> Leaders and big people don't take time to know us.

> Who teaches us to cope in all the crap we face day in and day out?

> We sometimes chill at our community youth club, and would share some of our stuff with our youth leader.

> If we make a mistake, we are quickly condemned.

No one is taking time to hear us, and the answers we have.

The church thing is a joke.

No thanks to social services, youth service and the police who just lack the know-how to deal with us.

What is the point working at school? There won't be any jobs for us.

The community don't belong to us.

Of course we are scared to go into another man's zone, that's why we need to carry our tings.

Before they do it to us, we'll do it to them.

We feel that the friends we grew up with is now our enemies because they live in a postcode that we can't rep.

All this repping ting are rubbish.

Yes, it's serious and total madness, and will get worse if we don't come together to deal with it.

Man's been killed over what? Do people know what it's like out the streets?

How many more of our friends have to die before this madness stops?

We are fed up of hearing that Black young people are at the bottom of the pile and that there is more of us in prison than university. Let us set up this council to change things.

We are treated as if our experience counts for nothing, we have seen more guns and knives than most, surely that should count for something?

We help each other to cope.

Love, respect, care and supporting each other is what we need help with.

We trust those who take time to understand what we are about, not those who just come to get information about guns and gangs and other stuff, and then just disappear.

We have to cope in all the crap we face day in and day out even when we are hurting.

We can help to clean up some of the mess on Road, just give us the time, space, training and money and see what we do.

This world is a challenge to churches and leaders who express a call to inner city ministry. The challenge is to live out our claim to be people of God, led and powered by the Spirit. We are called to live out Jesus' proclamation of the year of the Lord's favour (Luke 4:19) and the reign of God here and now (verses 21–22). We are called to look for God in the lives and words of those who are oppressed and imprisoned, those who hunger and thirst for justice (Matthew 5:6).

Where is justice for youth?

I suggest that the situation we presently live in is one of injustice. It is the result of big shifts in business and politics. These things shape the lives of our communities. Cities and towns have their own biographies and the prospects available to young people are decided by people with power and influence. The current generation of young people grew up in a struggle against disaffection, despair and hopelessness. Their parents faced the harsh effects of the Conservative Party's 'opening up' of Britain to the 'disciplines' of the market. That New Labour promised something better meant nothing. They saw that public authorities consistently failed their parents and grandparents. They saw their struggle to obtain better services from education, health and social care, police, prison and employment professionals all too often end in frustration. They saw 'schemes' come and go without any real impact: a few jobs and much disappointment. They saw the break up of communities and experienced poor schooling, social exclusion, and poor housing and health services. They knew that the colour of their skin and their 'postcode' shaped their lives, as it did their parents and grandparents. Two and, in some cases, three generations shared this isolation, discrimination and struggle. Often these things distorted the development of communities, families and individuals as they tried to cope with the stresses and demands of rapidly changing and worsening times for those at the bottom of the pile.

A lack of trust in authorities and public services and even the church is a reasonable and rational response. Before we condemn, we need to ask why young people are blamed for a situation they did not create? Why are their actions, if not lives, presented as the 'problem'? Why are their communities 'no go' areas where crime is rife and life cheap? My experiences and the research above suggest that many young people are abused, beaten, conned and robbed by governments, local authorities, public services, voluntary and private organisations, the media and businesses. Like the man on the Jericho road, they are left on the roadside (Luke 10:30). Is it any wonder, then, that churches, community groups, local authorities and national government lack the will to engage with those communities or their young people? Is it any wonder that communities see the powerful and the religious as part of the problem? (Luke 10:25–37).

In Birmingham, for example, the powerful drew up and imposed so many plans and solutions. Often, they discarded these schemes once the funding ran out, or the political crisis calmed. Their interest came and went based on political expediency rather than making lasting changes in the quality of people's lives. These plans failed to deliver the goods and served to demoralise those who put their hope in them. The failures contributed to the view of these communities as almost beyond redemption. The issue of gun crime further illustrates the theme and is the defining issue for how our cities and towns and our young people are viewed and how they view themselves. I've seen too many victims of violence to minimise their suffering or make cheap debating points out of it. However, the recent media spotlight on gangs, guns and knives is the latest in a long series of moral panics that distort our views of neighbourhoods and neighbours. The focus is on the 'sensational' destruction of people's lives.

The killing of gang members is not 'news' ('that's what they do') unless 'innocents' are caught in the crossfire. The breakdown in community relations and neighbourhood safety is not 'news' ('Who really cares?') unless there's a riot or we can talk about intra-ethnic hostility. Youth disengagement is not 'news' ('they deserve to be in prison') unless there is violence. Is this what our young people deserve? Here are some of today's headlines from my local paper (*Birmingham Mail*, 13 May 2008) picked entirely at random that relate to young people. This is not scientific, but does raise some questions:

Teen 'shoved boy of 8 on to railway'

Suspect [in murder of schoolboy, Jimmy Mizen] 'flees hunt'

Girl's cliff plunge

Boy, 6, is hit by bus

Please, give me an ASBO

A class act with stories

Town teenagers have their say

Just the tonic for children's ward

There seem to be two types of children – the innocent individual, who deserves our compassion, help and contributions, and the guilty individual, who deserves all they get and a lot more. The world of the headlines is a simple one, with clear distinctions between good and evil. It is very different from the place where our young people's voices came from? It is very different from the place described by the research studies I cited. It seems to me that we can use the research of the 'road' (rather than the media) to assess our situation and to glean possible solutions.

This perspective will allow us to see what the media rarely spotlights: the existence of different types of violence. We are familiar with hitting and hurting. However, there is a concept of 'institutional violence', where the actions or inactions of organisations can distort, damage and destroy lives and environments just as surely as knives, guns, drugs and fists. No one need be responsible for 'institutional violence'. It often occurs when agencies, businesses or governments fail in their 'duty of care' and regard people, areas and issues as 'expendable' or 'exploitable'. The young people we heard from earlier show how it feels to be at best 'collateral damage' and victims of 'friendly fire'. What was sad about some of my conversations with young people was that they felt that there was no hope; in fact some (youngsters between ages of 14 and 18) felt that they would not live to see their twentieth birthday.

At a conference on gun crime in Birmingham in 2004, Home Office minister, Caroline Flint stated:

> Legislation and enforcement alone will not solve gun crime. Key
> to our work is building strong communities who will support our
> young people and divert them away from a life of crime. Although
> a number of positive initiatives have been developed to tackle gun
> crime locally, the wider picture is more mixed and an improved

strategic multi-agency response is needed to meet the on-going challenge.

(Flint 2004)

Let us be clear on what she said. She said: that laws and the police do not stop gun crime; that current alternative solutions do not really work; that our communities do not keep our people from crime because they are not strong enough; and that the solution is in better communication between agencies. The minister's words highlight two things: that current thinking seems a little confused and fails to provide effective solutions; and that government policy offers little in terms of a realistic understanding of how to help people live decent lives and maintain strong communities. Yet, the minister presents these communities as needing professionals to protect them from their own children and young people. However, issues around young people, community safety, gangs and drugs have already pulled together a range of statutory agencies, including the Police, Drug Action teams, Connexions, employment and regeneration professionals, social care, health, social, youth and probation services. Given this inter-agency work, plus all the time, money and effort poured into building sustainable and just communities, it is reasonable to ask why there has been so little impact. It is reasonable to ask who is responsible for this persistent failure of policies to improve the lives of our young people – we already know who pays the price.

The church must respond

For many un-churched young people with friends in church, the church has failed to understand the real context of community and the challenges young people face each day. Again, I strongly argue that the churches in our communities should provide quality services and guidance for those who need transformation and reformation, where prisoners are set free, the blind are given their sight and the oppressed are released (Luke 4:18). It is clear that the church has a responsibility to affect individuals who are socially excluded, and seeking an identity and direction. Some of our churches and leaders are reconsidering and reprioritising their activities to be able to connect with their community. They are taking seriously their roles as caretakers, peacemakers and justice-bringers. They are part of a movement in the global church. There are examples of work in Jamaica,

Hong Kong, Ireland, Colombia and the US, where church action builds and sustains life in the most difficult of circumstances.

As an example, I've chosen the experience of churches in Boston, USA, because it is an inspiring story that shows the journey of a group of Christian people, from shock to service. In 1992, the Boston Black community had a wake-up call. During a funeral service for a young murder victim, gang members chased a rival member into the church. He was beaten and stabbed. People were stunned. Following consultations with the police department, a group of churches took to the streets, chatting to youngsters and those involved in drug deals. They also had mini tent revivals for children and young people. The church, along with the police and parole officers, visited young people's homes. The result of this intervention was stunning: 'the Boston miracle'. There was a huge reduction in the youth murder rate. Between 1995 and 1998, no one under 17 was killed. The overall murder rate for the city dropped from 157 in 1995 to 37 in 1998. Another great accomplishment was that a mostly White city criminal justice system, distrustful Black residents and local church people found ways to work together.

The testimony of the young man I commenced with, gives us hope that young people who are transformed can be real advocates for churches and communities regarding the power of God to radically change lives. This is seen in the transformation of Saul (name changed to Paul after conversion) in Acts 9. It is worth noting that Saul's conversion brought challenges to him and those associated with him. This context has to be a consideration for churches seeking to engage with young people, affected by a criminal lifestyle. As with the people in our cities, conversion brings consequences for those whose lives are changed and challenges to those around them. Paul the new convert was not free from suspicion and threats to his life, and the believers who supported and worked with him were in constant danger from the violence directed at him. It took time for relationships to develop and trust to grow. However, their experiences of living together through the persecution encouraged and enabled communities of believers to be established and nurtured across the Roman Empire.

Conclusion

If we are to face up to a realistic and holistic response to the issues raised in this chapter and to develop a paradigm for building strong communities, then we must refer to how Jesus expressed this in Luke 4:18. Let us therefore not negate the Spirit and the anointing of the Spirit. Paul acknowledged that it is possible for churches and their leaders to have little or no impact in community or the lives of people we today class as 'hard to reach', 'disaffected' and 'socially excluded'. In 1 Thessalonians 1:5 Paul said 'Our gospel comes to you not simply with words, but also with power, with the Holy Spirit.' Here, it can be argued that it is possible to have the words of a preacher or the church without power. Consequently, lives will not be changed or transformed under the influence of such ministry.

From our grassroots context, we have argued that the failure to examine what young people represent will minimise the response of our churches to be strategically and spiritually informed to act with power. This factor has maintained the persistent weakness of some of our churches to engage, support and maintain young people. I acknowledge the good work of groups, such as the Street Pastor Initiative, Peace Alliance, Bringing Hope and similar partnerships within the statutory and voluntary sector, and I have learnt from and with them. I am mindful of the need for a radical and dynamic model, which would lead to a process of positive change given the crisis we face in our communities. To that end, I suggest that young people should be fully involved in the shaping and implementation of support services that aim to be relevant and sustainable.

Despite all the negative perceptions relating to young people, the capacity to change for the better is indeed rooted in the Word of God that reminds us that Christians are called to be 'salt and light' in the world, which means our churches should be governed by principles and practices which bring hope for individuals, families, communities and the nation. I wish to leave you with a number of self assessment questions we might use in our quest for kingdom relevance:

- If I remain as I am, will I have impact?
- Do I know and understand me?
- Do I need to seek for direction and advice regarding my future?
- What do people say about my character and integrity?
- What is my greatest desire for my church and community?
- Do I need to change?
- What issues do I struggle with relating to being 'salt and light'?

References

Afari, Y. (2007) *Overstanding Rastafari – Jamaica's Gift To The World*, Jamaica, Senya-Cum

Aldred, J. D. (2005) *Respect: Understanding Caribbean British Christianity*, Peterborough, Epworth

Beckford, Robert (2004) *God and the Gangs,* London, Darton, Longman and Todd Ltd

Beckford, Robert (2006) *Jesus Dub Theology: Music and social change*, Oxford, Routledge Taylor & Francis

Bird, M. and Hilborn, D. (eds) (2002) *God and the Generations – Youth, Age and the Church Today*, Carlisle, Cumbria, Paternoster Press

Black Youth Project, *Exploring the Attitudes, Actions and Decision Making of African American Youth by Highlighting their Lives, Ideas and Voices*:
www.blackyouthproject.com, University of Chicago Centre for the Study of Race, Politics and Culture

Cone, James, H. (1986) *Speaking The Truth – Ecumenism, Liberation, and Black Theology,* Michigan, William B. Eerdmans Publishing Company, p.113

Davis, Ken (1996) *How to Speak to Youth and Keep Them Awake at the Same Time*, Grand Rapids Michigan, Zondervan Publishing House

Edwards, Joel (1992) *Let's Praise Him Again: An African-Caribbean Perspective on Worship*, Eastbourne, Kingsway Publication

Edwards, Joel (2008) *An Agenda for Change: A global call for spiritual and social transformation*, Grand Rapids, Michigan, Zondervan Publishing

Flint, Caroline (2004) 'Connected: Together we can tackle gun crime' Paper presented at the Home Office Conference, Birmingham, 19 and 20 January

Glynn, M. (2004) *Hard to Access Young People and Drugs Support Services In Birmingham*, A Birmingham City Council Drug Action Team Publication

Grant, Paul I. (2006) *Saving Our Sons – Strategies and Advice For The Parents Of African Teenage Sons*, Nottingham, Navigator Press

Grant, Paul and Patel, Raj (1992) *A Time To Act*, Nottingham, Russell Press

Grant, Paul and Patel, Raj (1990) *A Time To Speak*, Nottingham, Russell Press

Granville, G. and Laidlaw, J. (2000) *A Partnership of Trust: Young offenders supporting older people in care settings – an example of social inclusion through intergenerational practice*, Stoke-on-Trent, The Beth Johnson Foundation

Hopkins, Cheryl (2006) 'A Brighter Future For Children And Young People –The Birmingham Strategy', Birmingham City Council

House Of Commons Home Affairs Committee (2007) *Young Black People and the Criminal Justice System*, London, The Stationery Office Ltd

Light, Alan (1998) *Tupac Shakur*, London, Plexus Publishing Limited.

McDowell, Josh and Hostetler, Bob (1994) *Right from Wrong – What you need to know to help youth make right choices*, London, Word Publishing

McMillan, M. (2001) *Growing Up is Hard to Do – Young people and sexual health, Young people's health project*, Lewisham

Neilson, A. (2008) *Child Prisons Are 'Hotbeds of Violence'*, A Howard League Publication, Cambridge, Blackwell Publishing Ltd

Parston, Greg (2005) *Lost in Transition – A Report of the Barrow Cadbury Commission on Young Adults and the Criminal Justice System*, London, Barrow Cadbury Trust

Peterson, Eugene H. (1994) *The Message: New Testament*, Colorado, NAVPRESS
Wilson, David and Rees, Gwyther (2006) *Just Justice: A study into Black young people's experiences of the youth justice system*, London, The Children's Society

10 Education and the Black Church

Cheron Byfield

For decades the discourse on the education of Black children has been monopolised by the underachievement dialogue. Unsurprisingly, the upshot is that Black children, particularly Black boys, have become synonymous with the concept of underachievement. Black children in the UK start school as one of the highest achieving groups of children, but leave school as one of the lowest achievers. The long term effect of underachievement is particularly devastating, especially for Black males, as it partially accounts for them being overrepresented amongst the unemployed, in mental institutions and in prisons but underrepresented in universities and in skilled and semi-skilled occupations. Countless theories have emerged over the years to account for this phenomenon, most focusing on psychogenic and sociogenic explanations – for example, Black people are intellectually inferior to others (Herrnstein and Murray 1994), cool pose, a survival strategy employed by Black boys for coping with racism (Majors and Billson 1992), colour-blind educational policies and practices (Tomlinson 1977), the socio-economic class of Black students (Swann Report 1985) and racism (Watt et al. 1999).

The portrayal of Black children from a deficit standpoint provides an imbalanced picture of Black children. There are many Black boys and girls who achieve against the odds. This article therefore seeks to address this imbalanced picture of Black children by focusing on the more positive aspect of Black children in education and the role the Black churches have played in contributing towards their educational success. Thus, although the rewards of Christianity are often seen in the context of the afterlife, the reality is that the church has been instrumental in the education of Black children, thus engineering rewards in this present life.

Indeed, the Black churches are the oldest and largest Black social institutions in the UK. They are the anchoring institution in the Black community and one of the few institutions owned and operated by the Black community. Within many of these churches education is linked both to the formation of ideological beliefs and to social involvement. The Black churches have a legacy of addressing the educational needs of Black children; collectively they act as a bridge to enable Black students to participate more fully in the wider society.

Sunday School, church teaching and church culture continues to play an instrumental role in the educational achievement of many children who are exposed to such provisions. In examining these phenomena, this article shall be drawing upon the findings of the research undertaken into the educational success of Black boys (Byfield 2008a and 2008b) as this provides illuminating data on the positive influence of the Black churches on their educational achievement. Data will be presented on students who were either Christians, churchgoers or beneficiaries of positive action educational programmes run by Black churches who then successfully negotiated their way through the school system into universities. These students were from very diverse socio-economic backgrounds and family structures. They were from both new and old universities, mainly the University of Wolverhampton, Birmingham Central University, and the University of Oxford, and were studying a variety of degree disciplines. In order to maintain their anonymity, pseudonyms will be used for the participants who are quoted. In addition, this article will briefly outline two case studies – the National Black Boys Can Association and the Seventh-day Adventist Church. These highlight the diversity of pioneering social action educational initiatives that have been developed by Black churches which impact on the education of Black children.

Sunday Schools, Christian teachings and church culture

Christian teaching has been found to play a significant role in shaping the mindset and world view of children. Within many Black churches, Sunday Schools – sometimes described as the department which caters for people from the cradle to the grave – are the bedrock within many Black churches. One student commented:

> I attribute a lot of my success to Sunday School. We had to read the Bible a lot, and in the Bible there is a lot of thou's and thee's, just as there is in Shakespeare. So when we did Shakespeare at school, we were already familiar with the language; this gave us a head start to many others in our class.
>
> (*Tony, Birmingham Central University*)

Clearly, Tony saw direct educational benefit to the regular Bible reading of the King James Version. Interestingly, his regular exposure to the Bible enabled him to become familiar with the language which was also used in the great writing of historical authors such as William Shakespeare whose work is still widely read in schools. This gave him an advantage over his peers for whom the language appeared to be foreign.

The Bible is endowed with a plethora of parables, a popular reading resource for children that have helped to shape the educational values of some students.

> Christianity has made me aware of my responsibility to make use of the talents I've been given by God. I love the parable about the master's coins, where the master distributed differing amounts of coins to his servants. He expected them to invest whatever he had given them and to yield an increase. However, the one who got one coin chose not to invest it, unlike the one who had been given several coins. When the master returned, he was angry with the one who had not traded on what he had given him, so he ended up taking it away from him and giving it to the servant who had traded well with his talents. I believe that God has given me talents which I need to trade on, i.e. I have been given certain potentials which I need to realize. I believe it is a greater crime of those who do not achieve because they waste their potential through slothfulness, laziness or lack of interest, than it is for those who do not achieve because they don't have the potential to achieve. It's a waste to bury what God has given you, no matter how small it is; that's just not good enough!
>
> (*Henroy, University of Oxford*)

Henroy's testimony of the influence of this parable on his life is quite profound. Henroy did not limit the application of the parable to Christian works but extended it into the educational sphere.

Many of the students used words such as *'focus'*, *'direction'* and *'guide'* when describing the role of Christianity in their educational achievement. For these students, Christianity provided them with direction and kept them focused and positive. Indeed one student remarked:

> I believe that if you keep on trying, you will succeed eventually, and even if you do not succeed, there will be something that you're meant to do.

> *(David, University of Oxford)*

David's faith put him in a 'win win' situation; his academic pursuit would either lead to academic success, or to something else that he was destined to do. His faith, therefore, gave him a quiet sense of confidence that his endeavours would not be in vain.

Specific reference to prayer and the role that it played in their lives was made by several students.

> I didn't worry about things as much. If there was anything troubling me, I'd pray about it. It gave me a sense of being in control. I sing in this acapella group that tours around the world; a lot of us are Christians, so we pray together. If anyone is having problems or feeling down, we'll take time out after rehearsals and pray and talk about it. I always prayed about my education and exams.

> *(Stephen, University of Oxford)*

For many practicing Christians, prayer is a genuine form of communication with God. The reciting of prepared prayers is rarely part of public or private worship amongst Black Christians, rather the content of their prayers is personally constructed at the point of utterance. Indeed, prayer was perceived by these students as a mechanism by which they could draw strength and solicit support from their direct, beneficial relationship with God (Pattillio-McCoy 1998). Within the Black community, prayer is a valued form of capital (Pattilio-McCoy 1998), but as Carter (2003) asserts, the importance of this and other non-dominant forms of capital is unfortunately overlooked in the work of theorists such as Bourdieu (1983). Prayer, nonetheless, is prevalent in the everyday life of Black Christians. For many students, God is like a fortress that they turn to when they face adversities. Their strong belief in the activity of deity in everyday life – not just in life after death – leads them to pray to the deity for his intervention in their lives. Hence, religion gave these students solace, confidence and strength when they needed it and provided them with a sense of accept-ance and belonging.

Many of the students held the view that Christianity developed their character, endowed them with moral values and shielded them from adverse situations. Typical comments made by these students were:

> Christianity has contributed to my success because it has kept me out of trouble.
>
> *(Trevor, University of Oxford)*

> Without God, I wouldn't be here. Christianity has given me depth of character. I've looked at situations that my friends are in and know that I too could have been in them had it not been for God.
>
> *(Sam, University of Wolverhampton)*

> Being a Christian has developed my character. Because we are taught and live by Biblical principles – like the 10 commandments, which instruct us not to lie, steal etc – we develop character and discipline. Also, because we have to sit still in church for quite a long time this develops discipline in us. When we had events like conventions – these are huge collective church events which start in the morning and finish at 10 p.m. at night – we had to be disciplined [laughed], we just couldn't run up and down in church without getting into serious trouble with our parents. A lot of kids are not used to being in that kind of environment where they have to behave themselves for that length of time, but from the age of 2 or 3 years old, I had to. This helped to develop my character and caused me to be more disciplined. Church has also helped me to stay out of trouble. Being a committed Christian, I don't get caught up into gang culture or a lot of things that my friends are drawn into, i.e. going out to parties and having late nights. This

allowed me to have more time to devote to my education and to focus on the more important things in life.

(*Tony, Birmingham Central University*)

For many of these students, Christianity served as a preventative measure stopping them from getting involved in crime, gangs, drugs and other immoral practices. In addition, it served as a source of strength and as a survival mechanism in the face of peer pressure and other adversities. Hence, instead of adopting a pathological response to adverse situations, they were able to employ an adaptive strategy. Religion was an underlying driving force that kept them out of trouble and kept them on track to achieving educational success.

A popular theory found in the literature to explain boys' underachievement is that Black boys have low self esteem (Osborne 1997a) although more recently scholars have demonstrated that it is Black male *students'* self esteem that is low – how they perceive themselves within the school context – rather than their general self-esteem (Spencer 1991). The students in my study generally tended to be highly resilient, socially skilled, intellectually competent, self-reliant and self-accepting. Amongst the mélange of factors that had a positive influence in their lives which prevented them from developing low self-esteem, was their strong sense of racial identity and their religious beliefs.

The church: a place for skills development and nurturing

Several students saw a connection between regular Bible reading and the development of key educational skills. For some, during their early childhood, the Bible was the story book used by their parents and also the medium used to teach them how to read. For others, the Bible was a significant mechanism by which other key educational skills were developed. One student commented 'the Bible studies thing was huge; it was good practice for critical reasoning and vocabulary building'. Bible reading not only instilled work ethics in these students, but it also extended their intellectual capacity by introducing them to a wide range of conceptual frameworks, extended their vocabulary and developed their critical reasoning skills. Similarly, Channer also found that church exposed her respondents to the philosophical and psychosocial aspects of life, taught them self discipline, and through encouragement, developed their work ethic (Channer 1995 p.135).

Students also made reference to the social skills they developed through regular church attendance. Church attendance enabled them to develop certain disciplines which were also needed within the school classroom; for example, the development of the ability to sit still and listen for a long period of time. Black churches traditionally have longer services than White majority churches and hence children in attendance have to sit still for long periods of time. Glaeser and Sacerdote (2001) argue that sitting still and listening is a skill required in both going to church and going to school and that this, in effect, is likely to train children to listen and sit still for a considerable length of time. Church was also perceived by these students to have influenced their lives in other profound and encompassing ways. For example, it provided them with a strong personal, social and community identity, offered social and psychological benefits, and gave them a sense of belonging, reassurance and self validation (Byfield 2008b, Channer 1995, Rhamie and Hallam 2002). Historically, Black churches are renowned for the care they give to their members (Calley 1965).

Churches with a strong education culture

Some students considered the influence of their church to be a significant factor in the advancement of their education. Those who belonged to churches with a strong pro-education culture testified how their churches both nurtured and developed relevant skills of value within the school marketplace. They made comments such as 'we were pushed to get an education in our church' and 'educational achievements were always acknowledged in our church'. In addition, several students made reference to having access to positive role models within their church congregation. Black churches have a disproportionately high number of Black professionals compared to the Black community as a whole, and this phenomenon created a virtuous circle, as these professionals served as role models to the children within their churches. As one student commented 'I am inspired by seeing so many Black professionals in my church'. These students aspired to be like the people who inspired them and valued the opportunity to interact with these professionals that being part of the church community gave them.

However, amongst this cohort of students interviewed for this research, few considered their churches to have a pro-education culture. Indeed, much can be learnt from our Black sister churches in the USA, who generally, are far more advanced in responding to the educational needs of Black children. One American student I interviewed talked about how his church put up on the wall all the names of the graduates from elementary school through to graduate school each year, published their names in the anniversary book, and put up the pictures of the high school graduates accompanied by a little profile about them and details of the college they were going to. Sometimes they would call the students out to the front of the church and introduce them one by one and inform the church of what they were doing. Another USA student talked about the excellent educational provision in his church. His church had an education ministry with a board of teachers; each teacher had a subject specialism. Once a week they would meet for academic tutoring in a homework club followed by Bible studies and then choir rehearsals. During the academic tutoring session the Board of Teachers would help the high school students, and whilst they were doing their work they would help the middle school kids that were struggling. So they got help and had to help as well.

Beyond the four walls

Although seemingly they lag behind their US counterparts, there is increasing awareness amongst the churches in the UK that they exist to serve, not just their members, but also their wider community. Church organisations such as the African Caribbean Evangelical Alliance have been instrumental over several years in lobbying to effect change for Black children at educational policy level, and individuals from Black churches are represented on initiatives such as the REACH project – a governmental initiative to raise the academic achievement of Black boys. In addition, some churches have become proactive and highly instrumental in taking positive action to address the educational needs of their children by setting up programmes which supplement the educational provision of mainstream schools. Educational programmes such as those implemented via supplementary schools, Seventh-day Adventist Church schools, and projects such the National Black Boys Can Association constitute a response by the Black churches to their experience of racism in schools.

Case study: The National Black Boys Can Association

The National Black Boys Can Association, is a subsidiary of Excell3, a Black-led Christian based educational charity which was founded by Black professionals from the Birmingham-based Acocks Green Church of God of Prophecy denomination in 1999. Although the organisation has also developed the WISE project to cater for educationally disadvantaged children generally, in this article I will be focusing on its flagship project, the National Black Boys Can Association and its network of locally based Black Boys Can projects. The National Black Boys Can Association, under the patronage of Lord Morris of Handsworth OJ, seeks to raise the academic aspirations and achievement of Black boys throughout the UK.

The Association has not only attracted a number of schools and universities to running Black Boys Can Projects, but its non-denominational approach has also attracted a range of churches to join the network including the Church of God of Prophecy, New Testament Church of God, Apostolic Church, Baptist Church, New Testament Assemblies and Elim Pentecostal. From its humble beginnings in 1999, the National Black Boys Can Association has grown to national significance. Its growth was spearheaded by the front page coverage it received in 2001 in the *Times Educational Supplement* as being the organisation with a 'Can-do culture'. The Association works at both national strategic level as well as grassroots level.

At the national strategic level, the National Black Boys Can Association lobbies government and policy makers to effect change in the education of Black boys. Its work has featured in ministers' televised speeches and policy documents on education as an example of best practice, and it has participated in the Ministerial Question Time for young people. It has been invited and sponsored by the Labour Party, Conservative Party and Liberal Democratic Party to make a cross-party presentation to MPs at the House of Commons. In 2005 it became one of the eleven National Strategic Partners for the Department for Communities and Local Government and sits on several governmental working parties and policy groups. It has contributed to national strategic documents such as the Breakthrough Britain Report and the Conservative Party's education Green Paper, 'Raising the Bar, Closing the Gap'. In addition, it has influenced key reports on school exclusions such as 'Getting It, Getting Right' (DfES 2006) and also contributed to the REACH report.

At grass roots level, the National Black Boys Can Association supports organisations, community groups, churches, schools and universities to set up Black Boys Can projects. These now exist in most major cities throughout England. Their strategy for raising the aspirations and attainment of Black boys is based upon their four-pillar strategy of empowering the boys, empowering parents, engaging the community and supporting, challenging and working with mainstream education. Boys are empowered through a training and development programme and their work is accredited through the Excell Awards, a nationally recognised qualification as well as linking with national initiatives such as the 'Reading is Fundamental' project. Through the Black Boys Can National Youth Council, boys' voices are heard at every level and they play an active role in major events and conferences, for example, as co-chairs. For parents, the programme includes events such as parenting conferences, parenting forums, parenting skills training and mediation support.

A number of parenting handbooks have been published including *Empowering Black Parents to Empower their Sons ... a Handbook for Parents of Teenaged Black Boys*, as well as the DfES commissioned *Help Your Children to Learn – Information for African Caribbean Parents*. In addition, Trentham Books has published the positive international research study into educationally successful young Black males undertaken by one of its co-founders, entitled *Black Boys Can Make It ... How they Overcome the Obstacles to University in the UK and USA*. The National Black Boys Can Association also runs Black Boys Can projects in schools as well as providing schools with training and consultancy services. Joint projects are held with, and services provided to, other educational establishments including local authorities, universities and the National Union of Teachers.

One of the distinctive perceived benefits of Black Boys Can programmes is their pedagogy which promotes: positive student self-esteem, academic values and skills, life and career planning, and strategies for overcoming barriers Black boys face in pursuit of success. Its pedagogy supplements the mono-culturalistic state schools curriculum. Clive, for example, who attended one of the Black Boys Can projects, perceived the programme to be an 'eye opener'; he recalls:

> My mum and my Sunday School teacher encouraged me and my
> brother to go to Black Boys Can. It was a nice environment. It
> influenced my thinking about my ability to achieve and opened up
> new possibilities for me. We covered many areas ranging from
> Black culture to goal setting, and we learnt to cook as well! What

I found most amazing was the lessons we had on the Black presence in the Bible. That was the first time I ever learnt about Black people in the Bible so I found it fascinating. I also enjoyed lessons on Black inventors – some I had learnt about though TV and Black History Month, but a lot of it was new to me. I think we should cover these types of subjects in school. Our parents don't teach us these things because they didn't know either; they learnt British History at school, not Black history.

(*Clive, University of Wolverhampton*)

Clive's reference to the environment of Black Boys Can is a typical feature often noted in other studies about community interventionist programmes. Chevannes and Reeves (1987, p.151) describes the environment of such programmes as having a strong group solidarity based on common experiences of being Black in a White society, thus providing an environment for 'insulating, protecting and supporting the individual against the unpredictability of White behaviour and constant difficulty of interpreting outcomes in a context of widespread White prejudice and discrimination'.

Case study: Seventh-day Adventist schools

One of the central missions of the Seventh-day Adventist (SDA) Church is to help in the development of the spiritual, physical and mental well-being of people. This is done through its health, development aid and educational programmes. With regard to its global education programme, the church has involved over 100 institutions of higher education, nearly 1500 secondary schools and 5000 primary schools world wide. The church has nearly 1.5 million students enrolled in its institutions world wide. Many of these institutions enrol non-Adventist students as well as employ many non-Adventist teachers. The main criterion is that people are generally happy to comply with the main Christian principles and ethos of this institution.

There are ten SDA schools in England and Ireland and about 46% of all students are non-Adventists. Eight of these are primary schools and two are secondary schools. In addition, the church operates an institution of higher education – Newbold College – where students study for degree programmes accredited both in the UK and USA. Students from all over Europe attend Newbold College where they can study theology in order to formally qualify to become a minister in the church. In addition, New-bold students can earn degrees in Business Studies, English and History. All the primary and secondary schools, except John Loughborough in North London, are part of the independent schools sector where students pay fees in order to attend. There are primary schools in Plymouth, Bracknell, Walthamstow, East Dulwich and Birmingham. The schools follow the national curriculum and are regularly inspected by OFSTED. John Loughborough, which is a secondary school, follows the national curriculum and students there take the GCSE examinations. Harper Bell Primary School in Birmingham and the Theodore McLeary Primary School have both received very good inspection reports by OFSTED in recent years.

In England the schools reflect the cultural mix of the populations that make up the general Adventist church population, in which Whites are now a minority. In schools like Harper Bell and John Loughborough, the overwhelming majority of the students are of African Caribbean back-ground. In this respect, the schools, whilst adhering to the national cur-riculum, reflect the nature of the ethnic composition of the community. What the children learn is relevant to them in two ways: firstly, there is a spiritual perspective which strives to enhance their personal development. Secondly, some of the teaching material is culturally inclusive and relevant and draws upon the experience of Black people within a British context. Above all, because of the closely knit community environment, much of the teaching is delivered by staff who are academically and culturally competent and in some instances, actually know the children and/or their parents either from the community or the church. This helps to create a very positive learning environment for the children. According to Dr Keith Davidson, Education Director of the British Union Conference of Seventh-day Adventists, where the schools have strong leadership and an ethos of high expectations embedded within a spiritual context, students tend to develop a greater sense of 'purpose which drives them away from the path of disaffection'.

Sending children to schools is not the only way to educate them, however, and so the church has a world wide Pathfinder programme in which young people aged 10 to 16 are trained in a wide range of skills that will help them to fulfil their opportunities in later adult life. Young people are trained in leadership skills and citizenship issues, in addition to environment and nature studies. Young people complete tasks and each year produce a portfolio of evidence in order to demonstrate their competence in particular areas. They are called upon to lead worship services and other activities in front of audiences of varying sizes which helps to develop important communication and confidence-building skills. Most importantly, what all this demonstrates is that the Seventh-day Adventist Church in Britain is playing a major role in addressing the educational needs of children. This helps to dispel the myth that schools with large numbers of Black students are not likely to achieve satisfactory results in the primary and secondary education system in Britain.

Future challenges and opportunities

Clearly Black churches can, and many indeed do, play a critical role in the education of Black children. Children's connectedness to God, a concept I have termed, 'Divine Capital' (Byfield 2008b) enhances children's self confidence, provides them with a sense of direction, enables them to remain focused in the face of peer pressure and other adversities, helps to develop their character, endows them with moral values and shields them from adverse situations and associations. Above all, through prayer, they are able to draw strength and solicit support from God. The churches are also an arena in which children can gain and trade on their social capital – giving them access to positive Black role models, providing them with a strong personal, social and community identity, offering social and psychological benefits, and giving them a sense of belonging, reassurance and self validation. Churches often already provide, often unwittingly, opportunities for children to develop educationally relevant social disciplines, even though the link between school and the repository of social capital they acquire in church is often overlooked; and hence not as effectively transported into their educational endeavours.

Undoubtedly, in many respects the church community is a rich source of cultural capital. The type and level of support churches provide is diverse, ranging from encouragement and acknowledgment of educational achievement to providing direct academic support. Churches are instrumental in enhancing the cultural capital of students through connecting them with educated individuals from various professions and by providing them with educational support and instruction at church. Parents need to be encouraged to make more use of Bible reading in the home as Bible reading not only builds their child's spiritual development, but also helps to develop their reading skills, exposes them to historical language, extends their vocabulary and intellectual capacity, introduces them to a wide range of conceptual frameworks, develops their critical reasoning skills, and instills the work ethic in their children.

Churches that develop a pro-education culture generally do not happen by accident; they were engineered. The plight of Black children in the UK is of great concern, and Black churches collectively has to shift gear from being mainly spectators – observing the problem – to becoming major participators in providing solutions to the problems. Black churches in the UK have done well, but a lot more needs to be done and every church can do something, no matter how small. I wonder how many pupils in our churches could say 'We felt supported by the entire congregation'. This was the comment of one of the USA students I interviewed as part of my international research study. There are resources and empowerment opportunities within the Black churches which can be utilised to redress the underachievement of Black children. The National Black Boys Can Association for example, through its community franchise operation, offers resources and training to churches that want to start their own Black Boys Can project. In addition, the organisation has developed Blackpupils.com, an educational and personal development internet site for Black boys and girls, parents, schools and the community. This resource is readily available for churches to subscribe to.

The Department for Communities and Local Government, through its REACH project, are promoting a Black male role modelling programme. Although the role modelling project is somewhat controversial, there is nonetheless a plethora of positive Black males within the Black churches that can, and indeed should be, supporting Black boys within their churches and in their local community. There are both formal opportunities, through REACH, to get involved, as well as informal self initiated opportunities to support boys in your church and community. Furthermore, in recent years the government has been encouraging the establishment of a new breed of independent schools, known as academy schools. Academy schools are failing schools which can be taken over by companies including faith based organisations. Academy schools are non-fee paying, non-selective schools. Our White sister churches have become actively involved in bidding for these schools, but few Black churches are positioning themselves to seize these opportunities.

Excell3, the umbrella organisation for the National Black Boys Can Association, is now an approved academy sponsor supported by the Church of God of Prophecy and the Council of Black Led Churches. It has positioned itself to get involved in the academies movement. Although competition for these schools is fierce and the financial requirements are high, collectively the Black churches, by working together, can positively respond to this opportunity presented through the academy schools programme. However, Black churches are likely to face opposition in sponsoring academy schools, therefore, much lobbying needs to take place before this opportunity can be realised. Trust schools are also another new pedigree of schools being established by the government in response to failing schools. Trust schools are not independent schools, but they provide opportunities for Black churches to become trustees of schools and to affect the educational outcomes for children.

Conclusion

Black churches in the UK are often perceived as being irrelevant. Whilst this certainly is not the case, there is undoubtedly much more that many Black churches can do with regard to the education of Black children. There are opportunities for Churches to operate at different levels: at national strategic level – lobbying to effect change; at school level – seizing the opportunities available through government school initiatives to sponsor academy schools, or become involved as trustees in trust schools, or indeed as school governors. At community level, Black churches can get involved by offering to support children within the community, or at a church level, by heightening educational expectations and achievement and providing pupils with a wealth of capital which they can use to their academic advantage.

At whatever level churches choose to get involved, they can, through provisions of social, cultural and Divine Capital provide pupils with a psychological and social framework within which Black pupils can make sense of their purpose in life, whilst simultaneously providing them with emotional and spiritual support to maximise their potential here on earth.

References

Bourdieu, P. (1983) 'Forms of Capital' in Richardson, J. G. (ed) *Handbook of Theory and Research for the Sociology of Education,* New York, Greenwood Press

Byfield, C. (2008a) *Black Boys Can Make It – How they Overcome the Obstacles to Universities in the UK and USA*, Stoke on-Trent, Trentham Books

Byfield, C. (2008b) The Influence of Religion on the Educational Achievement of Black Boys: a UK-USA Study, *British Journal of Sociology of Education*, 29 (2), p.189–199

Calley, M. J. (1965) *God's People –West Indian Pentecostalism Sects in England*, Oxford, Oxford University Press

Carter, P. (2003) 'Black Cultural Capital, Status Positioning and Schooling: Conflicts for Low-Income African American Youth', *Social Problems*, 50 (1) pp.136–155

Channer, Y. (1995) *I am a Promise: The School Achievements of British African Caribbeans*, Stoke on Trent, Trentham Books

Chevannes, M. and Reeves, F. (1987) 'The Black Voluntary School Movement: Definition, context and prospects', in Troyna, B. (ed.) Racial Equality in Education, NY, Routledge

Glaeser, E. and Sacerdote, B. (2001) *Education and Religion*, National Bureau of Economic Research, Harvard Institute of Economic Research, Paper no 1913

Herrnstein, R. A. and Murray, C. (1994) *The Bell Curve: Intelligence and Class Structure in American Life*, New York, Grove Press

Majors, R. and Billson, J. (1992) *Cool Pose: The Dilemmas of Black Manhood in America*, New York, Lexington Books

Osborne, J. W. (1997a) 'Race and Academic Disidentification', *Journal of Educational Psychology*, 89, pp.728–735

Pattilio-McCoy, M. (1998) 'Church Culture as a Strategy of Action in the Black Community', *American Sociological Review*, 63 (6) pp.767–784

Rhamie, J. and Hallam, S. (2002) 'An Investigation into African Caribbean Academic Success in the UK', *Race, Ethnicity and Education*, 5, (2) pp.151–168

Spencer, M. (1991) 'Adolescent African American self esteem: suggestion for mentoring programme content', Conference Paper Series. Washington, Urban Institute

Swann, Lord (1985) *Education for All: Final Report of the Committee of Inquiry into the Education of Children from Ethnic Minority Groups*. Cmnd 9453, London, HMSO

Tomlinson, S. (1977) 'Race and Education in Britain 1960–77: An Overview of the Literature', *Sage Race Relations Abstracts*, 2 (4) pp.3–33

Watt, D., Sheriffe, G. and Majors, R. (1999) 'Mentoring Black Male Pupils', Unpublished manuscript, City College Manchester

11   *Health and the Black Church*

Lincoln Sargeant

Religion and health

For many in the Black community the Black Church plays an important role in building and strengthening social networks. It is therefore possible that the church can have a significant role in people's health and wellbeing by building social capital within the community. The majority of the research on the subject of religious involvement in health comes from the US. In general there is a well established association between religious affiliation, or church attendance, and better physical and mental health compared to people without religious involvement (Felix et al. 2003; Mitchell and Weatherly 2000). Religious affiliation can have a direct influence on lifestyle practices and can make smoking, alcohol abuse, illicit drug use and unsafe sex less common. Association may be mediated through family structure and community mores. It is worthy of note that personal faith expressed, for example, through prayer is associated with better mental health (Mitchell and Weatherly 2000).

A study of African American women found that private expressions of faith had a greater impact on mental health, resulting in fewer depressive symptoms than on self-reported general health and chronic conditions. Frequency of church attendance was also positively associated with health, but the prevalence of chronic diseases was higher among church members than among women with no affiliation. Social networks were found to mediate some of the positive aspects of religious involvement on health in this study (van Olphen J. et al. 2003). The great challenge for the

Black Church, however, is whether it has a role to influence health among people who have no formal affiliation or do not attend church services. With falling trends in church attendance the influence of the Black Church on health would have to reach beyond its regular members to the wider community if it is to have a significant impact. The church as a facilitator for the development of private devotion may help members to cope with the challenges of life and thus maintain mental wellbeing. The church as a facilitator of bonding social capital can ensure that members are part of caring social networks that can provide social, economic and psychological support to manage ill health. This role is particularly important as many adherents of the Black Church are ageing and living with potentially disabling long term conditions.

However, the Black Church in the UK should consider its role in building and fostering community social capital. In the context of experiences of interpersonal racism and perceptions of racism in the wider society the Black community has a mistrust of official institutions. The church may be consequently one of the few community organisations that have credibility in the Black community, both among church members and non-members alike especially where these communities are predominantly Christian. Where Black communities are made up of people of different religious backgrounds co-operation between church, mosque and temple becomes necessary to bring the whole community together to tackle health issues.

There are some broad areas that might define a role for the Black Church in promoting and maintaining health. The first is to act as a repository of health information and as a catalyst for change where preventive practices need to be adopted. The role of the church in promotion of sexual health especially among young people is well recognised (Nweneka 2007). Awareness of major diseases within the local community can position the church to help control these conditions. An example of a broad based approach to health promotion is evident in the Seventh-day Adventist Church through the Health Ministries department. Though not historically a Black denomination, there are several large churches in London with a Black majority membership. Each church is supported by the South England Conference of Seventh-day Adventists to deliver health promotion activities in areas including: Healthy Eating, Healthy Weight, Breathe Free (to help stop smoking), Heart Health, Sexual Health, and Drug Awareness.

Tuberculosis though still relatively uncommon in the UK remains an important public health threat. Early diagnosis and treatment is important not only for the patient but because it also reduces spread. Some three out of every four new cases of tuberculosis are reported in people who were not born in the UK. Non-UK born Black Africans accounted for the second largest number of new cases reported in 2006 (Health Protection Agency 2007). The Black Church can help to raise awareness of tuberculosis without creating the stigma that a targeted government programme might elicit.

The burden of hypertension and diabetes is high in the Black community (Zaninotto et al. 2007). High proportions of people with these conditions are undiagnosed or inadequately controlled. As a result they develop complications such as deteriorating vision and kidney function, strokes and heart disease. The church has a role to raise awareness and to empower patients to optimise the management of long term conditions. In particular, the Black Church can help their communities to tackle salt intake in the diet which is a major risk factor for raised blood pressure. Some people are unable to read food labels and are thus unaware of their salt intake. In similar fashion diet plays an important role in preventing overweight and obesity but the relevant knowledge to manage caloric intake may be lacking among those at greatest risk. The church can help to make relevant health education available in their communities by drawing on the relevant expertise and by providing models of optimal health behaviour.

In addition, the Black Church can act as a focus for community involvement in influencing health care planning decisions. A sense of disempowerment may prevent the people in greatest need of health care services from having a voice in the planning of these services. Access to health care is affected not only by geography and transport but also by cultural distance between service providers and users (Mclean et al. 2003; Szczepura 2005). Lack of knowledge about the processes by which health policies and strategies are formulated, or distrust of those processes can act as barriers to optimal health care provision for the Black community. The church can help to bring communities together to articulate their health needs and priorities and can facilitate the collective voice in making these wishes known to the powers that be.

The advocacy role of the Black Church is particularly evident around mental health issues. Black majority churches have worked with Black

Mental Health UK since its formation in 2006 to 'focus on empowering African Caribbean communities to improve the Black service user experience and reduce the over representation of Black people at the coercive end of psychiatric care.' The Black Church is well positioned to be an active third sector player in delivering services to enhance the physical and mental wellbeing of the community. One area of interest is community mental health care provision where the church may be better placed to detect mental illness in the early stages and facilitate referral to the appropriate health care providers. Another area is in provision of personal social care for the elderly and people with disability. The church has a long tradition of informal care and can work effective with the statutory sector in extending care to vulnerable people in the community to allow them to continue living at home rather than in care institutions. Many of the largest Black majority churches provide professional counselling services. For example, Kingsway International Christian Centre (KICC) operates Hopeline, a telephone counselling service, and Jesus House provides a pre- and post-natal counselling service for expectant mothers (Blossom Ministry). Most churches have visitation ministries to the sick.

The context

There were 1.15 million Black people in the UK according to the 2001 Census, including nearly 0.6 million from the more established Black Caribbean population and nearly half a million Black Africans. The Black population is concentrated in London, with 78% of the Black African population living there, as well as nearly two-thirds of the Caribbean-origin population (61%). These populations are more youthful in age structure than the White population, which means that Ethnic Minority population growth will remain rapid over the coming years (Szczepura 2005).

Any discussion of health among Black and Ethnic Minority (BME) groups in the UK must confront the almost inevitable comparison with the majority White population. The gap in health outcomes between BME communities and the general population is a major focus of UK government policy that aims to reduce these health inequalities. While this attempt is laudable, the focus on health inequalities may mean that a health problem in the BME community could be neglected if it is not deemed to be an important cause of health inequality. The observation that people of African descent have lower premature death rates from coronary heart disease (CHD) compared to the general population (Zaninotto et al. 2007), may mask increases in death rates from the condition within these minority populations (Abbotts et al. 2004). For those with an interest in the health of people of African descent, the most useful information would come from data on the major causes of illness and death in these populations. These data would enable monitoring of trends so that appropriate public health action can be taken and effective measures can be targeted at high-risk groups within the Black population. Unfortunately, such data are rare in the UK. The description of health among Black people in Britain is often based on a comparison with the general populace.

The examination of health in Black populations must first attempt to account for patterns of health and disease within these populations without undue reference to other populations. In addition to the scarcity of data from the UK and other developed countries with Black minority populations, there is also the challenge that the health experience of subgroups within the Black population may be very different. Black populations, like their White counterparts may be segmented by gender, age and socio-economic status. All of these variables will have substantial influences on health. However, other factors are also important. The health experience of Black people born in Britain differs from that of their parents who migrated from the Caribbean and Africa. In addition, the health of recent migrants can be expected to contrast with that of people who have settled in Britain for decades. Added to this is the complexity of ethnic groupings within the Black population. The Office of National Statistics gives three groupings for Black or Black British: Black Caribbean, Black African and Black other (Office of National Statistics 2003). Some people who might be considered Black may identify themselves as Mixed. It is evident that these categories are inadequate to capture the full diversity of ethnic groups commonly referred to as Black, but they are a useful starting point.

Ethnicity is a multi-faceted and changing concept that includes several aspects. These include country of birth, nationality, language spoken at home, parents' country of birth in conjunction with country of birth, skin colour, national/geographical origin, racial group and religion (Office of National Statistics 2003). Although 71% of Blacks reported Christianity as their religion in the 2001 Census, almost one in five reported no religion or did not state their religion. Furthermore, being religious was also related to country of birth. Those born in the UK were less likely to be religious than their immigrant parents born abroad (Office of National Statistics 2006). It can be reasonably assumed, given current trends in church attendance and religious adherence, that a substantial proportion reporting Christianity as their religion would not attend church services regularly.

Ethnicity and health

There is an implicit assumption when the health experiences of different racial or ethnic groups are compared. Ethnicity and race are assumed to explain the observed gap (Kaufman and Cooper 2008). Race is sometimes used as a surrogate for biologic variation but this is misleading. Most biologic attributes vary continuously in populations. For example, the height of adult men will vary around an average. To classify someone as tall or short presupposes a decision to establish criteria for this classification. For example, it might be decided that anyone who is six feet or more will be classified as tall but these criteria would be based on value judgements rather than on the features of the biologic factor, height. If 'tall' is defined as being 6 feet or more, then someone who was 5 feet 11¾ inches would not be classified as tall. However, without measurement it would be impossible to tell.

Genetic research has shown that there are no biologic attributes that can be used to classify people into mutually exclusive racial groups. There is more variation within so-called racial groups than between them. These research findings have confirmed the well established fact that race is a social rather than a biologic construct. The assignment of a racial or ethnic label even if self-identified is based more on social than physical attributes. Even when physical attributes such as skin colour are used to define racial and ethnic groupings the social milieu may be more influential in determining how individuals and the wider society relate to racial and ethnic identities (Kaufman and Cooper 2008).

Blood pressure levels among people of Black Caribbean origin in the UK are higher than other ethnic groups. The prevalence of hypertension among Black Caribbean men in England in 2004 was 38% compared to the general population of 32%. However, the prevalence among Black African men was 25% and this was lower than Irish men living in England at 36% (Zaninotto et al. 2007). An international study comparing hypertension prevalence across populations of European and African descent found that there was wide variation within both European (25% to 57%) and African (14% to 44%) populations. Furthermore, when viewed against White populations the prevalence of hypertension in Blacks is not unusually high (Cooper et al. 2005).

A study of hypertension in Black populations in Africa, the Caribbean and the United States found that prevalence was lowest in rural Africa, intermediate in the Caribbean and highest in the US. However, the average blood pressure was similar in the 25 to 34-year-old age group. Blood pressure rose more steeply with age in the US compared to Africa and there were consistent associations between blood pressure levels and obesity and salt intake in all populations (Cooper et al. 1997). Studies like these illustrate the point that focusing on difference between ethnic groups can mask important insights about prevention within an ethnic group. Hypertension although more common among Black Caribbean people living in the UK is not related to race or ethnicity per se. More importantly, the rise of blood pressure with age is not inevitable in Black populations. As in White populations, salt intake and obesity are critical risk factors and dealing with these will reduce blood pressure levels in Black people.

While race and ethnicity are not useful at defining biologic explanations for health and disease they do provide clues to understanding factors that can be influential. Ethnicity may influence lifestyle choices such as diet. Traditional diets may confer protection or harm in a different environment especially where average physical activity levels may vary (Rankins et al. 2007). Attitudes toward health and health-seeking behaviour can also be influenced by ethnicity. There is some evidence that obesity has a more positive impact on the self esteem of Black African girls compared to Black Caribbean and Black British teenage girls (Viner et al. 2006).

The association with ethnicity and health cannot be fully explained without taking account of the mediating role of socioeconomic status and its correlates. The UK Labour Force Survey of summer 2002 found an unemployment rate among Black people of 15% compared to 5% among Whites (Smith 2002). Black claimants for Job Seeker's allowance had longer claim periods compared to White counterparts (Grierson 2007). Black Africans and Black Caribbean people are two and a half times more likely to live in deprived areas compared to White people in the UK. These areas tend to be in London and other cities especially in the West Midlands (Tinsley 2006).

In addition to health disadvantage that is conferred by living in deprived areas, the issue of racism must be considered when examining the role of ethnicity and health. Black Caribbean respondents to the 1999 Health Survey for England were asked about their experience of interpersonal racism and perception of racism in the wider community. These experiences and perceptions were associated with a doubling or tripling of the risk of common mental disorders and psychosis (Karlsen et al. 2005). Studies of African Caribbean participation in local community networks in the UK found that levels of participation in voluntary organisations and community activist networks were low. There was serious distrust between statutory and community sectors, and reported disillusionment and disempowerment with the African-Caribbean community (Campbell et al. 2002, 2004).

Hence while bonding social capital may exist through social connections within the Black community there is less bridging (social connections between individuals who are dissimilar) and linking (social connections across different levels of social status) of social capital. Community level social capital may influence health in several ways. Social networks facilitate sharing of health information and adoption of preventive practices. Communities that have high levels of voluntary participation may find it easier to organise to influence how health services are planned and delivered for their communities. Strong social networks also provide psychosocial support and enhance resilience in the face of illness (Scheffler et al. 2008).

Specific health concerns in the Black community

Sexual health

Although it is difficult to monitor sexual health among young people of Black African and Black Caribbean descent, there is evidence to suggest that teenage conceptions and pregnancies are higher in Black communities compared to others of similar deprivation but different ethnic profile. Girls and young women of Black and Black British ethnicity are also over-represented among abortions for under-18s. Data on mothers giving birth under age 19, identified from the 2001 Census, show rates of teenage motherhood are significantly higher among mothers of 'Mixed White and Black Caribbean', 'Other Black' and 'Black Caribbean' ethnicity (Department for Education and Skills 2006).

There is considerable variation within the Black community when it comes to the attitudes and behaviour regarding sex and relationships of young people. However, some generalisations are supported by research done in East London and Birmingham. In a study of students from secondary schools in East London 25% of teenage men and 11% of teenage women reported having had sex. Among those who had sex, initiation was before age 13 in almost 2 in 5 of the students. Compared to White peers, Black Caribbean young men were more likely to have had sex, and were more likely to have had initiation at or before age 13 but were more likely to use contraception. Young men who reported frequent religious observance were less likely to have had sex. However, having initiated sex they were more likely to have unprotected sex (Coleman et al. 2008; Sinha et al. 2007; Teenage Pregnancy Research Programme 2005). Regular smoking, drinking and experimenting with drugs were associated with increased risk of sexual activity in both young men and women. Depression among teenage girls was a risk factor for sexual activity and low self esteem was associated with unprotected sex (Teenage Pregnancy Research Programme 2005).

In addition to increasing the risk of teenage pregnancy, unprotected sex is also a risk factor for the transmission of sexually transmitted infections, Hepatitis B and HIV/AIDS. These conditions have dire consequences for the physical and mental health of young people and in the case of teenage pregnancy for the next generation as well.

The Black Church has an important role in the health education of parents, young people and the wider community. Education must involve more than transmission of facts but must also seek to influence attitudes. Teenagers describe difficulties talking to parents about sex, but belief that parents would disapprove of a physical relationship was protective against having sex. Teenagers, however, sought information and advice from other relatives and trusted peers. Hence the knowledge and attitudes of the community about sexual matters may have profound influences on individual behaviour. This is true not only for teenagers but adults as well.

The Black Church should also be proactive in ensuring that access to sexual health services in the local community is optimised. In particular, availability of condoms is an important measure to reduce sexually trans-mitted illnesses and teenage pregnancy. People, and especially teenagers, may experience a disconnect between what is identified as acceptable behaviour by their religion and their day to day practices. This conflict may help to explain why teenagers who report regular religious observance are more likely to have unprotected sex having started being sexually active (Teenage Pregnancy Research Programme 2005). The Black Church has a role not only to advocate ideal sexual behaviour but also to assist those who make other choices to reduce the potential adverse consequences.

Mental health

The incidence of schizophrenia and other psychoses is very high among Black Caribbean and Black African people in the UK (Fearon et al. 2006). This is also true for common mental disorders such as depression and anxiety disorders (Weich et al. 2004). A considerable literature has devel-oped around the explanation for these findings especially as these mental disorders are not as common in the Caribbean. The raised levels of mental disorders in the Black community in the UK do not appear to be due to misdiagnosis or to excessive referral to mental health services. In fact the evidence suggests that mental health access is reduced in these communi-ties and diagnosis may be delayed (McLean et al. 2003). One consequence of this is that Black people with mental health disorders may be inad-equately treated and adverse consequences such as imprisonment may occur. African Caribbean people also suffer higher rates of involuntary detainment in secure psychiatric settings and greater police involvement in this sectioning process. Minority ethnic communities are far less likely to be offered 'talking therapies' such as counselling, more often offered medication, and tend to be prescribed higher drug dosages than their White counterparts (Callan et al. 1998). Pervasive cultural stereotypes permeate the way in which African Caribbean patients are more likely to be viewed as dangerous, threatening and irrational than their White counterparts (McLean et al. 2003).

Suicidal ideation was no more common among the Black Caribbean population compared to British White but the risk of lifetime suicidal ideation is higher among those born in the UK as opposed to migrating as an adult. Being unemployed, unmarried, having mental illness or having difficulty getting on with others were associated with increased risk of suicidal ideation. Importantly, experience of racial abuse or attack doubled the risk of lifetime suicidal ideation compared to the White population (Crawford et al. 2005). Dissatisfaction and mistrust of mental health services lead to the low utilisation of such services and this may in part explain the relatively poor outcomes for Black people with mental illness. In addition, mental health services may not be responsive to the specific needs that result from the cultural, religious and socioeconomic context of the Black community. Although people from the Caribbean speak English there are cultural nuances that are easily misunderstood by those who do not share a similar background. The expressive extrovert manner of communication may also be perceived as threatening.

The Black Church can play an important role in helping to overcome the stigma associated with mental illness within the Black community. The church is recognised as an important informal social support system within the Black community but the burden of mental illness may not be apparent among the leadership of the church. Religious attitudes to mental illness can delay diagnosis or promote resistance to treatment. Church members may feel ashamed to admit to having symptoms of psychological stress or mental illness because of the perception that mental illness is incompatible with religious experience. Mental illness may also be interpreted as demon-possession without referral to professional mental health practitioners for an opinion.

Informal support offered by church groups though not geared at mental health promotion is nevertheless a vital resource. It is important to note that people with mental health problems, and especially recent migrants, do not necessarily see themselves as suffering from sickness but rather from a range of social, political and economic circumstances. It has been noted that typically when most refugees are asked what would help their situation they are much more likely to point to social and economic factors rather than psychological help. By providing for these social and economic factors the Black Church may indirectly be promoting mental health. However, there is a need for specialist health care provision. The church has a role to help articulate the needs of the local community for culturally appropriate services, but may also be a direct provider of 'talking therapies'.

There is scope for partnership working between the Black Church and the NHS to deliver community mental health care services. An example of this type of partnership was highlighted in a BBC news report (BBC News 2001) which described a 'drop in' centre for mentally ill people staffed by mental heath and social workers that operated once a week at the New Creation Christian Centre church in Leyton, East London.

Chronic diseases

Estimates from nationally representative samples indicate that one in three Black Caribbean people has hypertension while one in five men and one in three women are obese. These estimates are higher than the general population as is the prevalence of diabetes – 6.4% among men and 7.3% among women. Despite these high estimates of cardiovascular risk factors, mortality from ischaemic heart disease is lower among people of Black Caribbean and West African origin. Stroke mortality, however, is higher. In general, Black people have a more favourable blood lipid profile compared to the general population (British Heart Foundation 2008; Zaninotto et al. 2007).

The frequency of diabetes in the Black community leads in turn to the high burden of diabetic complications – heart disease, visual impairment, kidney failure and lower limb amputation. Hypertension and diabetes also occur frequently together in this population leading to heart failure and stroke. There is now convincing evidence that adequate control of these conditions can greatly reduce the risk of complications and the disability associated with them (Holman et al. 2008a, 2008b). Screening for specific diabetic complications such as diabetic retinopathy can detect these at an early stage where treatment can limit the damage and preserve sight. In addition, the risk of diabetes and hypertension can be greatly reduced by managing weight and increasing physical activity. Physical inactivity is common; estimated at between 28.5% and 37.6% among Black Caribbean people (Zaninotto et al. 2007). Prevention of weight gain is the preferred strategy for preventing hypertension and diabetes but weight loss of 10% of body weight among overweight and obese people is highly effective. These targets are feasible while a return to ideal body weight is difficult to achieve and maintain.

Obesity is also related to some cancers that are common in Black populations. Of particular interest is prostate cancer where rates are very high. There are screening programmes in the UK for several cancers – breast, cervical and colon cancer. Cancer prevention begins with awareness of cancer risk and adoption of specific preventive measures. Effective measures include at least five portions of fruit and vegetables daily, regular physical activity, weight loss or maintenance of ideal body weight, smoking cessation where applicable, safe alcohol intake and uptake of screening. The Black Church can make a difference by ensuring that health education is done in a culturally appropriate manner. The church can partner with the health service to maximise the reach of health messages within the Black community. It can also help to inform social marketing approaches to health promotion in the Black community. As for other conditions the church can partner with the NHS to ensure that culturally appropriate services are available in the Black community to optimise prevention of long term and other complications.

Ageing

The first waves of migrants from the Caribbean population are ageing as are other migrants from that period. The prevalence of physical and cognitive frailty increases with age and as a result older people develop disabilities that prevent them from living independently as they age. Some have opted to return to their countries of birth but a substantial number have remained in the UK. Prevention strategies can be effective for specific conditions that are common among older people. These include stroke rehabilitation and falls prevention. However, where the scope for prevention is limited, as for example in dementia, provision needs to be made to support through health and social care.

Informal carers, who are often relatives, provide the majority of social care for older people. However, more formal arrangements may become necessary as disability levels or health status deteriorates. Older people may be unable to return home after an acute deterioration in health and provision for nursing/residential care and, if indicated, palliative care must be made. Frail members of the community are especially vulnerable as family structures change so that the extended families that are still typical of their countries of origin can no longer be relied on in the UK to care for elderly family members. As such the church may play a direct role in providing personal social care especially when elderly community members have needs but do not reach thresholds for formal provision. The church can partner with government and other voluntary agencies to develop policies that encompass more than health and social care provision in order to encourage older people to be active participants in society. Among these broader areas as housing and transport policies and legislation the church can promote independent living as well as help to secure the rights of older people's good health, and financial and physical security.

Stewardship of the body and care for the vulnerable

An emphasis on personal health and the imperative to care for the sick and vulnerable are embedded in Christian theology, tradition and practice. Paul speaks of the body as the temple of the Holy Spirit and admonishes his readers to glorify God in the body as well as in the spirit (1 Corinthians 6:19, 20). Illicit drug use and alcohol abuse would be seen by the Black Church as incompatible with wholesome Christian practice. Extramarital sexual relations and smoking are generally frowned upon. Vegetarianism is advocated by Seventh-day Adventists but there is no general position on diet, physical activity or other aspects of healthy living that are specifically advocated as part of routine church teaching. Nevertheless, advocacy of healthful living would be seen by the Black Church as necessary for glorifying God.

In Philippians 4:4–9, Paul sets out a prescription for peace of mind stressing an attitude of rejoicing in all situations and describing the things that Christians should focus their minds on. Research literature supports a link between personal faith and better mental health status, in particular lower rates of depressive symptoms. While personal faith has positive effects it can lead to a simplistic view of, particularly, mental health. The causes of mental illness are complex and varied. The focus of a person's thinking or attitudes to life may play a role but cannot explain why a given person may develop a specific mental illness. If mental illness is perceived as a failure of personal faith this may add to the stigma of the condition and thus delay diagnosis and treatment. The Black Church can do a great deal to help the Black community to relate to mental illness as they would to any physical illness. Black clergy should embrace the role of health educators and leaders in mental health promotion. They should be aware the early symptoms of mental illness and be willing to refer to professional services if necessary.

The gospels describe in detail the healing ministry of Jesus. This pattern of ministry to the whole person, physical as well as spiritual was evident in the early Christian Church. Acts 2:45 indicates that members shared their possessions so that everyone's needs were met. Acts 6:1–7 demonstrates the arrangements that were made to ensure that the widows in the growing church were properly cared for. Jesus speaking of the judgement said in Matthew 25:31–46 that the criteria would be based on how people treated the 'least' among them. This included the sick.

The foundations for service in the community are therefore well established in the Bible and the Black Church has had a tradition of meeting the needs of its members and the wider community. The UK welfare state through the NHS has provided access to healthcare free at the point of need to the whole population. There has consequently been less of a role for the church in meeting health needs in the UK as opposed to other countries without a similar healthcare system. However, cultural barriers and the perception of racism leading to mistrust may reduce access by members of the Black community. This has been the case in mental health access. Furthermore, the church through the fostering of social networks and building social capital in communities plays an often unheralded role in promoting mental and social wellbeing. These social networks are also important for delivering informal care to frail and vulnerable members of the community such as the elderly and people with disabilities.

Partnerships for health

The NHS has recently restructured in order to facilitate the changes necessary to deliver a more responsive service. A key framework for achieving this is through commissioning. The NHS will seek to determine the health needs of communities and commission care to meet these needs. This process envisions strong partnership with the community to define health needs and priorities but also seeks for service providers who can deliver to the necessary service specifications (Department of Health 2005)

A basic requirement is good information on the size and composition of the Black community and the health problems within it. In a 2003 address to the World Health Organization (WHO) staff, Director General Jong-Wook Lee highlighted the importance of data about the population: 'To make people count, we first need to be able to count people' (Lee 2003). Communities can change rapidly as a result of migration and patterns of health can be similarly affected. Census data are collected once a decade and do not provide the current information needed by the health service and other sectors to plan responsive services. The Black Church needs to be an advocate for better health information in local communities. A report by the New Local Government Network entitled 'Managing New Migration' has made suggestions for reforming the way population statistics are collected to address some of the challenges that communities face with rapidly changing populations (Clifton 2007).

While this report was prompted by migration from Eastern Europe the recommendations if implemented can benefit Black and other minority communities that have been underserved because of lack of information on the needs of these communities. UK government policy has repeatedly stressed partnership working at a local level to identify and respond to needs. A Treasury Review of 2002 identified the barriers that prevent the voluntary and community sector from engaging fully to ensure that government targets for reducing inequalities were met. Specifically, BME organisations often lacked resources, including premises, staff, skills, time and funding; had limited access to support; and suffered from low involvement in civic matters, regeneration and key partnerships related to racism and discrimination, real or perceived (Ellis and Latif 2006).

Although the Black Church faces many of these barriers there are also opportunities to increase its role in facilitating civic engagement and social inclusion for the communities they serve by partnering with other churches, community and voluntary organisations, the NHS and relevant government agencies to improve health. This requires a broadening of vision and a willingness to engage in strategic partnerships that may be unusual for the Black Church. However, the Black Church is one of the best placed institutions within the Black community to be a strong advocate for healthy public policy at a local level. It has the potential to be a champion for ensuring that health services are responsive, of high quality and culturally appropriate. There are also areas, such as mental health promotion, where the church can be competitive as a provider of health services.

References

Abbotts J., Harding S., Cruickshank K. (2004) 'Cardiovascular risk profiles in UK-born Caribbeans and Irish living in England and Wales' *Atherosclerosis*, 175(2): pp.295–303

BBC News Online. Black Churches 'can help mentally ill', 11 January 2001 http://news.bbc.co.uk/1/hi/health/1112189.stm (Accessed 24 October 2008)

British Heart Foundation, British Heart Foundation Statistics Website, http://www.heartstats.org/homepage.asp (Accessed 24 October 2008)

Callan A. and Littlewood, R. (1998) 'Patient satisfaction: ethnic origin or explanatory model?' *International Journal of Social Psychiatry*, 44(1): pp.1–11

Campbell C., Cornish F., Mclean C. (2004) 'Social capital, participation and the perpetuation of health inequalities: obstacles to African-Caribbean participation in 'partnerships' to improve mental health', *Ethnicity and Health* 9(4): pp.313–35

Campbell C., Mclean C. (2002) 'Ethnic identities, social capital and health inequalities: factors shaping African-Caribbean participation in local community networks in the UK', *Social Science and Medicine*. 55(4): pp.643–57

Clifton, M. (2007) 'Managing New Migration: A local approach to a global phenomenon', *New Local Government Network*

Coleman L.M. and Testa A. (2008) Sexual health knowledge, attitudes and behaviours: variations among a religiously diverse sample of young people in London, UK, *Ethnicity and Health*, 13(1): pp.55–72

Cooper R., Rotimi C., Ataman S., McGee D., Osotimehin B., Kadiri S.(1997) 'The prevalence of hypertension in seven populations of west African origin', *American Journal of Public Health*, 87(2): pp.160–8

Cooper R.S., Wolf-Maier K., Luke A., Adeyemo A., Banegas J.R., Forrester T. (2005) 'An international comparative study of blood pressure in populations of European vs. African descent', *BMC Medicine*, 3:2

Crawford M.J., Nur U., McKenzie K., Tyrer P. (2005) 'Suicidal ideation and suicide attempts among Ethnic Minority groups in England: results of a national household survey', *Psychological Medicine*, 35(9): pp.1369–77

Department for Education and Skills (2006) *Teenage Pregnancy Next Steps: Guidance for Local Authorities and Primary Care Trusts on Effective Delivery of Local Strategies*

Department of Health (2005) *Commissioning a patient-led NHS*

Ellis J.and Latif S. (2006) *Capacity building Black and minority ethnic voluntary and community organisations*, Joseph Rowntree Foundation

Fearon .P, Kirkbride J.B., Morgan C., Dazzan P., Morgan K., Lloyd T., (2006) 'Incidence of schizophrenia and other psychoses in Ethnic Minority groups: results from the MRC AESOP Study', *Psychological Medicine*. 36(11): pp.1541–50

Felix A.K., Levine D., Burstin H.R. (2003) 'African American church participation and health care practices', *Journal of General Internal Medicine*, 18(11): pp.908–13

Grierson K. (2007) Ethnicity data for Jobseeker's Allowance claimants, Economic and Labour Market Review, 1(2): pp.26–9

Health Protection Agency Centre for Infections (2007) Tuberculosis in the UK: Annual report on tuberculosis surveillance and control in the UK, London

Holman R.R., Paul S.K., Bethel M.A., Matthews D.R., Neil H.A. (2008a) '10-year follow-up of intensive glucose control in type 2 diabetes', *New England Journal of Medicine*. 359 (15): pp.1577–89

Holman R.R., Paul S.K., Bethel M.A., Neil H.A., Matthews D.R.(2008b) 'Long-term follow-up after tight control of blood pressure in type 2 diabetes', *New England Journal of Medicine*, 359(15): pp.1565–76

Karlsen S., Nazroo J.Y., McKenzie K., Bhui K., Weich S. (2005) 'Racism, psychosis and common mental disorder among Ethnic Minority groups in England', *Psychological Medicine*, 35(12): pp.1795–803

Kaufman J.S., Cooper R.S. (2008) 'Race in epidemiology: new tools, old problems;. *Annals of Epidemiology*, 18(2): pp.119–23

Lee J-W. (2003) Address to WHO staff. Geneva, World Health Organization

McLean C., Campbell C., Cornish F. (2003) 'African-Caribbean interactions with mental health services in the UK: experiences and expectations of exclusion as (re)productive of health inequalities', *Social Sciences and Medicine*, 56(3): pp.657–69

Mitchell J. and Weatherly D. (2000) 'Beyond church attendance: religiosity and mental health among rural older adults'. *Journal of Cross Cultural Gerontology*, 15(1):37–54

Nweneka C.V. (2007) 'Sexual practices of church youths in the era of HIV/AIDS: playing the ostrich', *AIDS Care*, 19(8): pp.966–9

Office National Statistics (2003) *Ethnic group statistics: A guide for the collection and classification of ethnicity data*, London, Palrave Macmillan

Office of National Statistics (2006) *Focus on Ethnicity and Religion*, London, Palgrave Macmillan

Rankins J., Wortham J., Brown L.L. (2007) 'Modifying soul food for the Dietary Approaches to Stop Hypertension diet (DASH) plan: implications for metabolic syndrome (DASH of Soul)', *Ethnicity and Disease*, 17(3 Suppl 4):S4–12

Scheffler R.M., Brown T.T., Syme L., Kawachi I., Tolstykh I., Iribarren C. (2008) 'Community-level social capital and recurrence of acute coronary syndrome', *Social Science and Medicine*, Apr.66(7): pp.1603–13 (e-publication)

Sinha S., Curtis K., Jayakody A., Viner R., Roberts H. (2007) '"People make assumptions about our communities": Sexual health amongst teenagers from Black and minority ethnic backgrounds in East London', *Ethnicity and Health*, 12(5): pp.423–41

Smith A. (2002) 'The new ethnicity classification in the Labour Force Survey', *Labour Market Trends*, December

Szczepura A. (2005) 'Access to health care for Ethnic Minority populations', *Postgraduate Medical Journal*, 81(953): pp.141–7

Teenage Pregnancy Research Programme (2005) *Research briefing: Protective and risk factors for early sexual activity and contraception use amongst Black and Minority Ethnic adolescents in East London*, London, Department for Education and Skills and Department of Health

Tinsley J., Jacobs M. (2006), 'Deprivation and ethnicity in England: a regional perspective', Office of National Statistics/Regional Trends Report No.39

http://www.statistics.gov.uk/articles/RegionalTrends/Article3RT39,pdf

Van Olphen J., Schulz A., Israel B., Chatters L., Klem L., Parker E. (2003) 'Religious involvement, social support, and health among African-American women on the east side of Detroit', *Journal of General Internal Medicine*, 18(7): pp.549–57

Viner R.M., Haines M.M., Taylor S.J., Head J., Booy R., Stansfield S. (2006) 'Body mass, weight control behaviours, weight perception and emotional well being in a multiethnic sample of early adolescents', *International Journal of Obesity (London)* (10): pp.1514–21

Weich S., Nazroo J., Sproston K., McManus S., Blanchard M., Erens B. (2004) 'Common mental disorders and ethnicity in England: the EMPIRIC study', *Psychological Medicine*, 34(8): pp.1543–51

Zaninotto P., Mindell J., Hirani V. (2007) 'Prevalence of cardiovascular risk factors among ethnic groups: results from the Health Surveys for England', *Atherosclerosis*, 195(1):e48–e57

12 *Economics and the Black Church*
Christopher A. Johnson

This paper examines the nature and extent of faith economics and its applicability to Black Churches against the backdrop of a growing realisation that faith-based economic development activities play a significant part in urban regeneration. An observation on the evolution of Black Churches and their existing role-function, clarifies that faith-based activities encompass a wide range of cultural, economic, social and spiritual developmental activities and benefit from key partnerships with public sector, community development organisations and other faith institutions. The battle of ideas pertaining to religion versus commerce is historic, but with the advent of modern technology, the level of awareness has heightened and churches and their congregations are questioning not only their puritanical beliefs, but whether realism is being abdicated for 'naked' acceptance of faith as the monopoly of all human progress.

While there is little academic literature on faith economics in Britain, it appears that many religious organisations are engaged in a variety of economic and social activities. Much of our understanding of faith-based economic development efforts are evidenced via Black America, the popular press, and news media. And while such accounts offer important pieces of a story, the literature tends to be scattered, disjointed and descriptive rather than conceptual or analytical (Thomas and Blake 1996: p.137). Although African-led churches in Britain have offered a distinction between religious and commercial activities by combining a translated version of faith economics, it was Caribbean-led churches that pioneered the practice of self-help and self-reliance by mobilising resources in diverse communities including South Asians and Whites, to help bring about economic and social justice.

Background

Government policies of the 1970s and 1980s encouraged individual enterprise and though they also resulted in many social excesses, faith organisations played a significant part in this affair, by mobilising grassroots activity among inner-city residents who were experiencing economic deprivation and social exclusion. Successive British governments have tried to include faith groups in the implementation of urban policy. In the early part of this century, the term 'social enterprise' became commonplace, as policy-makers sought to offer faith organisations greater opportunities to participate in economic development in their respective communities. The birth of the Single Regeneration Budget (SRB) was a direct signal for church organisations to play a more pivotal role in local outcomes. Thus local authorities and regeneration agencies, finally acknowledged the importance of collaborating with faith groups throughout England, to access their vital resources for the benefit of achieving community regeneration targets (Single Regeneration Budget 1–6 (1994–2001), Cabinet Office; Ethnic Minority Business Initiative (1981)).

There are numerous Black Churches in England – located mostly in London, the Southeast, the Midlands and Home Counties, with congregants affiliated to various forms of Christian denominations. Much of this is derived from European influences imposed on generations of Black people, starting with slavery and indentureship, through to colonisation and independence. The added American influence has resulted in churches assuming a Pentecostal outlook in terms of worship and other evangelical rituals.

Statistics from the Christian Research Association show that over the last five years Black Church membership has risen by around 18% compared with a 5% drop for churches nationally (Fig 1). 'Across the UK churches are closing more than they're opening. The growth rate we are seeing in the UK largely comes from the ethnic minority groups' (UK Christian Handbook 2002/2003).

Figure 12.1 Impact of Black worshippers on mainstream churches in the UK

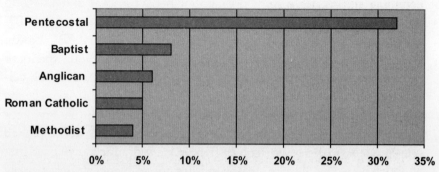

(Source: *UK Christian Handbook*, 2002/2003

In the main, churches provide spiritual and social support, whilst contributing to the regeneration of inner-cities where poverty and other forms of multiple disadvantages exist. A group of Caribbean men in their thirties expressed disappointment in their churches' lack of interest in encouraging commercial enterprise even during prayer and seminary sessions. A young 20-year-old entrepreneur admitted that some Caribbean pastors were afraid of 'losing control' of their congregation if they had to encourage followers to opt for self-employment. This view is common among regular church-goers too. A straw poll conducted in February 2007 showed the following:

- 100% felt that churches should include aspects of economics in their spiritual agenda;
- 60% signified intentions of starting a business;
- 60% considered being an active participant in a moral and spiritual campaign to deal with material and spiritual decay affecting the environment in which young people live;
- 25% were in business but needed support from their churches and/or recognised trade associations;
- 5% were prepared to form a network to champion specifically faith-based businesses

(Business Link Community Engagement Seminar, Black Business Association, West Midlands, February 2006).

Unlike Caribbean established churches, African faith groups tend to be more proactive when it comes to promoting entrepreneurship from a spiritual angle. The 2,000 strong Glory House Church in East London for example, is a modern organisation that serves African and Caribbean communities. In one year, the organisation had a turnover of nearly £1.5 million much of it in the form of donations by members giving around 10% of their income, otherwise known as a 'tithe' (John Cindy, BBC News, August 2005). Like Caribbean settlers of the 1950s and 1960s, the more recent African migrants also bring with them a deep-rooted church culture. Regarded as more than a place of worship, Glory House is a growing institution that has a dedicated mission of combined spiritual and economic empowerment. A large group of its congregants are accomplished entrepreneurs in their own right. Bishop Dr Joe Aldred acknowledged that although new churches are 'prospering' it is not an even picture nationally and the demographics are changing fast. He said, 'Some of these churches started by Caribbean immigrants in the 1950s and 1960s face decline. The church where I am pastor in Birmingham, if you go back 25 years was an overwhelmingly White Baptist church. Fast forward to today and 98% of its members is Black' (BBC News, August 2005).

As stated earlier, a few Caribbean church organisations in England such as the New Testament Church of God (NTCG) and the Pentecostal Credit Union (PCU) have demonstrated the creative fusion of religious expression and community enterprise spirit. On the one hand, Dr. Oliver Lyseight, founder of the NTCG, helped grow the church's congregation from a few hundred in 1953 to tens of thousands of followers today. The organisation has over 100 branches and two missions, with assets valued in excess of £20 million. Revd Carmel Jones is the founder of the PCU, an organisation that was created to fill a void in commercial lending for minorities who were exploited by rapacious money lenders and shady banks (Johnson 2008). Many of the churches' successes have been neither acknowledged or celebrated nationally even though they impact positively on urban regeneration in the English regions particularly.

Faith-based economic development

Understanding the importance of faith economics to religious organisations in modern Britain is a prerequisite when defining economic development in such a context. Economic development is the process of transforming assets into higher valued uses. Its aim is viewed as producing higher living standards and better quality of life, goods and services of high quality, greater variety, and lower costs, more and or better jobs, higher incomes, more productive enterprises, a more diverse economic base, advanced skills that will prepare workers for economic change, the opportunity to alleviate poverty and increase equity, a stronger tax base and the capacity for sustained economic development (Foster 1991).

Generally, faith-based community economic development may be defined as the involvement of faith-based institutions in projects aimed at reinvigorating their communities, establishing sustainable economic development initiatives, and attracting investments by building wealth creation and encouraging entrepreneurship. According to literature on the subject, there are several examples of faith-based economic development and they range from small organisational tasks such as asking groups of people to take part in feeding the elderly at luncheon clubs, to employment skills training for young people in poor neighbourhoods. Other diverse schemes include:

- Working with local authorities to help finance the maintenance of school buildings, and purchasing textual and other writing material for after-school clubs;
- Being part of commissioned studies to determine the availability of sports facilities for young people interested in a variety of sports and other recreational activities;
- Participating in small building projects such as social housing schemes for the elderly and the disabled.

But what do these definitions say about faith-based economic development? Several goals appear to be key for economic development such as employment, skills development and increased tax revenue. Yet, definitional boundaries are unclear regarding the role of faith-based groups in economic development, since their primary function is traditionally one of spiritual uplift, and the exemplification of a moral code for adherents and the wider society.

Activities such as the sale of religious literature to the public and offering guidance and counselling to married couples, constitute both economic and social welfare activities. Yet the definitional question depends on the nature of activities by church groups and their impact on congregants including the non-Christian community. For the purposes of this paper however, a broad idea of economic development is used, through examples of best practice, to show the effect faith organisations have on local development. Indeed, faith-based community development in the Black community offers several opportunities for neighbourhood improvement. Allied to their influence and presence within inner-city areas, religious groups operate within a coherent value system, and provide a framework necessary to carry out social reform. They also offer ready-made leadership and possibilities for strategic co-operation.

Still, there are few case studies on successful African and Caribbean faith groups in Britain such as the role of clergy leadership in economic development. There is incontrovertible evidence to suggest that these faith groups are involved in numerous activities such as:

- Welfare services for young people and older community members;
- Taking part in luncheon clubs;
- Renting church facilities for nursery education and skills training;
- Renting space to community groups to run small revenue projects.

In 1995 the London firm of ABi Associates established *Faith in Business* (FIB). South Asian entrepreneur, Vijay Amin, recognised a niche market for faith organisations and encouraged minority groups to access opportunities afforded by this newly-created supply-side route. To date, FIB has supported hundreds of African and Caribbean entrepreneurs in creating firms across London. Although these firms have a commercial outlook, owners have an unwritten moral and spiritual code of ethics. The FIB's initiative should be applauded although it needs to embrace a national remit.

Measuring impact

The failure to understand the value of faith economics to religious or spiritual organisations in the Black community in Britain is also a failure to recognise the necessity for further investigation into this modern practice. Since many faith groups are in deprived neighbourhoods, it will be interesting to examine both the geography and demography of congregants. This type of analysis can show an interesting mix of racial characteristics within congregations. It can also demonstrate the diversity of the clergy and members of the laity.

Indeed, the measurement of economic activity in each church is absolutely necessary to highlight different operational categories. Implicitly, these should be information and advice, guidance and counselling, training development, pastoral care, contracted social welfare services, housing provision, cultural events and other activities.

In a sample of twenty Black Churches in England, I identified key issues which should be included in measuring the impact of their contribution to faith economics in local communities.

Table 12.1 Organisation of economic development in Black Churches

Driving Force	Admission By
clergy	non-profit board
congregant	head clergy
external leader	committee
internal body	clergy/board
other church	church staff
denomination	other
Client Base	**Source of Revenue**
parishioners	sectional grants
neighbours	church budget
neighbourhood/city wide	private donations
Profit-making	**Grants/Foundations**
no	central government/regional government
yes	in-kind
	sell shares
	special fund-raisers

(Source: Adapted from Reese and Shields 1999)

For this process to be effective, the above criteria for selection should be carefully pre-researched since the overriding goal is to gain basic descriptive information about faith-based economic development efforts to support future research. A broad sampling of faith-based institutions within key deprived wards can also guarantee positive results and challenges. Since most African and Caribbean churches are in distressed neighbourhoods, researchers can access 'informed experts' who can identify different forms of economic development by religious organisations. Lay experts can identify periodic changes within 'active' faith-based organisations.

Assessing community needs

There are causal factors which characterise the diversity-needs of communities including congregations in the UK. If church organisations are to be effective conduits in enterprise and economic matters as a whole, they should plan strategically. Planning enables faith groups to mobilise the asset value of congregants in defining a strategic vision and aspirations, as well as considering the needs of the wider community. At the centre of Government's poverty development strategy, is the active involvement of grassroot organisations of which faith organisations play a crucial part. Therefore, faith organisations that are keen on pursuing economic development at grass root level should recognise that organised self-help is essential to the entire process. For it to work, certain factors affecting impoverished communities need considering.

According to Halpern (1995 pp.4–18), distressed communities are characterised by such problems as the following:

- Lack of adequate access to financial capital;
- Damaging effect of racial and social exclusion;
- Loss of jobs to the suburbs;
- Significant immigration of rural and newly arrived foreign migrants;
- The loss of community due to the fragmenting effects of ethnic pluralism and urban life, coupled with the shift of social functions from primary institutions such as family, church and neighbourhood to bureaucratic institutions;
- High school dropout, and lack of mobility for the poor;
- Heavy reliance on the grant-aid system;
- Poor or inadequate public services or lack of access to them;
- Ageing or deteriorating housing stock.

Despite slender resources and receding confidence among deprived communities, some faith-based organisations have helped create thriving enterprise initiatives. The establishment of the South London-based Black Business Initiative (BBI) in 2001 resulted from encouragement and extensive support from the church. Nigerian-born Sunny Lambe, a trained marketer and a devout Christian, views the BBI as a recognised community agency. Interestingly, even though a Peckham-based church was headed by a member of the White clergy, the level of support it gave the BBI astounded Christians and non-Christians alike. Below is the number of activities that BBI is engaged; they include:

- Job training
- Enterprise support
- Capacity building
- Information and advice
- Pastoral care
- Youth development
- Grant application support
- Annual award ceremonies
- Supplementary school provision
- Newsletter production

From a community-asset base perspective, there is a need to focus on new forms of collaboration for community-building strategies. The involvement and utilisation of residents in programme planning, decision-making and evaluation are essential to faith economics involving churches. Congregants are well-suited for developing a community assessment as the Pentecostal Credit Union attests even today. Working in partnership with either congregations or other community partners, churches can map the assets of congregants and the wider community through the (social) financial evaluation method.

The accomplishment of faith-based organisations is thus built on the importance they attach to a consistent pattern of community asset mapping, as seen in Figure 12.2.

Wealth-creation opportunities

Churches in the Black community are known to respond to the needs of their congregation and by extension, other communities. However, these require careful assessment to determine the extent to which there might be a distinction between the requirements of existing congregants and non-church goers. Generally, very few churches discriminate when providing welfare services to the poor and needy. Perhaps it is time that faith organisations assume a greater role in community regeneration; that is, the supply-side dimension, an important element of (practical) faith economics.

Figure 12.2 Creating a Community Assets Map

◆ Step 1: Identify the people who will conduct the survey and compile the data. Ideally, community residents should do most of the data collection. It may be possible to get student volunteers from a local college to help organise and interpret the data.

◆ Step 2: Gather information on households among the congregation and the skills of other residents.

◆ Step 3: Identify the abilities and skills of each member of the congregation.

◆ Step 4: Identify community capabilities (community activities in which residents have participated).

◆ Step 5: Record the experiences and skills of entrepreneurs.

◆ Step 6: Collect personal information from people interviewed for future contacts.

◆ Step 7: Organise and interpret the information that has been collected.

◆ Step 8: Write up a summary of what has been learnt about the community.

It may be possible to get some technical support from a local college or community-based organisation in the preparation of a report.

(*Source:* Reese and Clamp 2000, p.12)

In building on the BBI's example of service provision, other faith-related organisations can invest in the following:

• *Business operations* – development of free-standing businesses exclusive of church regulations and or control. The role of this type of operation should be to identify, train and empower local community workers.

• *Job Training* – initiate a range of modest tutorial programmes in a co-operative effort with businesses to fund education for young people. Small congregations should be involved in the development of computer labs to serve the education and mentoring needs of young people.

- *Mixed Social Services* – these are described more commonly as job training and referral services for young women, church ministers, community schools, cultural groups and others related to social welfare activities.
- *Financial Activities* – the creation of credit unions is a case in point; this formal institution can grant low interest loans to church members to set up micro enterprises. This fund can be matched by reputable charities' contribution to a special fund aimed at promoting social enterprises in the faith sub-sector.
- *Citizenship Education* – churches can offer extensive services and support to new migrants and refugees. Such provision could be classified as 'social' service or welfare, especially since many support efforts establish the individuals and families within the new economy.
- *Cultural Development* – churches could also help to bridge the gaps in cultural misunderstanding among diverse communities. By investing in neighbourhood programmes, they can limit divisions particularly in areas where culture, dialect and other factors challenge the status quo of (permanent) settler communities.

In addition, mobilising the congregation is very important towards influencing wealth-creation activities. By nature, religious organisations are a beacon of stability in low-income communities. Often they are the only organisations capable of enabling disenfranchised residents to find the resolve to cope by using the spiritual compass as a guiding force. Another way of mobilising the community is through 'community ministry' which goes beyond charity. The aim here is for ministries to deal with economic and social issues affecting congregants who are at the mercy of the economic system and lack resilience because of poor education or a lack of financial resources. This type of evangelist orientation sees the church as an agent of change in the lives of both its congregants and the wider community in which it serves.

Ammerman (1997) identified four typical ways that churches orient themselves. Congregations with a 'civic' orientation work at being good, co-operative citizens of the community, helping out where they can, without significantly challenging the status quo. Their emphasis is on individual citizenship, in contrast to corporate action of the 'activist' congregations. This approach is evident among the clergy of African churches who adopt a 'pastoral-type corporate' approach in preaching and practising the gospel, according to their interpretation of faith and economics. Most Caribbean-owned churches tend to perceive their role as one of merely offering congregants 'spiritual nourishment'. Deploying their talents towards the deprived by empowering them economically and strategically to overcome material deprivation, is not considered a top priority. The objective of maintaining practical forms of faith versus economics-orientation remains an ongoing challenge for pastors, ministers and lay preachers who are inclined to adhere to the traditional role of sermonising.

Today, Black Churches have in their ranks a growing and restless young entrepreneurial population who also possess leadership qualities. These congregants need positioning within and without the congregation for the common good. For instance, there are some young people especially those in their twenties, who attend university, work part time, carry out once a week mini-enterprise tasks and on Sundays, are busy teaching Sunday Schools. These talents need to be properly harnessed within a framework of faith economics so that these emerging leaders could be a force for future good. Their attempts could maintain the credible image of faith organisations in Britain, not only as 'Bible-based seminaries' but as institutions of faith economics both in principle and practice. The Seventh-day Adventist Church is one of the more proactive faith organisations that engage their congregation in the enterprise, as well as spiritual, route. Entrepreneur and lay preacher, Lee Williams who is a firm believer in the 'crystallisation of the spiritual and the economic', observed that churches must do more to build the capacity of their members, particularly young people who have the makings of being successful entrepreneurs, given the right guidance and support.

> Wealth creation is crucial to Black communities in general, and our young people need ongoing support if they are to take over from us in the foreseeable future. Church leaders must recognise that they can no longer ignore the economic imperative or the material reality of our universe, since the spiritual and material are intertwined. Passages of Scripture are clear on what is expected of us as God's children and it is our duty to interpret the Holy Word with conviction, purpose and a sense of reason and

consistency. Capacity building is crucial in all of this and it is necessary for faith organisations to achieve their goals through this means. More churches should evaluate their congregants on a regular basis, organise classes or training sessions around entrepreneurialism, by inviting specialists and practitioners in various fields of business and industry so that members of the congregation who have an inclination towards enterprise, can be encouraged to do so without feeling daunted by the very idea of going into business.

(Intervieview with Lee Williams 2007)

Williams' philosophy is informed by other second-generation Caribbean entrepreneurs who are practising Christians and who are deeply moved by the need to adopt a more modernistic approach to religion, politics and economics. Several are involved in industry networks such as trade associations and enterprise sub-groupings, in their attempt to learn, teach and lead a 'pastoral-type of economic activism'. Such a model is advantageous in mobilising the resources of congregants and others as it allows a collective sharing of space to develop projects alongside various regeneration initiatives in England. Wealth creation is no longer a negotiable option in the world of ideology and intricate financial arrangements. It is imperative that Black Churches and their congregations endeavour to adapt the principle of spiritual dynamics. Leaders ought to recognise the importance of a practical, collective and holistic approach to progress, through faith economics.

As was alluded to at the beginning, mainstream or White-owned faith institutions such as those found in the Jewish community, are well-endowed spiritually and financially. Their sphere of influence in public, private and civic life is renowned throughout the British Isles. Besides Jewish synagogues, Hindus and Sikhs use temples, Muslims Masjids and mosques, and other faith groups use their 'houses' of worship to celebrate both their 'Godhead' and share their 'communitarian economic bread'.

Even though the belief system or methods of worship might appear different and sometimes mind-boggling, there are important elements that Black churches and their congregations can adopt in small measures. There is nothing immoral in organising groups of women and young people to discuss ideas about wealth-creation after Saturday or Sunday school or after prayer sessions. This activity can help infuse awareness of wider economic issues via spirituality. Selective prayers from the Book of Psalms or other passages of scripture for example, can help reinforce the importance and relevance of faith and economics as a pathway of peace, happiness, prosperity and stability for human beings generally.

Black Churches can maximise the advantage of limitless ideas and human capital to initiate different wealth-creation activities such as the following:

- Intensive training for young people and women interested in pursuing a career in enterprise;
- Strengthening partnership with public agencies to assist more Black businesses with technical information, advice and enterprise support;
- Help statutory bodies to measure the performance of minority firms and social enterprises;
- Encourage the building of micro-cottage industries within the church by mobilising low-income congregants to convert allotments into mini-commercial agricultural production or homestead units;
- Buy in the skills of retired Black machinists, carpenters and other skilled congregants to develop faith-trade schools for young men and women who have a leaning towards a technical vocation;
- Set up quasi-resource centres of excellence and bid for 'Loan Revolving Fund' schemes for 'enterprising congregants' who wish to start a business or expand existing firms;
- Host annual enterprise exhibitions, fairs and seminar worshops to enlighten the congregation and the wider community about the churches' role in faith economics in a modern urban regeneration setting.

Conclusion

This paper explored the concept of faith economics within the context of African and African Caribbean people's practice of Christianity, and the growing realisation of the importance and relevance of blending religion with commercial imperatives. This gives primacy to the often-recited excerpt from the Lord's Prayer, 'Give us this day our daily Bread'. It was acknowledged that, as a modern institution, the Black Church is still evolving and it will probably take another generation of church leaders and their followers to adopt an American (type) version of 'spiritual enter-prise'. While some African-based churches have gone beyond the spiritual affirmation or Evangelical tradition, Caribbean-founded churches are yet to develop a missionary zeal, embracing dual spirituality that is blending the 'human face' of materialism with faith.

In mid-2007, I was invited to address a Seventh-day Adventist Church convention which had a business element. It attracted in excess of 200 congregants and other attendees. About 75% of participants were below the age of 30 and seemed interested in the idea of business start-ups. There was a mixture of African, Caribbean, South Asian and other minority ethnic congregants. Weeks later, members of the congregation 'beseeched' my help and support for their business ideas. Some had existing businesses but needed advice on a way forward since they did not receive much assistance from traditional enterprise agencies.

There is no dedicated agency that provides technical information, advice and broad-based enterprise support to faith-based organisations in the UK. Recently, a manager from Business Link, when questioned by a Christian gospel artist about support for faith organisations, said this:

> In the new scheme of things, we now have Business Link advisers who are experienced and knowledgeable on matters pertaining to commercial and social enterprise start-ups.

> *(Young Entrepreneurs Business Networking*
> *Meeting, Business Link: Black Business Association,*
> *30 January 2008, West Midlands)*

For decades, the survival of mainstream or White churches has been dependent on a certain amount of commercial activity. These range from the sale of academic-religico merchandise, educational tourism, renting space to student societies and other recognised community groups, to developing social enterprises.

So that, land, property and other tangible assets owned by university churches for instance, are managed and protected by a trusteeship sys-tem; these assets are duly operated in a commercial manner, with revenue ploughed back into institutions. The time is opportune for the leadership of Black Churches to appropriate this model of resource ownership and management, since currently, most faith-based organisations have a set of ad hoc arrangements or loosely co-ordinated management committee systems that deals with limited enterprise-related matters.

In concluding this paper on faith economics, it would be remiss if I didn't offer a few more pertinent recommendations, particularly for the benefit of Black Church-goers, but for non-Christians alike.

(a) Churches should conduct an annual audit of congregants/parishioners to determine their various occupational and vocational persuasions;

(b) Pastors/Ministers should encourage congregants to be self-reliant and co-exist in their communities by developing the requisite entrepreneurial skills;

(c) As part of their liturgical or evangelical outreach work, churches should organise business seminaries, thereby complementing existing traditional spiritual activities;

(d) Churches should work with enterprise agencies, social organisations and professionals to develop joint enterprise programmes;

(e) Churches should use their influence and moral authority to promote entrepreneurship among children and young persons who attend Sunday School and church-related sessions;

(f) The clergy should use facilities to re-brand the principle of 'Christian economics' to enable congregants to realise their potential and progress (hidden) enterprise ambitions.

As a new concept, faith economics could be used to optimise the effect churches seek to spread the gospel. Black Churches should embrace innovations around 'supply-side' economics, thereby becoming complementary providers of networked services for the infirmed, indigent and other disadvantaged people. By following this approach, the prevailing affirmation, 'Give us this day, our daily bread,' will no longer be construed as a simplistic recital creed, but instead be valued as a practical mechanism for utilising the God-given talent of every man, woman and child in the Christian family and beyond.

References

Ammerman, N.T. and Farnsley, II, A.E. et al. (1997) *Congregation and Community*, New Brunswick, NJ, Rutgers University Press

Black Business Association/Business Link meetings:

Young Entrepreneurs Business Networking Meeting (30 January 2008) BBA and Business Link West Midlands

Business Link Community Engagement Seminar (February 2006) BBA, West Midlands

Ethnic Minority Business Initiative (1991) London, HMSO

Foster, R.S. (1991) *Local Economic Development Strategies for a Changing Economy*, Washington DC, International City Management Association

Halpern, R. (1995) *Rethinking the Inner City*, New York, NY, Columbia University Press

John, Cindy (2005) 'Black worshippers keep the faith', BBC News, 1 August

Johnson, Christopher A. (2009) 'Social Enterprise', in *British Caribbean Enterprises*: A century of challenges and successes, London (self-published)

Reese, L.A. and Shields, G. R. (1999) 'Economic Development Activities of Urban Religious Institutions', *International Journal of Economic Development* (Wayne University USA) 1(2): pp.166–200

Reese, T. David and Clamp, Christina A. (2000): *Faith-Based Community Economic Development: Principles and Practices*, Federal Reserve Bank of Boston

Single Regeneration Budget (1994–2001), 1–6 Cabinet Office

Special Meeting for Christian Entrepreneurs (February 2006) Black Business Association, West Midlands

Thomas, J.M. and R.N. Blake (1996) Faith-based Community Development and African-American Neighbourhoods, in W.D. Keating, N. Krumholz, and P. Star Lawrence (eds) *Revitalising Urban Neighbourhoods*, University Press of Kansas, pp. 131–143

UK Christian Handbook, Religious Trends 2002/2003

Williams MBE, MD, Lee, (June 2007) Interview. Universal Service Solutions, England

13   *Climate Change and the Black Church*

Chris Andre-Watson

Welcome to a Green World!

'Don't throw that out the window', shouted Heather as I was about to discard the hungrily devoured remains of a box of Kentucky Fried Chicken and chips out of the car. 'It's not biodegradable.'

'It's not bio ... what?' I garbled back, freezing mid-action as I attempted to repeat the seemingly unpronounceable word.

'It's not biodegradable.'

Heather Pinnell, a fellow journalist on the newspaper I worked for before starting in Baptist ministry then began enlightening me on the joys of environmentalism. This was incredibly progressive considering this was in the early 1980s, years before the first green consumer revolution when strangely named products like 'Ecover' began appearing on supermarket shelves. Two decades on, I compost our household waste, recycle everything that can be recycled, fit energy-saving light bulbs wherever they might be fitted and take public transport in order to reduce my carbon footprint. Now words such as biodegradable, eco-friendly, green-house gases, carbon offsetting and low emission zone, trip off the tongue with the expertise that my early foray into 'enviro-lingo' lacked.

Today we are bombarded with a plethora of eco-edicts extolling the virtues of the green life. Adverts urge us to recycle, to switch to green electricity or to click off our standby switches to save energy. Food packaging is covered with a bewildering array of symbols designed to prick our consciences but which require the brains of a cryptologist to decipher. Pop stars and celebrities covered in bling jewellery, apparently unembarrassed by their own conspicuous consumption, call on the rest of us lower down the social order to save the planet or feed the world.

Even politics is attempting to rediscover its conscience after years of being driven by the economics of global capitalism. Politicians are wrestling with the debate over renewable energy, carbon offsetting and environmental degradation. In 2006 the government's *Stern Review on the Economics of Climate Change* (Stern 2006) was a pivotal moment in putting environmental issues at the heart of political thinking and making the link between green and capitalist ideologies. Years of ignoring the moral arguments for addressing climate change were overturned when the bill for inaction was finally calculated. Green issues are no longer the preserve of 'woolie-jumpered', tofu-eating, tree-hugging, eco-warriors going by the name of Swampy. Now Disney has also joined the planet-saving bandwagon with its recent hit film *Wall-E*, the story of an environmental robot left behind after the Earth has suffered a catastrophe brought on by over consumption.

Yet despite this monumental shift in thinking and discussion the environmental issue seems to have barely registered on the Richter Scale of Black theological thinking or churchmanship in the UK. I recently met and talked with Revd Katie Kirby, CEO of the African and Caribbean Evangelical Alliance, about the level of interest of the Black Churches on this issue. She said no UK Black Church had ever approached her on the subject of climate change. The question is why?

Being Black and green

In June 2008 the London Cruise Terminal in Tilbury was the site for the sixtieth anniversary of the arrival of the *Empire Windrush* which signalled the beginning of large scale migration from the Caribbean to the United Kingdom. It was an opportunity to reflect on that period, acknowledge the struggles and the triumphs of the Windrush generation and provide an opportunity to think about the future. It was out of those struggles and triumphs that the Black Church as we know it emerged. It is that experience that has had such a defining influence upon it. A siege mentality largely beset the church that was about surviving the harshness of British life. It was a corral instinct that sought strength from being together, that preserved a particular view of life and culture and was about hunkering down rather than engaging with the wider community. A theology that emphasised personal piety over political engagement and an over-realised eschatology born out of centuries of persecution and a yearning for a better world further added to the Black Churches marginalisation.

However Black Churches in the last decade have seen unparalleled growth in the UK. Whilst the national church and traditional denominations have been in steady and some say terminal decline, Black Churches have undergone something of a renaissance aided by African immigration. No longer perceived as small elderly congregations filled with hat-wearing older women, many Black Churches run super-slick highly successful operations that would not look out of place on the FTSE 100 index. Names such as Kingsway International and Ruach Ministries are multi-million pound operations. Their 'suited and booted' leaders like Matthew Ashimolowo and John Francis are international figures with large congregations that are eyed with envy by politicians seeking the Black vote. Leaders like Les Isaacs of the Street Pastors initiative and Nims Obunge of The Peace Alliance have the ear of leading political figures. Even on a smaller scale, a trip down the Old Kent Rd in South London will reveal new churches with ever more elaborate names meeting wherever there is space. But even within more traditional settings, Black passion and presence has revived dying inner-city congregations and given tired old denominations a new lease of life.

Out of this has emerged a new generation of Black theologians and leaders such as Anthony Reddie, Kate Coleman, David Muir, Joel Edwards and Robert Beckford. There is a growing confidence within the Black Church as it is genuinely being seen as a key player in addressing some of the issues that beset the Black community. But few of these have turned their considerable talents and creative energies to the issues of creation care. Instead they have concentrated on issues that have bedevilled the Black community and the Black Church. The emphasis until now has been on recovering an afro-centric hermeneutic, paradigms for Black political engagement, Black ecclesiology, the slavery debate and womanist theology. Socio-political issues such as the breakdown of the Black family, Black youth crime, educational underachievement and poverty have also been the order of the day.

A visit to any Black majority church would reveal that preaching emphasises worship, God's character, miracles and healing, living in victory, the power of prayer and sexual morality. That is not to stereotype Black Churches but to recognise that these are probably the issues their congregations have to deal with on a regular basis. In terms of the American psychologist Maslow's hierarchy of needs the Black Church is moving from survival mode into the areas of personal development, creativity and purpose and seeking to extend its influence beyond the perceived traditional Black Church cul-de-sac of spiritual power, prayer and piety. From this summary it would not be too difficult to reach the conclusion that you cannot be Black and green. Yet it does not have to be this way nor should it be this way. Any understanding of the issues will reveal that those most impacted by climate change will have a black or brown face. Just a brief summary of the environmental and economic impact of climate change on places such as Africa reveals the cost of inaction.

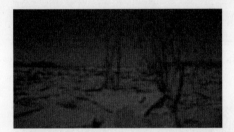

Figure 13.1 Droughts will be more frequent

- The African continent is warmer that it was 100 years ago. The six warmest years in Africa have all occurred since 1987 with 1998 being the warmest year (Pak Sum Low (ed.) 2005, p.30)
- Climate change is predicted to disrupt crop yields and reduced African GDP by a tenth in years ahead. In a continent that is already struggling to feed itself images of famine stricken Africans will become even more frequent
- The search for food, water and survival will result in mass migration (Christian Aid 2007, *Human Tide*)
- Mali is a country on the frontline of climate change. Droughts are predicted to double in the coming decades in the Sahel region which covers this country and stretches from Senegal to Somalia (*Christian Aid News* 2005)
- In 2007 widespread flooding in Uganda, Ghana, Sudan and Ethiopia affected 7,500,000, destroying homes and harvest washed away. This is expected to happen more frequently as temperatures continue to rise
- The glaciers on Mount Kilimanjaro and Mount Kenya are melting at an alarming rate threatening many villages that rely on the snows to

renew their drinking wells. Mount Kilimanjaro is expected to lose its remaining ice caps by 2020 and Mount Kenya has lost 90% of its glaciers already (*Christian Aid News* 2005, p.15)

• By 2080 it is likely that 1.1–3.2 billion people will be experiencing water scarcity, and between 200–600 million will be hungry (IPCC Intergovernmental Panel on Climate Change, 2007)

• Nor are the West Indies immune. 2007 was a record breaking year for hurricanes. Five storms in the hurricane season between June and November reached category five; the highest category possible. This was the first time since records began that more than one storm had reached that category in a single season.

The facts and predictions paint an apocalyptic future and misery for millions. Whilst there are clearly pressing issues that the Black Church and its leaders must address today all those efforts will be wasted if tomorrow is not secured as well.

Figure 13.2 The world's poor face more floods

Me Tarzan – You Jane!

In 2005 the global *Live 8* concert once again set out to raise the plight of the poor in Africa, and mobilise a populist movement that would prick the consciences of the G8 nations. One of the notable omissions from the line-up of the British leg of the concert was that of Black UK musical talent. It seemed when it came to the saving of Africa Black people had little to contribute, or were not talented enough. Once again it would be the efforts of White men such as Bob Geldof to rescue Black people from disaster. This and many other examples such as the commemoration of the Abolition of Slavery where White contribution to the abolition movement seemed to down-play Black involvement in their own emancipation are symptomatic of a condition known as the 'Tarzan Syndrome'. This is the belief that such is the cultural, economic, scientific, intellectual and political superiority of White people that even in the deepest, darkest most remote jungle, traditionally the domain of primitive Black folk, the White man is King and Jane is Queen.

As the argument goes, it is by the ingenuity of 'White power' that the dark and animalistic forces of the jungle are subjugated. It is also a challenge to what is perceived as Black male physical power that even a White man who cannot string a sentence together is more powerful than the natives of the jungle. Even when White intruders enter the jungle to plunder its wealth and resources it is up to Tarzan to stop them. The African native caught in the middle between these two axes of power is but a passive recipient of their benevolence or malevolence. Books and films such as *King Kong*, *Planet of the Apes* and more recently *Congo* all have traces of this assumption in one form or another. Tarzan is also the one that is seen to be in tune with nature, able to converse with the animals that befriend him and regularly come to his aid. In Tarzan and Jane films White man is seen as living in harmony with nature, the first man and woman ruling the Garden of the Eden.

The evidence that global warming is the fault of carbon emissions from the Western industrialised world illustrates that that assumption is as fictitious as Tarzan himself. Nevertheless Tarzan does have a role to play in the jungle. It is scientific research funded by Western wealth that is revealing the full impact of climate change on Africa and other parts of the 'two-thirds' world. In Tarzan the jungle does have an ally and it would be naive to presume that Africans could address the challenges of climate change alone. The mission agency I currently work for, the Baptist Missionary Society (BMS) World Mission, has a long history of working in Africa. BMS works in Angola, Congo, Guinea, Uganda and South Africa but it recognises that it has limited engagement with African diaspora communities in this country and is actively seeking ways to form stronger links with the growing Black Church. BMS has recognised that the baggage of its history could identify it with the Tarzan stereotype. Its endorsement of the Baptist Union of Great Britain Council's apology for slavery demonstrates its commitment to challenging this notion and on 15 November 2007 the BUGB Council unanimously approved an Apology for the Transatlantic Slave Trade. BMS World Mission seconded the statement.

And just as Tarzan was Lord of the Jungle, White man must once again don his loin cloth and be prepared to flex his ecological muscles. Make no mistake the debate over climate change is about muscle. Ultimately the climate change debate is not a moral or ideological debate even though it is being played out in this way to give it an almost religious credibility. The climate change debate is fundamentally about economic, commercial and political power; the preservation of that power and the long term battle for a share in the earth's dwindling resources.

It is for this reason that the Black Church and community urgently needs to mobilise itself because the future of the planet is being decided by White Western world leaders who have little vested interest in the welfare of the Black world. This may smack of paranoia but history demonstrates that the wealthy White world will sacrifice Black people in order to further its own need and preserve its status. The half-hearted attempts by global governments to meet their stated promise to fulfil the Millennium Development Goals, is evidence of this continuing apathy and self interest. The current global meltdown and recession will only contribute to a further retreat from the promise to halve poverty by 2015. And while the world celebrates the election of the first US Black President in Barack Obama, we are all aware of the 'Herodian' backlash whenever a new kid emerges on the block. Nonetheless it is time to remind Tarzan and Jane that they are not the only Kings and Queens in this jungle.

Unleashing the Incredible Hulk

To the outside world Doctor David Banner is just an eccentric and reclusive scientist. Just don't get him angry. Underneath that mild-mannered exterior is a green-skinned behemoth by the name of 'The Hulk' just bursting to get loose. The identities of the doctor and the Hulk are deeply interwoven. Though they may manifest differently in external appearance, they are one and the same sharing the same DNA and psyche. Inside the Black Church is a 'green' monster waiting to be released. Not in the conventional sense of an uncontrollable beast, but as a creative and powerful force for good. Like the Hulk the issue of creation care and the environment is locked within the DNA of its host and it is time to release it.

A brief summary of the biblical story reveals how the environmental theme is an intrinsic part of the text. The opening chapters of Christian scripture are a rapturous homage to our creator God and the value and purpose of creation. Quite how the Christian community has all but ignored the ecological message within this overture to creation is staggering. However critics of Christian theology suggest that the edict given to Adam to 'fill the earth and subdue it' has resulted in the justification for exploiting the planet (Genesis 1:28). In the subsequent story of 'the fall' we are reminded of God's judgment and our estrangement from the land (Genesis 3:17–20). This is a theme repeated throughout the Old Testament as the apostasy of God's people has consequences for the environment (Deuteronomy 28:16–19). Indeed evidence of their repentance will be seen in the healing of the land (2 Chronicles 7:14). Noah's building of the ark and his preservation of the animals during the flood has a vital message for us today about our treatment of wildlife (Genesis 6–8). The call of Abraham and the conquering of Canaan, a 'land flowing with milk and honey', are stories rich with creational symbolism.

The environmental theme finds resonance within the creation theology of the Psalms, typically expressed in the triumphant affirmation of Psalm 24: 'The Earth is the Lord's and the fullness thereof ...' It is echoed in the courtroom drama of Job where he is silenced in the face of God's creative powers (Job 38–41). Jesus' demonstration of his power over nature in calming the storm continues the theme in the New Testament (Matthew 14:22–32). He is part of the triumvirate of co-creators in the beginning with the Father and Holy Spirit (John 1:3). In Paul's Epistles the creation is a sign of God's general revelation and of his eschatological hope (Romans 1:20, 8:18–22). By the time we reach Revelation, the creation motif reaches its climatic denouement with the creation of a new Heaven and Earth, serving as conclusive evidence that the material world is integral to the work of salvation and no side story (Revelation 21:1). Like parts of the evangelical church, the Black Church has largely ignored the issue of ecology despite claiming to be biblically based.

Even with these rich exegetical resources waiting to be mined, one of the major hurdles to overcome in engaging the Black Church constituency with the issue of climate change is the language of climate change. Much of the debate has been shrouded in scientific techno-jargon. In Western urban civilisation the environment has become rationalised, industrialised and demystified. The Black Church rooted in a spiritual and an over-realised eschatology is deeply suspicious of the materialistic and anti-God view represented by the scientific world. 'We are living in the end times now therefore we cannot do anything about it because it is all in God's hands anyway', so the argument goes. That antagonism to the scientific world and the sense of fatalism needs to be addressed in order to engage fully with the issues. One way in which the connection between green issues and the Black Church can be made is to explore the theme of land and our relatedness to it.

As the former minister of a predominantly Caribbean Baptist Church in Brixton for ten years, one of the great calendar events was the Harvest Festival celebration. A bounteous display of fresh fruit and vegetables, some of it grown on local allotments, took pride of place on the church stage. Harvest was such an event in the church that it once featured on the BBC One cookery programme *Feasts for a Fiver*. Most of the food would then get distributed to the 'shut-ins' and to the Trinity Hospice in Clapham. Whilst the staff at the hospice appreciated the annual contribution, one year they asked if they could receive packet and tinned food instead as they could store them for longer. But that year when I suggested that we had a tinned-food harvest there was virtual uproar. What I had failed to understand, appreciate and value was that for many of these people, harvest took them back to that simple subsistence living that they had now left behind.

Most of the congregation came from rural communities and had been transported to the cities but their 'roots' were still tied to the land. Many still owned a piece of land that they planned to build on and cultivate once they returned 'back home'. In the interim their tiny urban plots over-crowded with attempts to grow tomatoes, potatoes, sweet peas and corn would have to suffice. The same is true for many African churches too where people would have been familiar with the cultivation and selling of their own produce. In Kenya 80% of the population depend upon agriculture for their living. However, now caught up in an urban environment, that connection to the land and the seasons has largely been lost. The mechanisation and commercialisation of the food chain has added to that sense of distance. Nonetheless it's a connection that needs to be rediscovered as a way of engaging the constituency in the issue of climate change and creation care.

A little book called *Planet Wise* by Dave Bookless (2008) is helpful here in setting out a basic biblical framework for understanding the significance of, and our relationship with, the land. It is a theme that is significant in the Bible but gets overlooked despite a surprising number of references to it. Bookless reminds us that we are part of a triangular relationship that includes God and our environment and the heart of the subject of climate change is our broken relationship with all three. The book is even being printed on environmentally friendly paper so you should not feel guilty purchasing it. Drawing on Bookless for inspiration here in Table 13.1 is a framework of texts and discussion questions that could be used in church for addressing the issues.

However of even greater significance and resonance for African Diaspora churches is the inspiration that can be drawn from the African Earth-keeping Movement. In a fascinating book M. L. Daneel (2001) describes the earth-keeping movement that arose in Zimbabwe, which draws on traditional Shona eco-religious spirituality and ritual practice and Christian enviro-theology, in a bid to address the impact of environmental degradation caused by climate change, and human exploitation of the natural world. Daneel argues that the cosmological worldview of the Shona people and their sacred appreciation of the natural world provides a mobilising critique of the anthropocentric consumerism of Western spirituality which is harming the planet. This religious and ecological movement is regarded as the next phase in 'chimurenga': Zimbabwe's colonial liberation struggle. After political emancipation comes environmental liberation which sets about restoring ecological harmony. Not only does this provide a repudiation of Western rationalist assumptions about the world but helpfully gives African and Black Churches an opportunity to reclaim some of their valuable cosmological insights that have been lost in the transition into an urban context. The 'trick' will be the ability to overcome the suspicion of African spirituality that has been in imbibed from a Western Christological viewpoint.

Table 13.1 Framework for biblical discussion in church

Theme	Text	Issues	Discussion questions
Humans and the Land	Genesis 2:7	Even the name Adam which means 'from the ground' reminds us that though we are distinct we are not separate from creation.	What impact does relatedness to, but distinctiveness from the environment mean for creation care?
Prosperity and the Land	Genesis 1:28	Many Black Christians are refuting the assumption that Black suffering and poverty are the results of God's judgment.	Are some sections of the Black Church guilty of preaching a gospel of consumption?
Steward-ship of the Land	Gen 1:28	Prosperity teaching needs to be anchored in social and environmental responsibility if it is not to become a gospel of greed.	How can Black Churches balance wealth creation and creation care?
Possessing the Land	Gen 12:1	The subject of land possession should be something that is close to the hearts of the Black Church and community. It tackles themes of dispossession, powerlessness, conflict, colonialism, migration, drought, famine and the exploitation of resources particularly within Africa.	In what ways has the Black community been dispossessed from the land and in what ways can that reconnection be made?
Worship and the Land	Deuter-onomy 7:25	The land produces the offerings which are given to God in worship but the land is not to be worshipped as a deity. This separates Christianity from the fertility, new age and wicker cults.	What is distinctive about Christian environmentalism as opposed to other forms of environmentalism?
Eschatol-ogy and the Land	Revelations 21:1	God has an eternal purpose for the land and the environment. It is not disposable. A renewed heaven and earth may still bear the evidence of the damage done to it.	If God has an eternal purpose for creation what should our attitude be towards it?

The future is bright. The future is green

In the face of the challenges that lie ahead, the Black Church needs a major re-education of its congregations. Those churches with the capacity to help need to be looking at ways they can be more involved in shaping the political agenda around climate change, ensuring that the UK Black voice is heard. Yet even with this it has to be acknowledged that there is not much spare capacity to address the problem and that any involvement at this stage may well be limited.

Black congregations also have a number of practical problems that could impact on measures they may seek to implement to address climate change. For instance many Black Churches do not own their own buildings so have little input in how these buildings are maintained. It would be difficult for those in that situation to introduce measures to reduce energy consumption. Many of these churches are often dependent on the host organisations to make decisions about building use. Black Churches will need to ensure they are not just end users of buildings but are involved in committees that make decisions about building use and regulations. Those larger churches that are able to build their own building need to be aware of new regulations regarding the energy efficiency of their buildings and be prepared to incorporate some of the latest eco-technology into their designs and not just to be concerned about the aesthetics.

One of the problems for the larger churches and their plans to develop larger buildings is that they end up with substantial commuting congregations. Many worshippers will travel right across town to attend a thriving worship centre. The carbon footprint of the average Sunday worshipper to a gathered congregation for instance would be enough to destroy a small portion of the Amazon Rain Forest. But it is their very size which makes these churches attractive and gives them the economic clout. They may not be willing to trade lower carbon emissions for the loss of influence in having smaller satellite congregations.

However there are some positive benefits for developing an eco-consciousness. Black Churches need to be preparing their congregations for the green economy and the vista of opportunities that will arise from this ecological future. The future is green. The coming green revolution will open up new career opportunities for the high-flying Black worshipper. Traditionally career opportunities have been limited to local government, the medical and legal professions, IT, accountancy and the music world. Now having environmental credentials on your CV could become increasingly important to a prospective employer. Careers are opening up in environmental planning and law, conservation, corporate strategy, construction, design, civil engineering, renewable energy and new technology. The Black community is already being left behind in the IT race. It seriously risks being left behind again with all the implications for employment and poverty. The Black Churches have demonstrated that some of the leading figures within the community have emerged from within its ranks.

Difficult though it is, the Black Church needs to harness what energy and enthusiasm it has to begin to take the first faltering steps into the issue and like me more than twenty years ago begin to pronounce the unpronounceable. At BMS we are also in the early stages of that process ourselves by carbon offsetting our overseas air travel. In one year £2,600 was donated to Climate Stewards (a branch of A Rocha, a Christian international nature conservation organization, www.climatestewards.net) which will provide 2,116 trees, the equivalent of 5.3 hectares of new forest.

The green toolkit

In addressing the environmental issue, Black Churches have an arsenal of resources at their disposal. The number of books and websites on the issue is now overwhelming. The web is perhaps the most immediate and accessible places for finding resources on the creation care issue. Table 13.2 gives some of the sources used for this chapter and some of the web sites.

Table 13.2 List of resources

An Inconvenient Truth (2006)
Al Gore, former American presidential hopeful, pulls no punches in this challenging and informative documentary that would be great to show the whole church

www.christianaid.org.uk
An invaluable website stocked with reports and campaigns that government takes seriously

www.tearfund.org
Tearfund is a Christian relief and development agency working with a global network of local churches to help eradicate poverty. They have produced some useful reports found on their policy and research tab

www.stopclimatechaos.org
This site is for the coalition of the UK's largest group of people dedicated to action on climate change and provides a campaign your church can sign up to

www.foe.co.uk
Friends of the Earth were amongst the first to sound the alarm about climate change and the environment, another useful site for information and campaigning

www.arocha.org
A Rocha is a Christian environmental and nature conservation movement. Click here for a resource pack which can be used in church worship or Bible studies

www.earthscan.co.uk
Earthscan is the leading publisher in English on climate change, sustainable development and environmental technology for academic and professional, and also policy and general readers. For the serious reader

www.climatestewards.net
Climate Stewards is an arm of A Rocha set to enable carbon offsetting. Money given to Climate Stewards will fund projects

www.bmsworldmission.org
Future Shape? is a six-part mission study resource being developed by BMS. Available on the website

www.occ.gov.uk
The Office of Climate Change (OCC) works across Government to support analytical work on climate change and the development of climate change policy and strategy. One for the serious 'greeney'

Conclusion

The UK Black Church scene has seen unparalleled growth and development within the last decade. It has become a powerful mobilising force within and for the Black community, addressing many of the issues that affect it. However, climate change is another item on its growing agenda. This must not be regarded as burdensome, but as an opportunity to extend the influence of the Black Church. There is the opportunity to speak into the policy decisions that are being formulated that will affect the whole world – particularly the poorest parts of the world. There needs to be a powerful and eloquent advocate who will speak on their behalf. There is the benefit in rediscovering an afro-centric ecological spirituality that has been lost in the transition from rural to urbanised communities. The Black Church also needs to prepare its people for the emerging green world which will radically impact their lifestyles. And while we can sing 'He's got the whole world in his hands' with confidence in God's plans for the future of the world, He also calls us to join with Him in its preservation and its transformation.

References

Bookless, Dave (2008) *Planet Wise*, London, Inter Varsity Press
Christian Aid News (Spring 2005), Issue 35
Christian Aid (May 2007) *Human tide: the Real Migration Crisis* www.christianaid.org.uk/indepth/705caweekreport/index.hymn
Daneel, M. L. (2001) *African Earthkeepers, Volume I, Interfaith mission in earth-care*, Unisa Press, copyright University of South Africa
IPCC Intergovernmental Panel on Climate Change (2007) *Impacts Adaptation and Vulnerability, Draft of the Technical Summary, Working Group II Contribution to the IPCC Fourth Assessment Report*
Stern, Lord Nicholas (2006) *The Stern Review on the Economics of Climate Change*, www.occ.gov.uk/activities/stern.htm
Sum Low, Pak (ed.) (2005) *Climate Change and Africa*, Cambridge University Press

14 Challenges Facing Black Church Leadership

Joe Aldred

I am not the first to attempt to identify and articulate some of the key challenges that face the Black Church, in particular its leadership, in Britain; and I certainly will not be the last. Indeed, the volume in which this paper appears contains a range of challenges. However, here I want to sketch out seven that I regard as key as we draw towards the close of the first decade of the twenty-first century. This paper first emerged in 2008 as an inaugural lecture given to mark the opening of the New Testament Church of God's National Leadership Centre, based in Northampton, England. This is a personal perspective birthed out of close involvement in the Black Church in Britain where I am a bishop in one of the Black-led denominations. I come to this task humbly and prayerfully, suspecting that nothing of what I have to say is new to some – nothing new under the sun, says Solomon – and certainly it is not rocket science. However, I hope that my insider perspective counts for something as together we face up to the challenges of the twenty-first century. I begin by saying something about my topic.

Challenge

In contemporary parlance, we can tend to view the word 'challenge' as a somewhat passive term. However, in its root meaning, 'challenge' implies an invitation or summons to do something, like take part in a contest (*Collins English Dictionary*). When the Philistine champion, the giant

Goliath of Gath challenged Saul and the men of Israel to 'choose a man for yourselves, and let him come down to (fight) me' (1 Samuel 17:9), that was a challenge that demanded a response; which eventually David made and spared King Saul's and Israel's blushes. A challenge demands a response, and if a response is not forthcoming, the contest is awarded in favour of one's opponent. So when today we speak of the challenges facing the Black Church we are not referring to something passive, hypothetical, or ephemeral; rather, we refer to matters that confront the Church and which demand a response. And the Church fails to respond at its peril.

Black Church

In the British context, the 'Black Church' is essentially a Black Pentecostal Church. In the first place this refers to those churches that are led and 'membered' in the majority by people of African and Caribbean heritages (some Asians consider themselves part of this definition too). Black skin colour is important in the British context because it is symbolic of a particular sociology, history and experience lived in relation to the adversity of White racism (Lartey 1998, p.7–9). Black is therefore more than skin deep. Second, 'Black Pentecostal Church' belongs to the movement that is rooted in the experience that is iconized by Azusa Street and related revivals, that emerged around and after 1900; of which the five enduring identifying theological marks, according to the *Dictionary of Pentecostal and Charismatic Movements* are: i) the works of grace – justification and sanctification, ii) baptism in the Holy Spirit, iii) premillennialism, iv) healing, and v) miracles (Burgess and McGee 1993, p.2).

Black Pentecostalism in Britain derives from this tradition and according to Christian Research's *2005 English Church Census*, is among the fastest growing congregation within an overall declining national church attendance; with, for example, the New Testament Church of God showing an increase of 37% in Sunday attendance between 1998 and 2005 (Brierley 2006, p.33). But before we get carried away, it is worth remembering that African and Caribbean people total just 2% of the overall population (*1991 Census*) and furthermore not all Black churchgoers are Pentecostals. Mixed heritage account for 1.2% of the population some of whom are African or Caribbean and another ethnicity or nationality. By extrapolating from Brierley's figures, we can suggest that in 2005, 51% of the

300,000 Pentecostal churchgoers were Black. There are at least that many Black worshippers in the historic and other independent churches in Britain.

Leadership

There are many theories on and about leadership, all of which have lessons for the Black Church, but here I highlight only a few popular ones. Some highlight the difference between a leader and a manager; some say leadership can be learnt, others say it is innate. Some say God anoints you at appointment, others insist the anointing precedes the appointment. The purists speak of directive and participative leadership, task or people orientated leadership, transactional and transformational leadership, team leadership, and much beside.

Probably the biggest issue concerns whether leadership can be taught. And here the likes of John Maxwell (1998) believe profoundly that leadership can be learnt, and he provides, amongst other aids, a book called the *21 Irrefutable Laws of Leadership*. It states quite simply, follow them and people will follow you. Another of Maxwell's (1999) books is *21 Indispensable Qualities of a Leader*, with the promise that if you cultivate them you will become the person others will want to follow. Clearly for Maxwell, the laws of leadership need to be closely matched by endearing qualities. It may be instructive to highlight two examples from the ministry of Jesus that illustrate his attitude to leadership: 'I am among you as the One who serves' (Luke 22:27); 'he calls his own sheep by name and leads them out' (John 10:3). Jesus was as much at ease leading 'among' as well as being 'out in front' of his flock. Which of these models current Black Pentecostal leadership mirrors is open to conjecture, but unquestionably Black Church leadership is currently under increasing scrutiny!

The twenty-first century

I want to use four terms to describe the twenty-first century: post-modern, post-colonial, post-denominational and post-Christendom.

Post-modern

John Drane (2000, p.129) observes that Western civilisation, based upon European Enlightenment values, has three philosophical facets:

rationalism – which asserts that the only things worth knowing are what we can think about in particular analytical and abstract ways; *materialism* – which asserts that the only things worth thinking about are those we can see, touch and handle; and *reductionism* – which asserts that everything can be understood by taking them to pieces. These three concepts of rationalism, materialism and reductionism constitute the basic philosophical foundation of post-modernity. It describes also the abolition or erosion of conventional certainties, replacing them with a new pluralism in an exciting world of endless possibilities and uncertainties. Walter Breuggemann (1993, pp.vii–3) argues that a post-modern climate recognises that there is no given definition (of anything) and that rival claims must simply be argued out. Conversely, modernity was when everybody knew their place and stayed there; the slave, the servant, and the poor knew their place beneath the slave master, the lord of the manor and the rich, and stayed there. Brueggemann calls this a period of 'certitude and domination', and cites Karl Marx, who astutely observed, that the ruling ideas of each age have ever been the ideas of its ruling class. Since I and my sort were never part of that ruling class, I do not clamour for the return of modernity, I merely observe that everything is up for grabs in this the post-modern era.

Post-colonial

A second signifier of the twenty-first century is the term 'post-colonial'. This identifies a period after imperialistic colonial rule, particularly in relation to Britain and her former colonies in Africa, Asia and the Caribbean. However, as Michael Jagessar and Anthony Reddie (2007, p.xvii) point out, post-colonialism is not about the demise of colonialism as 'post', or past, since it embodies both 'after' and 'beyond', its not just about historical chronologies, but more about adopting a critical stance, oppositional tactic or subversive strategy. Within post-colonialism, is, according to R. S. Sugirtharajah (2002, p.25) an ongoing battle for emancipation, and a continuing battle to dismantle imperial institutions and dominating structures. And so, this post-colonial space is a problematic one, because as Musa W. Dube (2002, pp.51–75) points out, our current relationships involve the colonised and the coloniser, the ruler and the ruled, the centre and the periphery, the first world and the 'two-thirds world'. There are even resonances here in the relationship between some Black churches and their 'colonial' General Headquarters.

Post-denominational

A third signifier of the twenty-first century is described by the term 'post-denominational'. As in the other two themes, post-denominational does not describe the absence of denominations, rather it describes a time when the power and rule of sectarian denominationalism is under serious question and strain as Christian belonging depends upon new and alternative factors. I remember when I sang with gusto, 'Church of Prophecy, Church of Prophecy is my belief, Church of Prophecy till I die; I was born and bred in Church of Prophecy and I'll die on the Prophecy side.' I would not display the same denominational blind loyalty by singing that now. Post-denominational describes a period when the old certainties of sectarian boundaries are waning and some have all but vanished. The names are still there and new ones emerge everyday, but the people so gathered under these various banners are increasingly seeing themselves as part of the *ekklesia*, less as the property of a denomination (Gasque 1979, pp.1–13).

It may be that one way to understand our post-denominational times is by applying Rick Warren's 'spiritual surfing' theory. Here, people look for where the wave of God is and surf there, rather than join those trying to build waves (Warren 1995, p.13). It may also be the case that denominational ties have been replaced by the cult of personalities and that Christians now divide their loyalties between denominations, personalities, ministries, and ecumenical streams. What is not in doubt is that things are not what they used to be. As Hans Kung (1995, p.3) puts it, the future has already begun; and, he further argues, even if the church wanted to, it cannot stand aside from this world-wide reorientation which heralds a new era. Kung does however offer this hope, 'what looks like a serious crisis may mark the moment of new life; what looks like a sinister threat may in reality be a great opportunity'.

Post-Christendom

If this is a moment of opportunity, then it occurs against a background of not just post-modernity, post-colonialism and post-denominationalism, but also post-Christendom. Although it is true that Christianity is growing in the 'two-thirds world', it is also true that in the Western 'one-third world' where we live, Christianity as the contemporary cornerstone of custom, morals and culture is a thing of the past or is at best on the wane. In its place are myriad faiths and spiritualities and a rampant, strident atheism: the 'death of God' brigade. John Drane (2000, p.175) asserts simply but profoundly that we are in the midst of a paradigm shift of massive proportions. Drane reminds us that when the nineteenth-century philosopher Friedrich Nietzsche spoke of the death of God he implied the disintegration of the entire religio-philosophical basis upon which Western civilisation had been built. He describes this regressive process in the following way: that in the earliest times humans sacrificed each other to the gods, then later they sacrificed their instincts and nature to the gods, and in a third and final stage they sacrificed God leaving nothing to worship save stone, stupidity, gravity and fate.

I hope I am not painting too gloomy a picture of our times; I am merely attempting to present a picture of the context in which today's leadership operates. What is clear is that at the start of the twenty-first century, everybody's ideas are as valid as anyone else's; the gloves are off and the fight is on to throw off the yoke of colonial rule and its religious cousin, coerced denominational hegemonic allegiance; and Christianity has lost its privileged place in western society. This is the moment at which Black Church leadership has been called upon to make a difference. But before addressing my seven key leadership challenges I want to make further, not unrelated reference to the times in which we live.

A nation that has rejected God

Sometimes I feel like I live in the nation upon which woe has been pronounced because we have forgotten God, we now call evil good and good evil, darkness light and light darkness, bitter sweet and sweet bitter (Isaiah 5:20). Sometimes it feels like the time referred to in Romans 1:18–21 '... for the wrath of God is revealed from heaven against all ungodliness and unrighteousness of men, who suppress the truth in unrighteousness ... because although they knew God they did not glorify him as God ...'. I scarcely need to remind anyone of the spiritual, social, political and economic chaos we are in locally, nationally and internationally. There are numerous international political and economic wars and intra-national tribal conflicts, approximately 10% of the world consume 90% of the world's resources, with millions dying in abject poverty; the phenomenon of globalisation means that multi-nationals backed by unfair trade arrangements keep the rich rich and the poor poor. A report by Iain Duncan Smith, titled *Breakdown Britain* (2006), highlights issues such as family breakdowns, educational failure, worklessness and economic dependence, addictions and indebtedness among our ills; then there is the little fact that many of our children are lost, being killed and killing each other on our streets. With what have we replaced in the lives of our youth the Christian morals our society has displaced, for example?

Is it any wonder that some now view the church and particularly the Black Church as the last hope of redemption for this country? As someone said to me recently, it's only the church that can help us now! And some of our own have articulated what a few of these challenges are; let me name three. First, Robert Beckford (2000) continues to argue that the Black Church must develop a political theology and praxis, and not allow notions of transcendence through rapturous music, singing and preaching to foster political ignorance and naivety. Second, Anthony Reddie (2003) has argued for the Black Church to develop an education programme that is liberative, providing people with the tools to survive in a racialised environment. We do not need education that simply create clones, and obedient denominational cadres. Third, Mark Sturge (2005) has laid down the challenges of credibility and integrity, relevance, confidence, spiritual impact, inspiring young people, and punching our weight in the public square. Many others from inside and outside have challenged the Black Pentecostal Church, yet, it remains to be seen whether the Black Church has the stomach for the fight. Has the Church the will to move beyond maintenance to mission? On the assumption that my part-rhetorical question attracts a 'yes', I now want to name seven clear challenges that I believe demand answers. I posit them in the hope that the leadership of Black British churches will facilitate an articulate and spiritual response. In the twenty-first century, it really is up to us!

1. The Black history challenge

The history challenge that is before us begins with the repeated biblical imperative to 'remember'. For example, Exodus 13:3 'And Moses said to the people: "Remember this day in which you went out of Egypt, out of the house of bondage; for by strength of hand the LORD brought you out of this place ..."' Here, as elsewhere, the root meaning of remember is to 'mention'. So, the historic challenge to remember requires that the Black Church finds ways to mention important people, happenings, and things. This calls for a change of vocabulary and iconography because what we say, iconise and celebrate illustrates everything about the value we place or do not place on what has gone before, and their influence on our future direction. The Jamaican hero Marcus Garvey has said that history is the landmark by which we are directed into the true course of life (Jacques-Garvey 1977, p.1). However, it is not only important that history is told, it matters who tells it. Richard Reddie (2007, p.33) reminds us of an African proverb that says, 'until lions have their own historians, the story of the hunt will always glorify the hunter'. History is almost always his-story, and he is almost always the victor; rarely does the victim's story get told. Black Pentecostal leaders of a people whose history goes largely untold, or gets told badly, have a responsibility to develop a vocabulary and an iconography that mentions and marks their history appropriately. Equally, a focus on history must include a new vocabulary about the historical Jesus, a first century Palestinian Jew, not an eighteenth-century European with blond hair and blue eyes.

2. Our responsibility to rootless African Caribbean youth

I am in little doubt that a key problem affecting young people today is a lack of identity linked to a lack of familiarity with their history: where they come from, the morals, spirituality and values upon which those communities were built, the heroes and sheroes upon whose shoulders they stand, and the struggles and victories they fought and either won or lost but learned from. The identity needs of young Black people place upon Black leadership a historical challenge. Indeed, as Robin Walker (2006) has recently articulated, the history of the human race needs to be re-told, properly. The bicentenary year of the parliamentary act to abolish the Slave Trade, 2008, was for the most part, a timely reminder of how history can be revised and retold. At the start of 2007 when asked who they most associated with ending the enslavement of Africans, overwhelmingly people, Black and White, named William Wilberforce. However, marking the bicentenary made manifest a better balanced historical recounting of this epoch of human tragic-history.

We now know that the story of the enslavement and liberation is not primarily one of White European poacher turned game-keeper, but that resistance in many forms was waged by the enslaved themselves during and after capture (Reddie 2007, p.110). We now know that Black people and White people worked tirelessly to end that shameful episode in human history. That millions of Africans lost or gave their lives and that many lived to tell their own stories, chief among them Olaudah Equiano (2003). Through the co-operative leadership of government, ecumenical bodies, human rights organisations and individuals, no longer have Black children in schools to hang their heads in shame when they see pictures of their enslaved ancestors. Rather, they can hold their heads high in the knowledge that the reason they are here is because their fore parents were made of such sturdy stuff, physically and in character that they survived that onslaught of man's inhumanity to man.

The Church history challenge

The Black Pentecostal movement forgets at its peril the importance of its complex history; a history that unless explained, leaves successive generations rootless and in a crisis of ecclesiological identity. The history of Black Pentecostal churches, need to be told, properly, including, for example, the spat back in the 1920s between the White US headquarters of what we now know as the New Testament Church of God and Church of God of Prophecy; and other similar incidences. We can no longer afford divisive history-telling such as those told in *Upon this Rock* (Davidson 1973) and *Like a Mighty Army* (Conn 1977), which serve to divide us; for only when I had read them *both* for myself did I get a balanced view of the major dispute that split those forerunner organisations, and which resonates still today. The historical challenge requires us also to recount the way in which race has played a significant part in Black Church development, dividing Christians along Jim Crow lines. And so that history does not repeat itself, leaders need to help the church to understand that the strong and privileged have not always defended the dignity of their vulnerable fellow believers in Christ (Michel 2000). The story of the consequential subversive activities of the early Black Church pioneers needs to be told so that today's Black Church recognises the source of its liberation and on whose historic shoulders it stands.

Some tough historical questions need to be asked and answered; such as, how and why was William Seymour abandoned by the movement he established? Why was it that as late as 1958 Oliver Lyseight's appointment as National Overseer of the New Testament Church of God in England required a change in the governance regulations of the Church of God, Cleveland (Aldred 2005)? And why does the Black Church have such a history of fragmentation leading to a struggle for ecclesiastical harmony in Britain? Is there something in the Black Church's DNA that is predictive of splits? Will the Black Church ever come together sufficiently to tell one comprehensive, compelling story of 'how we got over'? And who are the real antecedents of the Black Church in Britain? There is a Black Church history challenge to respond to.

The theological challenge

The next challenge before us is a theological one. Some years ago I mentioned to a fellow young brother that I was contemplating studying theology. To this he replied that he did not think we should do theology, we should just stick to the Bible. Black Pentecostals have long needed to lose their theology-phobia. Theology, it has been variously pointed out is what we all do when we reflect upon God and the world Christians believe God created. It is a mistake to trivialise the need to properly engage in reflections on a community's faith. If we are going to think about God, we had better think deeply and well. If we are going to share our thoughts with others, we had better check and double check that what we are saying is as correct as we know how to make it. It is truth that sets people free, not flawed but well-rehearsed dogma. As Paul told Timothy, 'study to be diligent to present yourself approved to God, a worker who does not need to be ashamed, rightly dividing the word of truth' (2 Timothy 2:15).

James Cone (1993, pp.70 and 71) states that,

> Theology is the critical side of faith, and without it faith loses its
> distinctive identity … if a church has no theologians, then it
> cannot be genuinely self-critical and thereby seek to overcome its
> shortcomings and weaknesses. Black churches have not
> encouraged the development of theology alongside strong
> emphasis on preaching.

Cone's focus is the Black Church in the United States, however, there is a strong resonance with the Black Pentecostal Church in Britain. This misplaced distrust of the insider certainly chimes with my experience. But the Black Church should trust its own more, not less, to critique itself. This way confidence and trust, and a certain theological quality assurance becomes a constant companion.

Theology in the academy: the external challenge

The theology challenge of the Black Church is both external and internal. Its greatest fear seems linked to academic theological studies. I understand the fear, especially after I heard the joke about the young priest who took his Bible with him as he went to Oxford to study theology and graduated wondering what to do with it! But we need to bridge the gap between us in the church and our colleagues in the academy, especially those in the field of Black Theology. There is in Britain a thriving Black Theology community that operates at arms length from the Black Pentecostal church. With others I have been there at some important points in our journey, including my spell as founding Chair of the *Journal of Black Theology* in Britain, launched in 1998 (Jagessar and Reddie 2007, p.9). Repeated attempts have failed to attract significant Black Pentecostal participation, as readers or writers. The *Black Theology – An International Journal* is now a successful international academic journal, published three times a year, but it has given up attempting to solicit significant patronage from Black Pentecostal membership or leadership. The sobering reality is that the Black Church, largely Evangelical and Pentecostal, and Black Theology are not bedfellows.

It has been argued that the theological work done by 'Black Evangelicals' falls into the category of 'Black Christian religious experience', not Black theology (Jagessar and A. G. Reddie 2007, p.5). According to Reddie, 'Black Christian religious experience' is a 'folk orientated approach' which, whilst it arises from the Black experience, does not necessarily have a political or explicitly transformative agenda; or sees Blackness as a primary hermeneutical lens for re-interpreting the Christian faith. This apparently sets 'Black Christian religious experience' apart from Black theology since the latter begins with the material reality of the Black experience as its point of departure. I am not myself convinced of this distinction. However, there clearly is an ideological chasm that requires a bridge. Sitting in both camps, as I try to do, I suggest that a possible way forward is the recognition that both seek the liberation of the oppressed, one primarily through the lens of the Bible, the other primarily through the lens of Black experience. Our challenge is to use the tension between these two approaches creatively in the service of the Black Christian community.

Clearly, Black Pentecostals and Evangelicals need more academic advocates from that expression of faith. It is unhelpful that because Pentecostals in general and Black Pentecostals in particular, have been resistant to structural engagement with theology from the academy, the most authoritative theologians in the world on Pentecostalism, such as Professor Walter Hollenweger, tend not to be Pentecostals by persuasion (Hollenweger 1997). It is not that there are no Pentecostals doing theology, or that there is something innately wrong with non-Pentecostals doing Pentecostal theology, but herein lies a challenge for Black Pentecostal thinkers.

Theology in the Church: the internal challenge

It is probably a little unfair but not far from the truth to say that Pentecostals, especially Black Pentecostals, love doctrine, they do not love theology. Black Church doctrine tends to rely upon prescriptions agreed upon by people so long enough ago that present day leaders have not had to have to think them through. They just enforce them, often like the Pharisees and sometimes just as harshly. Unfortunately, a protectionist environment towards doctrines tends to discourage theological investigation and examination. This often leads to leaders coercing obedience but rarely supporting spiritual growth and independence among members. For example, Evangelical Christians instinctively object to homosexuality, but where do they make the theological case for that objection based on experience, scripture, reason, history, Christian tradition, and divine revelation? Where do Pentecostals reflect upon the different doctrinal emphases of Charles Fox Parham and William Seymour about initial evidence (Hollenweger 1997, p.20)? Where do they reflect upon prosperity teachings and tithing? What do they make of a two-stage or three-stage salvific process? Is it really the case that all they are allowed to do is passively accept and propagate only that which is handed down from on high, or can they innovate theological reasoning as befitting a people with lively minds and who follow a God that is past finding out? There is need for a space that does more than assent givens, but facilitates rigorous attention to biblical truth and a willingness to look again, and again, to see if the things we have been taught are true (Acts 17:11).

In Britain, Black theologian Robert Beckford (2000) has attempted some theological reconstruction of Black Pentecostal theology, focussing on how it can be politicised. Beckford makes the point that Black Pentecostalism is not a unitary system or homogeneous practice; rather, it is a dynamic tradition consisting of a legion of denominations and congregations; with the theological hallmarks of the experience of God, a dynamic spirituality, and empowering worship. This empowering worship however is not matched, in Beckford's view, by effectiveness in the political and economic spheres. Emmanuel Lartey's seven-item agenda for Black Theology in Britain is also something for us to consider. Lartey (1999, pp.79–91) posits the following: i) a biblical hermeneutical task that builds upon Black love of the 'Word', ii) a historical task that articulates the trajectories of Black people in the UK, iii) a philosophical and cultural educational task that unearths and articulates African and Asian philosophies, iv) a socio-economic task that emphasises the holistic nature of humanity, v) a political task that is committed to the struggle for justice, vi) a psychological task that connects with Black understanding thereby raising self-esteem leading to good mental health, vii) an aesthetic task that promotes Black arts in music, drama, dance, film and iconography.

To achieve that mentioned above, formal theological and ministerial training is of the utmost importance, not just for the benefit of gaining a certificate, but for a much higher purpose. Writing at the beginning of the twentieth century, African American W. E. B. DuBois (1994) reflecting upon the role of education in the rehabilitation of the Negro Race (*sic*) after the trauma of enslavement, reminds us about the real purpose of education and training. He describes the need for 'an education that encourages aspiration that sets the loftiest of ideals and seeks as an end culture and character'. My call is for home grown theologians to be encouraged to emerge from within the Black Pentecostal movement, people who are liberated to reflect and write, critically, people of such character that they assist in the process of developing an authentic Black British Pentecostal theology that helps the Church to remain as relevant in the twenty-first century as it was in the twentieth . Here I note the words of Bishop Eric Brown (2008) in the Leadership Training Centre prospectus, 'to lead effectively in the twenty-first century, leaders must be trained and well disciplined'.

3. The ecclesiological challenge

Another challenge that faces Black Pentecostal leadership is the ecclesiological one. Ecclesiology concerns the shape of church and according to Alister McGrath (1994, p.405), it asks questions like 'What sort of body is the church?' The Bible offers us many images of the church as a bride, the building of God, the people of God, a holy temple, the body of Christ, and as a multi-membered body (1 Corinthians 12:12). The early development of this complex entity was racked with controversies and persecution accompanied by rapid growth and expansion. An accompanying feature of the Church over these years, however, is a sense of order, organisation and authority. And whilst we must acknowledge that Black Pentecostalism emerged out of a non-conformist tradition, by people who were expressing both their dissatisfaction with the status quo and, simultaneously, following where God was leading; I do believe we have to ask ourselves if the present shape or shapelessness of Black Pentecostalism in Britain fits the biblical model, marked by diversity within a framework of order. Hans Kung (1967, p.263) makes the sobering point, albeit from a Roman Catholic perspective, that the nature and form given the church through God's eschatological saving act in Christ, was given it as a responsibility. This nature, he says, must be constantly realised anew and given new form in history by our personal action of faith. A challenge to the Black Church is this, how well does what we currently represent match the ecclesiological remit of one, holy, catholic and apostolic church? (McGrath 1994, pp.418–426).

The Black Church might ask itself questions about the ecclesiological discipline that has led to the existence of so many independent Pentecostal churches operating often in isolation from each other and from the rest of the Body of Christ? Conservative estimates suggest there are well over 300 differently named churches in Britain servicing the small Black constituency drawn from 2% of the British population, and approximately 6% of the British worshipping community. Does this pass for diversity, or fragmentation? The challenge for us is clear, it is the task of constructing a spiritual and rational argument for working closer together, and mergers of organisations may be necessary. Pentecostal leadership cannot afford simply to stand back and look on at the fragmentation. Someone must be willing to articulate a prophetic vision of our life together, now and in the future that inspires action towards greater unity. Since there is one church, the Black Church should exist in solidarity with the rest. In a time past in Israel, the sons of Issachar were said to have understanding of their times, to know what Israel ought to do (1 Chronicles 12:32). Does today's Black Church leadership know what to do?

4. The ecumenical challenge

The ecumenical challenge includes, for example Black/Black ecumenism, Black/White and multi-cultural ecumenism, internationalism ecumenism, working with ecumenical agencies, and some would even argue for consideration to be given to inter-faith relations between the three major Abrahamic faiths. We need to act because the unity prayed for by Jesus in John 17 continues to challenge and embarrass today's Church profoundly, and yet I often wonder how much the church understands it. In a transcendent sense that which God utters exists; what the Black Church is challenged by is how to express and actualise that which already is. If, as is often the case, we believe that unity means a single world-wide denomination with a single head, be that the Pope or other, then we will continue to strive for what some call the visible unity of the one universal catholic church. If on the other hand we perceive unity as something first and foremost of the spirit, then we focus less on visible disunity as something to fix and work towards keeping the unity of the spirit in the bond of peace, in a manner that leaves difference in tact. As Joel Edwards points out, the whole universe is one gigantic symphony of 'harmonising differences', from the vast expanse of our galaxies to the individuality of each delicate snowflake (Edwards 1999, p.114).

Unity in diversity is, I believe, implied in Jesus' prayer, 'make them one as we are one'. The place we pursue is a place of spiritual maturity and spiritual bondedness, of redeemed diversity, that is devoid of the three traits of divisiveness that Mark Sturge (2005) highlights; the lack of unity and joined-up mission, the undermining of trust, and the evasion of mutual acceptance. The scriptures put it like this, 'till we all come into the unity of the faith and of the knowledge of the Son of God, unto a perfect man'. Being one like the godhead is one, is well beyond what a single denomination in the world could bring. We know only too well how much fussing and fighting go on within single denominations to believe that that on a grander scale would solve anything! Whatever our theological stance on secondary, even sometimes primary issues, the place we seek is where in spirit we are so much one that the world sees you in me and I in you; that the world marvels and says, look, how they love one another.

It is by this that the world will know that we are who we say we are and be led to glorify God. This unity is counter-cultural and counter-intuitive because it crosses race, culture, clan, nationality and sectarianism. It's a unity predicated upon the person of Christ as God, Lord of all, the focus of our worship and work. The leadership task is to assist in raising up 'a living household (*oikos*) in which all God's children who have been beaten down or excluded by the powers of this world find their rightful place' (Kinnamon and Hope 1997, p.1). These ecumenists tell us that the magnitude of our task is illustrated by the fact that 'the churches involved in the ecumenical movement have not only been divided; they have been divided over what it would mean to be united'.

5. The social, economic and political challenge

Some years ago a former National Overseer of the New Testament Church of God, Selwyn Arnold (1992), published the result of his doctoral thesis that examined the church's response to social responsibility. Arnold challenged the Black Pentecostal Church to hold on to its belief in the concept of the afterlife whilst simultaneously developing policies, strategies and plans to attend to the everyday issues of people's lives in the here and now. His thesis was aptly titled, 'Why wait for tomorrow'. Echoing a demand from the Black community that Black Church leadership need to both preach to the people on Sunday and accompany them to the police station on Monday when their children get into the trouble, Arnold highlights the image of a minister who could walk into the shops where the drug-pushers were hanging out and would be recognised as someone from the church who was making a difference in the community. Then in 2003 Christian Aid in collaboration with the University of Birmingham published a report titled 'Am I my brother and sister's keeper?' to highlight the lack and the possibility of Black Church economic development (Howell-Baker and Brown 2003). Jesus' example of healing the sick, feeding the hungry, including the excluded and tackling head on oppressive powers seems an excellent pointer to the Black church's social, economic and political ministry in the world.

I note that in the early phase of the Black Church in Britain, the charge that they were insular, looking only after members and then only concerned with social welfare, not political activity, had some validity. However as Beresford Lewis (2008) in a recent unpublished thesis has sought to show, Black church leaders are heavily involved in various forms of political engagement. This growing level of involvement in strategic high level politics is emerging in numerous ways, significantly through the work of the Black Christian Leaders Forum. This new forum meets regularly with cabinet ministers and civil servants to advocate for the issues of import to the Black community.

As we look ahead, a key to the Black Pentecostal Church's socio-economic and political involvement in the world will be mobilising members for socio-economic and political engagement. However, to enable this, members must feel liberated to act. Galatians 5:1 illustrates how Christians easily become unsettled, and are therefore in constant need of guidance and support to stay in the freedom of Christ, freedom from the bondage of legalism. Unity and effective engagement in the world can only be achieved when people realise their freedom from man-made religious rules, from fear of self and other, liberated to be who and what God intended each and every one to be. Paul puts it simply; 'it is for freedom that we have been freed'. Here I believe we have a lot to learn from Black and Liberation Theology. James Cone (1975, p.11) reminds us that freedom is the structure of, and a movement in, historical existence.

Freedom has to be real and holistic, true to the past and the future. It's no good freeing a man from slavery then enslaving him in colonialism; no good freeing him spiritually by giving him the Bible whilst enslaving him by using the same Bible to encourage him into servitude. The indomitable human spirit that instinctively desires freedom will always protest against oppression and enslavement. That is why the enslaved sang,

> Oh Freedom! Oh Freedom!
> Oh Freedom, I love thee!
> And before I'll be a slave, I'll be buried in my grave
> And go home to my Lord and be free

> *(Cone 1975, p.11)*

If I may cite Cone again, he says freedom expresses God's will to be in relation to his creatures in the social context of their striving for the fulfilment of humanity (Cone 1975, p.139). Neither can the Black Church afford the luxury of narrowness in reference to humanity – it cannot mean Black humanity alone, since until all are free, none is free. Christians are called to a universal concept of mission to the world, not just to people who look like us. The social, economic and political challenge amounts to a call for total liberation and equality for all.

6. The leadership challenge

As mentioned before, there is no single definition, type or style of leadership. However, the stand-out feature of leadership is the ability to lead people into a fruitful future. People are always asking, 'Where are we going?' 'Where are you taking us?' And so, a key challenge for Black Pentecostal leadership is the 'vision thing'. The wisdom literature says simply, where there is no vision, the people perish (KJV), or where there is no revelation, the people cast off restraint (NKJV). That is, if leadership does not help people understand their context, their present and their future, they will behave with carelessness and abandonment. It is the discipline of the task or the journey that keeps us focussed and productive.

Another aspect of leadership that challenges the Black Church was highlighted in some limited research I commissioned in 2005. This showed that although Black Church membership is overwhelmingly female its pastoral ministry is overwhelmingly male, 83%. Probably even more alarming was the revelation that only 3% of pastoral ministry was under 40 years old, a whopping 80% between 40 and 65 years old, and 17% over 65. Taken seriously, these statistics signal real questions about succession planning. The Black Church's traditional system of leaders emerging and then being home trained leaves too much variability in the system. This needs to be supplemented by a commitment to high level training and development programmes, with top leaders mentoring others who are emerging and those in office. It is no coincidence that the great leaders of our time are educated people: Martin Luther King, with an earned doctorate; Nelson Mandela, a lawyer; Barack Obama, a lawyer; Condoleeza Rice, with an earned PhD and speaks fluent Russian; Diane Abbot, Baroness Amos, Baroness Scotland, David Lammy, Joel Edwards, and more, are university graduates. It is fine to get your education at the cross, as the saying goes, but you must then go on to study and train for ministry. So, as Black Church pioneers go off the stage one by one, where are their replacements?

The missiological challenge

The seventh challenge that I suggest lies before the Black Church is one concerning mission. I have never forgotten the many leaders I interviewed during my PhD research, who declared unequivocally that they believe God had brought Black Christians to Britain to bring about revival in a country in which the Christian church was in, or heading towards, an apostate state. Sadly, sixty years on it does not appear that mainstream Christianity has been rescued, but the mission to promote biblical authority, resist racism and refuse to compromise the gospel as Black churches understand it was and is very clear. Clear too was the churches' sense of mission to seek out and rescue the lost. Oliver Lyseight (1995) for example, makes clear in his autobiography that he was personally quite comfortable, but it was observing his fellow Caribbean people with nowhere to worship that motivated him to start the mission in Wolverhampton. However, having now passed that formative stage of mission, the Black Church has an over reliance on continued migration, rather than on gaining converts from the population on a whole. The question is, what shape must the ministry of the Black Pentecostal church be to be effective and relevant in the twenty-first century?

Mark Sturge (2005) devotes a section of his book, *Look What the Lord has Done* to discussing the future of Black majority churches. He concludes that he does not know what the future holds for this genre of church; nobody knows or can know. I suggest that whilst the future is in God's mind, it may be permissible to say that the future of Black Pentecostal churches depend on their missiological positioning. Having initiated churches that did not exist in Britain before, and by so doing, rescued people who did not find a home, or did not desire one in the historic churches, the second phase of these churches' existence was to become more sociologically, economically and politically secured and relevant. However, I suggest that a third phase of these churches' development ought to be mainstreaming themselves so that they minister to, and draw following from non-Black, non-African and non-Caribbean heritage communities. A mission predicated on a gospel and ministry to the world rather than one that is ethnic specific is more likely to underwrite our future existence in an increasingly sceptical and unbelieving Western world. We cannot continue to fish 2% of all the fish in the sea!

Conclusion

I have tried to set out some of the challenges that face the leadership of the Black Pentecostal Churches in the UK. In the face of all of these, the Black Church cannot afford to think small. It cannot think of Black Pentecostal churches alone, but of providing a ministry to the church as a whole. For Black Pentecostal Leadership in the twenty-first century, the task amounts to: 'preparing God's people for works of service, so that the body of Christ may be built up until we reach unity in the faith and in the knowledge of the Son of God and become mature, attaining to the whole measure of the fullness of Christ' (Ephesians 4:12,13 NIV). It is a tall order; is the Black Church up to it?

References

Aldred, J. D. (2005) *Respect: Understanding Caribbean British Christianity,* Peterborough, Epworth

Arnold, S. E. (1992) *From Scepticism to Hope,* Nottingham, Grove Books

Beckford, Robert (2000) *Dread and Pentecostalism – A Political Theology for the Black Church in Britain*, London, SPCK

Brierley, Peter (2006) *Pulling Out of the Nose Dive,* London, Christian Research

Brown, Eric (2008) *Leadership Training Centre Prospectus*, Northampton, New Testament Church of God

Brueggemann, Walter (1993) *The Bible and Postmodern Imagination*, London, SCM Press

Burgess, S. M., and McGee, G. B., (eds) (1993) Dictionary of Pentecostal and Charismatic Movements, Michigan, Zondervan Publishing House

Census (1991) http://www.statistics.gov.uk/cci/nugget.asp?id=273

Cone, James (1993) *My Soul Looks Back,* New York, Orbis Books

Cone, James (1975) *God of the Oppressed,* San Francisco, Harper.

Conn, C. W. (1977) *Like A Mighty Army: A History of the Church of God 1886–1976,* Cleveland Tennessee, Pathway Press

Davidson, C.T. (1973) *Upon This Rock* Vol 1, Cleveland, Tennessee, White Wing Publishing House and Press

Drane, John (2000) *Cultural Change and Biblical Faith*, Carlisle, Cumbria, Paternoster Press

Dube, Musa W. (2002) 'Reading for Decolonisation (John 4:1–42)' in Dube, Musa W. and Stanley, Jeffrey L. (eds), John and Postcolonialism: Travel, Space and Power, London, Sheffield Academic Press

DuBois, W. W. B. (1994) *The Souls of Black Folk*, New York, Dover Publications

Edwards, Joel (1999) *Lord Make Us One but Not All the Same,* London, Hodder & Stoughton

Equiano, Olaudah (2003) *Interesting Narrative and Other Writings*, London, Penguin Classics

Gasque, W. Ward (1979) 'The Church in the New Testament' in Ellis, David J. and Gasque, W. Ward, *In God's Community,* Illinois, Harold Shaw Publishers

Hollenweger, Walter J. (1997) *Pentecostalism: Origins and Developments Worldwide,* Massachusetts, Hendrickson Publishers

Howell-Baker, Maxine and Brown, Tonya (eds), (2003) *Am I My Brother and Sister's Keeper?,* London, Christian Aid

Jacques-Garvey, Amy (ed) (1977) *Philosophy and Opinions of Marcus Garvey* Vols I and 2, New York, Atheneum

Jagessar, Michael and Reddie, Anthony G. (eds) (2007) *Postcolonial Black British Theology: New Textures and Themes,* Peterborough, Epworth

Jagessar, Michael and Reddie, Anthony G. (eds) (2007) *Black Theology in Britain: A Reader,* London, Equinox Publishing

Kinnamon, Michael and Hope, Brian E. (eds) (1997) *The Ecumenical Movement: An Anthology of Key Texts and Voices,* Michigan, William B. Eerdmans Publishing Company

Kung, Hans (1967,1995) *The Church,* Tunbridge Wells, Burns & Oats/Continuum Publishing

Lartey Emmanuel (ed) (1998) *Black Theology in Britain: A Journal of Contextual Praxis, Issue 1,* Sheffield, Sheffield Academic Press

Lartey, Emmanuel (ed) (1999) *Black Theology in Britain: A Journal of Contextual Praxis, Issue 3,* Sheffield, Sheffield Academic Press

Lewis, Beresford (2007) Unpublished PdD Thesis, Birmingham University

Lyseight, Oliver (1995) *Forward March – An Autobiography,* Birches Printers, Willenhall

Maxwell, John C. (1998) *21 Irrefutable Laws of Leadership,* Nashville, Thomas Nelson Publishing

Maxwell, John C. (1999) *21 Indispensable Qualities of a Leader*, Nashville, Nelson Books

McGrath, Alister (1994) *Christian Theology: An Introduction,* Oxford, Blackwell Publishers

Michel, David (2000) *Telling the Story: Black Pentecostals in the Church of God,* Cleveland, Pathway Press

Reddie, Anthony G. (2003) *Nobodies to Somebodies: A practical theology for education and liberation,* Peterborough, Epworth Press

Reddie, Richard S. (2007) Abolition: The struggle to abolish slavery in the British Colonies, Oxford, Lion Hudson

Smith, Iain Duncan (2006) *Breakdown Britain*, London, Social Justice Policy Group, Interim report on the State of the Nation

Sturge, Mark (2005) *Look What the Lord Has Done,* Milton Keynes, Scripture Union

Sugirtharajah, R. S. (2002) *Postcolonial Criticism and Biblical Interpretation,* Oxford, Oxford University Press

Walker, Robin (2006) *When We Ruled,* London, Every Generation Media

Warren, Rick (1995) *Purpose Driven Church: Growth without compromising your message and mission,* Grand Rapids, Zondervan Publishing House

Contributors

Bishop Joe Aldred MMTh, PhD
Joe is Secretary for Minority Ethnic Christian Affairs with Churches Together in England and former Chair of the Council of Black-led Churches. He presents Chat Back with Joe Aldred on BBC Radio WM 95.6FM and is a contributor to BBC Radio 2's *Pause for Thought*. He is a bishop in the Church of God of Prophecy and operates ecumenically across the churches and faiths. He has authored and edited a number of books and articles and works with several organisations at grassroots and board level on community building, education and health.
Website: www.joealdred.com

Revd Carver L. Anderson MSocSc, RSW, CQSW, DipSW, DipTh, Cert-CII
Carver is the Co-Founder, Chair and Director of Shalom Consultancy. He is a trustee with Bringing Hope and the Churches Child Protection Advisory Service, and a committee member of Young Disciples. A former National Director of Youth and Christian Education for the New Testament Church of God in England and Wales, he continues to champion issues of youth development and empowerment. He has ministered across the UK and Europe, in Africa, Caribbean, and USA. He works as a social scientist within communities to initiate change and transformation.

Revd Chris Andre-Watson BD (Hons)
Chris originally trained as a journalist in London before being called into Baptist ministry. Having gained his theology degree at Spurgeon's College, he became the minister of Brixton Baptist Church. During his 10 year

ministry he was involved in a number of initiatives addressing issues facing young Black men, including establishing a mentoring programme called Face2Face and the Beacon Project. He now works for BMS World Mission and has been the regional coordinator for London and the South-east for the past four years.

Cheron Byfield BA, MSc, CFCIPD, MBA, DPhil
Cheron is co-founder and chairperson of Excell3 which houses the WISE project and the National Black Boys Can Association. She is founder and editor of Black Pupils.com, and author of *Black Boys Can Make It*. She has lectured in colleges and universities, and has worked at senior manage-ment level in Enterprise Development. A strong advocate for the educa-tion of disadvantaged children, she leads by example, having successfully obtained four degrees, including a doctorate from the University of Oxford.

Juliet Fletcher
Juliet is a Gospel Music specialist consultant and a recognised pioneer in British Gospel music. She is a Gospel singer and media producer for radio, TV, live events, and audio visual presentations. For over thirty years Juliet has scored numerous 'firsts' in the music industry including – founding the first commercial Gospel promotion company and pioneering the first BBC 'live broadcast' network radio Gospel show direct from leading Black Churches. She has worked with the BBC as an expert on Gospel and Soul music. She has produced live shows for Andrae Crouch, Chaka Kahn, Candi Staton and CeCe Winans.

Dionne Gravesande DipCII, DipTh, BA
Dionne is the Head of Churches and Education at Christian Aid. She takes the corporate lead on working with churches in the global north and south. She serves as a National Youth and Christian Education Board Member for the New Testament Church of God and is Chair of the African and Caribbean Evangelical Alliance Council. She is a Missions Coordinator at her local church in Northampton where she has been a member since 1994. Dionne's background is in youth and social care; she is a qualified counsellor and serves her local community as a school Governor.

Revd Les Isaac
Les is CEO of Ascension Trust which he founded in 1993. His mission is to train and develop individuals to serve the local community, city, nation and

nations of the world. His passion is to enable Christians to get involved and impact their communities and society. He co-founded the Street Pastors Initiative in 2003 which provides late night outreach service in high crime areas. He has led the roll-out of the Street Pastors Initiative across the country and abroad with over 2000 Street Pastors serving in 24 initiatives in London, over 100 nationwide and 1 in Antigua and Barbuda.

Christopher A. Johnson FFMSc, MBA, PhD

Christopher is an author and business management consultant. He is a former Commonwealth and Nuffield Press Fellow of Wolfson College, Cambridge University. An acclaimed researcher, author, editor and publisher, he has developed expertise in multi-industry sector strategy and commercial and social entrepreneurship. He is the author of *Journey Through Life*, an authorised biography of Randolph Beresford MBE, the first non-British born Mayor of a London Borough. He won the 2009 Obama Shield for his book: *British Caribbean Enterprises: A century of challenges and successes.*

R. David Muir PGCE, Dip.Th., BA (Hons), MA, PhD

David is a political scientist and a theologian. He is founder and director of Faith in Britain and former Executive Director for Public Policy and Public Theology and former executive director at the Evangelical Alliance. He has been a secondary school teacher and Principal of a community school. He was Head of Teaching, Research and Regional Development at the Commonwealth Institute. He has lectured at London University, the University of East London and was senior lecturer at London Metropolitan University where he taught Caribbean political economy and post-war Black British history. He worked with the late Sir Bernard Crick on citizenship education and on the report 'Life in the United Kingdom'. He has also been an independent adviser on the Home Office's Lawrence Steering Group (LSG) and Deputy Chairman of the Metropolitan Police Authority. David earned his doctorate from King's College, London University in Black Political Theology and Pentecostalism.

Keno Ogbo PGDip, BSc, MSc

Keno is a Strategist and Project Manager with particular expertise in setting up projects and initiatives. With Bachelor and Masters Degrees in architecture, she worked in housing development before playing a key role in the setup and development of the Peace Alliance, a national Charity founded to promote peace and anti-violent initiatives. She has a strong interest in the internet and web technologies and is founder of Spiraluniverse.org, a Christian community website dedicated to supporting organizations and individuals to profile their work. She is a visiting lecturer at the University of Hertfordshire Business School.

Pastor Jonathan Oloyede ChB, MB
Jonathan is a medical doctor by profession and a missionary to England and Europe. A Christian convert from Islam, he is founder and Senior Pastor of City Chapel, London, established in 2008. He is the initiator of the Year for London and National Canopy of Prayer. He is the catalyst for London's Global Day of Prayer and has a vision to see the United Kingdom saturated with prayer. The Global Day of Prayer London holds large annual prayer gatherings in stadiums across London culminating at Wembley in 2010.

Carl J. Ryan RMN, CertEd, BA (Hon), MPhil
Carl is a Registered Mental Nurse (RMN), lecturer and practitioner, CEO and lead tutor of the Ryteq Training Institute. Accredited by Greenwich University, Ryteq has provided courses in conflict management for over 20 years to a variety of health and non-health sector organizations. He also works in a variety of psychiatric and prison systems. He recently completed a research study into conflict management involving the use of manual restraint techniques in mental health locations, for which he received an award from the City University, London in 2008.

Lincoln Sargeant MFPH, MD, PhD
Lincoln is a Consultant in Public Health Medicine with NHS Cambridgeshire. He was previously Clinical Lecturer in Public Health and Epidemiology with the University of Cambridge. He is a medical graduate of the University of the West Indies, and lectured in Jamaica before migrating to the UK. He has a doctorate in Epidemiology from the University of Cambridge specializing in diabetes and obesity. His perspectives on the health of peoples of African origin is informed by his experience and training as a clinician, researcher and public health doctor.

Revd Mark Richard Shelton Saint
Mark is the Cultural Architect of the Christian church/movement Encounter. With over 15 years of preaching and ministry experience,

human rights leadership and corporate success, God led him from leadership in the African American church experience to pastoring two Caucasian churches. After years of rebuilding dying churches in America, God called him to London. He is an anointed communicator and theologian and has the rare blend of a seminary education and signs of the power of the Holy Spirit that equip him to effectively reach the world with the Gospel.

Julia Smith LLM, MA, MCIPD
Julia is a Director and founder of the Dispute Resolution Centre for Faith Communities and is an Employment and Equalities consultant at Julius & Co. Solicitors. She was the first Director for Women's Ministries in her church. She is a lay preacher and has ministered in Ghana and Rwanda. She has worked extensively with ecumenical initiatives such as Churches Together in Britain and Ireland. She had held senior management roles in national and local government and specializes in employment law, equality and diversity. She is currently pursuing a PhD in church conflict resolution.

Bibliography

Abbotts, J., Harding, S., Cruickshank, K. (2004) 'Cardiovascular risk profiles in UK-born Caribbeans and Irish living in England and Wales' in *Atherosclerosis* 175(2): pp.295–303

A Brighter Future For Children And Young People – The Birmingham Strategy, Birmingham City Council 2006

Afari, Y. (2007) *Overstanding Rastafari – Jamaica's Gift To The World*, Jamaica, Senya-Cum

Aldred, Joe (ed.) (2000) *Sisters with Power*, London, Continuum

Aldred, Joe (2001) 'The Black Church in Britain and Their Relations with the Ecumenical Movement' in Dahling-Sander, Herausgegeben von Christoph, Funkschmidt, Kai M., and Mielke, Vera (eds) *Pfingstkirchen und Okumene in Bewegung*, Frankfurt am Main, Verlag Otto Lembeck

Aldred, Joe and Parris, Garnet (2001) 'The Bible and the Black Church' in Rowland, Chris and Vincent, John (eds) *Bible and Practice*, Sheffield, Urban Theology Unit

Aldred, J. D. (2005) *Respect: Understanding Caribbean British Christianity*, Peterborough, Epworth

Ammerman, N.T. and Farnsley, II, A.E. (1997) *Congregation and Community*, New Brunswick, NJ, Rutgers University Press

Anderson, Roberts M. (1979) *Vision of the Disinherited: The making of American Pentecostalism*, New York, Oxford University Press

Arnold, S. E. (1992) *From Scepticism to Hope*, Nottingham, Grove Books Ltd

Aron, Raymond (1965) *Main Currents in Sociological Thought*, Vol.1, (translated by Richard Howard and Helen Weaver) Harmondsworth, Middlesex, Penguin Books

Asimolowo, Matthew (1993) *Tongues of Fire*, London, Mattyson Media Publication

Austin-Broos, Diane J. (1997) *Jamaica Genesis: Religion and the Politics of Moral Orders*, Chicago, University of Chicago Press

Bakke, Dr Raymond (1987) *The Urban Christian*, Nottingham, InterVarsity Press

Barrow Cadbury Trust (2005) Lost in Transition – *Report of the Barrow Cadbury Commission on Young Adults and the Criminal Justice System*, London

Bartleman, Frank (1980) *Azusa Street – Roots of Modern-day Pentecost*, New Jersey, Bridge Publishing

BBC News Online. 'Black churches "can help mentally ill"'. 11 January 2001. http://news.bbc.co.uk/1/hi/health/1112189.stm (Accessed 24 October 2008)

Becker, Ernest (1962, 1972) *The Birth and Death of Meaning: An Interdisciplinary Perspective on the Problem of Man*, Harmondsworth, Middlesex, Penguin

Beckford, Robert (2004) *God and the Gangs*, London, Darton, Longman & Todd

Beckford, Robert (1998) *Jesus is Dread: Black Theology and Black Culture in Britain*, London, Darton, Longman & Todd

Beckford, Robert (2000) *Dread and Pentecostal: A Political Theology for the Black Church in Britain*, London, SCM Press

Beckford, Robert (2001) *God of the Rahtid*, London, Darton, Longman & Todd

Beckford, Robert (2006) *Jesus Dub Theology: Music and social change*, Oxford, Routledge Taylor & Francis

Bird, M. and Hilborn, D. (2002) *God and the Generations – Youth, Age and the Church Today*, Carlisle, Cumbria, Paternoster Press

Black Youth Project, *Research Project Exploring the Attitudes, Actions and Decision Making of African American Youth by Highlighting their Lives, Ideas and Voices* : www.blackyouthproject.uchicago.edu, Chicago

Blair, Maud (2001) *Why Pick on Me – School exclusion and Black youth*, London, Trenthan Books

Blyden, Edward W. (1887, 1994) *Christianity, Islam and the Negro Race*, Baltimore, Black Classic Press

Bookless, Dave (2008) *Planet Wise*, London, Inter Varsity Press

Bossart, Donald E. (1980) *Creative Conflict in Religious Education and Church Administration*, Birmingham, Alabama, Religious Education Press

Bossart, Donald E. (1995) *Growing through Conflict. Reflect: A series of faculty reflections on contemporary issues*, Denver, Colorado, Iliff School of Theology

Bourdieu, P. (1983) 'Forms of Capital' in Richardson, J. G. (ed.) *Handbook of Theory and Research for the Sociology of Education*, New York, Greenwood Press.

Boyd-MacMillan, Eolene and Savage, Sara (2008) *Transforming Conflict*, University of Cambridge

Bradley, Ian (2007) *Believing Britain: The spiritual identity of 'Britishness'*, London and New York, I.B. Tauris

Breeze, D.J. and Dobson, B. (2000) *Hadrian's Wall* (fourth edition) London, Penguin Books Limited

Bridgebuilders (2006) London Mennonite Centre, London

Brierley, Peter (1991) *Christian England*, London, Marc Europe

Brierley, Peter (2000) *The Tide Is Running Out*, London, Christian Research

Brierley, Peter ed (2003) *U.K. Christian Handbook*, London, Christian Research

Brierley, Peter (2006) *Pulling out of the Nosedive: A Contemporary Picture of Churchgoing – What the 2005 English Church Census Reveals*, London, Christian Research

British Heart Foundation. British Heart Foundation Statistics Website. http://www.heartstats.org/homepage.asp (Accessed 24 October 2008)

Brooks, Ira V. (1982) *Where Do We Go From Here? A History of 25 Years of the New Testament Church in the UK 1955–1980*, Great Britain, Charles Raper

Broughton, Viv (1985) *Black Gospel : An illustrated history of the gospel sound*. Poole, Dorset, New York, NY, Blandford Press

Broughton, Viv (1996) *Too Close To Heaven: The illustrated history of gospel music*, London: Midnight Books

Brueggemann, Walter (1993) *The Bible and Postmodern Imagination*, London, SCM Press

Buber, Martin (1952) *Eclipse of God: Studies in the relationship between religion and philosophy*, New York, Harper & Row

Burgess, S. M. and McGee, G. B. (eds) (1993) *Dictionary of Pentecostal and Charismatic Movements*, Michigan, Zondervan Publishing House

Byfield, C. (2008) *Black Boys Can Make It – How they Overcome the Obstacles to Universities in the UK and USA*, Stoke on-Trent, Trentham Books

Byfield, C. (2008) 'The influence of religion on the educational achievement of Black Boys: A UK/USA study', *British Journal of Sociology of Education*. 29 (2) pp.189–199

Callan A , and Littlewood, R. (1998) 'Patient satisfaction: Ethnic origin or explanatory model?' in *International Journal of Social Psychiatry*. 44(1): pp.1–11

Calley, M. J. (1965) *God's People – West Indian Pentecostalism Sects in England*, Oxford, Oxford University Press

Campbell C. and Mclean C. (2002) 'Ethnic identities, social capital and health inequalities: Factors shaping African-Caribbean participation in local community networks in the UK' in *Social Science and Medicine*. 55(4): pp.643–57

Campbell, C., Cornish, F., Mclean, C. (2004) 'Social capital, participation and the perpetuation of health inequalities: Obstacles to African-Caribbean participation in 'partnerships' to improve mental health', in *Ethnicity and Health*. 9 (4): pp.313–35

Campbell, Lorna (2002) 'An Evaluation of Theological methodology at Work through a Critical Appraisal of *Jesus is Dread: Black Theology and Black Culture in Britain* by Robert Beckford', unpublished paper

Carter, P. (2003) Black Cultural Capital, Status Positioning and Schooling: Conflicts for Low-Income African American Youth, *Social Problems*

Cashmore, Ernest (1983) *Rastaman: The Rastafarian Movement in England*, London, Unwin Paperbacks

Centre for Studies on New Religions CENSUR-2000

Channer, Y. (1995) *I am a Promise: The school achievements of British African Caribbeans*, Stoke on Trent, Trentham Books.

Chevannes, Barry (1994) *Rastafari: Roots and ideology*, Syracuse, Syracuse University Press

Chevannes, M. and Reeves, F. (1987) 'The Black Voluntary School Movement: Definition, context and prospects', in Troyna, B. (ed.) Racial Equality in Education, NY, Routledge

Chike, Chigor (2007) Voices from Slavery, Milton Keynes, Authorhouse

Clarke, Peter and Byrne, Peter (ed.) (1993) *Religion Defined and Explained*, London, Macmillan Press

Clifton M. (2007) Managing New Migration: A local approach to a global phenomenon in *New Local Government Network*

Coleman, L. M., Testa, A. (2008) 'Sexual health knowledge, attitudes and behaviours: Variations among a religiously diverse sample of young people in London, UK', *Ethnicity and Health*, 13(1): pp.55–72

Comblin, Jose 'The Holy Spirit' in Sobrino, Jon and Ellacuria, Ignacio (eds), (1996) *Systematic Theology: Perspectives from Liberation Theology*, London, SCM Press

Cone, James (1975) *God of the Oppressed*, Minneapolis, Minnesota, Seabury Press

Cone, James (1970) *A Black Theology of Liberation*, Philadelphian and New York, J.B. Lippincott Company

Cone, James (1989) *Black Theology and Black Power*, San Francisco, Harper & Row

Cone, James, (1986) *Speaking The Truth – Ecumenism, Liberation, and Black Theology,* Michigan, William B. Eerdmans Publishing Company

Cone, James (1993) *My Soul Looks Back*, New York, Orbis Books

Conn, C. W. (1977) *Like A Mighty Army: A history of the Church of God 1886–1976*, Cleveland Tennessee, Pathway Press

Cooper, R., Rotimi, C., Ataman, S., McGee, D., Osotimehin, B., Kadiri, S. (1997) 'The prevalence of hypertension in seven populations of west African origin', *American Journal of Public Health*, 87(2): pp.160–8

Cooper, R. S., Wolf-Maier, K., Luke, A., Adeyemo, A., Banegas, J. R., Forrester T., et al. (2005) 'An international comparative study of blood pressure in populations of European vs. African descent', *BMC Medicine* 3:2

Copher, Charles B. (1993) *Black Biblical Studies*, Chicago, Black Light Fellowship

Cox, Harvey (1995), *Fire From Heaven: The rise of Pentecostal spirituality and the reshaping of religion in the twenty-first century*, London, SCM

Cox, Harvey (1965), *The Secular City: Secularization and urbanization in theological perspective*, London, SCM Press

Crawford, M.J., Nur, U., McKenzie, K., Tyrer, P. (2005) 'Suicidal ideation and suicide attempts among Ethnic Minority groups in England: Results of a national household survey', *Psychological Medicine*. 35(9): pp.1369–77

Curtin, Philip D. (1990) *The Rise and Fall of the Plantation Complex – Essays in Atlantic History*, Cambridge, Cambridge University Press

Daneel, M. L. (2001) *African Earthkeepers, Volume 1, Interfaith mission in earth-care*, Unisa Press, copyright University of South Africa

Davidson, C.T. (1973) *Upon This Rock Vol 1*, Cleveland, Tennessee, White Wing Publishing House and Press

Davies, Brian (ed) (2000) *Philosophy of Religion: A Guide and Anthology*, Oxford, Oxford University Press

Davis, Ken (1996) *How to Speak to Youth and Keep Them Awake at the Same Time*, Grand Rapids Michigan, Zondervan Publishing House

Dennis, Ferdinand (2000) 'Birmingham: Blades of Frustration' in Kwesi Owusu (ed.) *Black British Culture and Society: A Text Reader*, London, Routledge

Department for Education and Skills (2006) *Teenage Pregnancy Next Steps: Guidance for Local Authorities and Primary Care Trusts on Effective Delivery of Local Strategies*

Department of Health (2005) *Commissioning a patient-led NHS*

Dixon, Marcia in *Black UK Christian Directory 2008*, Bury St Edmunds, Black UK Publications Limited

Dobson, Edward G.,Leas, Speed B., Marshall, Shelly (1992) *Masterminding Conflict and Controversy,* Christianity Today International.

Drane, John (2000) *Cultural Change and Biblical Faith*, Carlisle, Cumbria, Paternoster Press

Dube, Musa W. (2002) 'Reading for Decolonisation (John 4.1–42)' in Dube, Musa W. and Stanley, Jeffrey L. (eds) *John and Postcolonialism: Travel, Space and Power,* London, Sheffield Academic Press

DuBois, W. W. B. (1994) *The Souls of Black Folk*, New York, Dover Publications

Dudley, Carl S; Zingery, Theresa; Breeden, David (2000) *Insights into Congregational Conflicts* and Faith Communities Today

Dunn, James (1970) *Baptism in the Holy Spirit: A re-examination of the New Testament teaching on the gift of the spirit in relation to Pentecostalism today*, London, SCM Press

Edwards, Joel (ed.) (1992) 'The Pentecostal Distinctives', in *Let's Praise Him Again: An African-Caribbean perspective on worship*, Joel Edwards, Eastbourne, East Sussex, Kingsway Publication, pp.75–83

Edwards, Joel (1993) 'The British Afro-Caribbean Community', in Martyn Eden (ed) *Britain on the Brink*, London, Crossway Books

Edwards, Joel (1999) *Lord Make Us One – But Not All the Same*, London, Hodder & Stoughton

Edwards, Joel (2000) *The Cradle, The Cross and the Empty Tomb: A faith we can be proud to proclaim*, London, Hodder & Stoughton

Edwards, Joel (2001) *Review of Dread and Pentecostal* (unpublished paper)

Edwards, Joel (2008) *An Agenda for Change: A global call for spiritual and social transformation*, Grand Rapids, Michigan, Zondervan Publishing

Ellis, J., Latif, S. (2006) *Capacity Building Black and Minority Ethnic Voluntary and Community Organisations*, Joseph Rowntree Foundation

Equiano, Olaudah (2003) *The Interesting Narrative of the Life of Olaudah Equiano, Or Gustavus Vassa, The African*, London, Penguin

Erasmus (1971) *Praise of Folly and Letter to Martin Dorp* (translated by Betty Radice, introduction and notes by A.H.T. Levi), Middlesex, Penguin Books

Fanon, Franz (1965) *The Wretched of the Earth*, Great Britain, MacGibbon and Kee

Fearon, P., Kirkbride, J.B., Morgan, C., Dazzan, P., Morgan, K., Lloyd, T.. (2006) 'Incidence of schizophrenia and other psychoses in ethnic minority groups: Results from the MRC AESOP Study', *Psychological Medicine*. 36(11): pp.1541–50

Felix A.K., Levine D., Burstin H.R. (2003) 'African American church participation and health care practices', *Journal of General Internal Medicine*. 18(11): pp.908–13

Foster, R.S. (1991) *Local Economic Development Strategies for a Changing Economy*, Washington DC, International City Management Association

Gasque, W. Ward (1979) 'The Church in the New Testament' in Ellis, David J. and Gasque, W. Ward *In God's Community*, Illinois, Harold Shaw Publishers

Gause H. R. (1973) *Church of God Polity*, Cleveland, Tennessee, Pathway Press

Genovese, Eugene D. (1971) *The World the Slaves Made: Two essays in interpretation*, New York, Vintage Books

Gerloff, R. (1992) *A Plea for British Black Theologies – The Black Church movement in Britain in its transatlantic cultural and theological interaction*, Frankfurt am Main, Peter Lang

Gerloff, R. (1999) 'Response' to Beckford in A. Anderson and W. J. Hollenweger (ed.) *Pentecostals After a Century: Global perspectives on a movement in transition, Journal of Pentecostal Theology* supplement, Sheffield Academic Press, p.65

Gerzina, Gretchen (1995) Black England: Life before emancipation, London, John Murray

Glaeser, E. and Sacerdote, B. (2001) *Education and Religion*, National Bureau of Economic Research, Harvard Institute of Economic Research, Paper 1913

Glynn, M. (2004) *Hard to Access Young People and Drugs Support Services In Birmingham*, A Birmingham City Council Drug Action Team Publication

Goodman, Denise W. (2000) *Congregational Fitness: Healthy Practices for Layfolk*, Alban Institute publication

Grant, Paul and Patel, Raj (1990) *A Time To Speak*, Nottingham, Russell Press

Grant, Paul and Patel, Raj (1992) *A Time To Act*, Nottingham, Russell Press

Grant, Paul I. (2006) *Saving Our Sons – Strategies and Advice For The Parents Of Afrikan Teenage Sons*, Nottingham, United Kingdom, Navig8or Press

Grierson K. (2007) 'Ethnicity data for Jobseeker's Allowance claimants', *Economic and Labour Market Review*, 1(2): pp.26–9

Halpern, R. (1995) *Rethinking the Inner City*, New York, NY, Columbia University Press

Halverstadt, Hugh F. (1991) *Managing Church Conflict*, John Knox Press Publication

Health Protection Agency Centre for Infections (2007) Tuberculosis in the UK: *Annual report on tuberculosis surveillance and control in the UK 2007*, London

Herrnstein, R. A. and Murray, C. (1994) *The Bell Curve: Intelligence and Class Structure in American Life*, New York, Grove Press

Hollenweger, Walter J. (1972) *The Pentecostals*, London, SCM Press

Hollenweger, Walter J. (1997) *Pentecostalism: Origins, Developments Worldwide*, Peabody, Massachusetts, Hendrickson Publishers

Holman, R. R., Paul, S. K., Bethel, M. A., Matthews, D. R., Neil, H. A. (2008) '10-year follow-up of intensive glucose control in type 2 diabetes', *New England Journal of Medicine*, 359 (15): pp.1577–89

Holman, R. R., Paul, S. K, Bethel, M. A., Neil, H. A., Matthews, D. R. (2008) 'Long-term follow-up after tight control of blood pressure in type 2 diabetes' *New England Journal of Medicine*, 359(15), pp.1565–76

hooks, bell and West, Cornel (1991) *Breaking Bread: Insurgent Black Intellectual Life*, Boston, South End Press

House Of Commons Home Affairs Committee (2007) *Young Black People and the Criminal Justice System*, London, The Stationery Office Ltd

Howell-Baker, Maxine and Brown, Tonya (eds) (2003) *Am I My Brother and Sister's Keeper*, London, Christian Aid

Jagessar, Michael and Reddie, Anthony (eds) (2007) *Postcolonial Black British Theology: New Textures and Themes*, Peterborough, Epworth

Jagessar, Michael and Reddie, Anthony G. (eds) (2007) *Black Theology in Britain: A Reader*, London, Equinox Publishing

Jacques-Garvey, Amy (ed.) (1977) *Philosophy and Opinions of Marcus Garvey Vols 1 and 2*, New York, Atheneum

Johnson, C.A. (2009) 'Social Enterprise', in *British Caribbean Enterprises*: A century of challenges and successes, London, Tropical Enterprises

Johnson, Douglas W. (1974) *Managing Change in the Church*, New York, NY, Friendship Press

Kalilombe, Patrick A. (1999) *Doing Theology at the Grassroots: Theological essays from Malawi*, Gweru, Mambo Press

Karlsen, S., Nazroo, J.Y., McKenzie, K., Bhui, K., Weich, S. (2005) 'Racism, psychosis and common mental disorder among Ethnic Minority groups in England', *Psychological Medicine*, 35(12): pp.1795–803

Kaufman, J. S., Cooper, R. S. (2008) 'Race in Epidemiology: New tools, old problems', *Annals of Epidemioliology*, 18(2): pp.119–23

Kee, Alistair (1990) *Marx and the Failure of Liberation Theology*, London, Philadelphia, SCM and Trinity Press International

Kee, Alistair (2006), *The Rise and Demise of Black Theology*, Burlington, Vt., and Aldershot, UK, Ashgate

Killingray, David and Edwards, Joel (2007) Black Voices: The shaping of our Christian experience, Nottingham, IVP

Kinnamon, Michael and Hope, Brian E. (eds) (1997) *The Ecumenical Movement: An Anthology of Key Texts and Voices*, Michigan, William B. Eerdmans Publishing Company

Kolakowski, Leszek (1982) *Religion*, Glasgow, Fontana

Lartey (ed.), Emmanuel (1998) *Black Theology in Britain: A Journal of Contextual Praxis, Issue 1*, Sheffield, Sheffield Academic Press

Lartey, Emmanuel (ed.), (1999) *Black Theology in Britain: A Journal of Contextual Praxis, Issue 3*, Sheffield, Sheffield Academic Press

Kung, Hans (1967,1995) *The Church*, Tunbridge Wells, Burns & Oats/Continuum Publishing

Leary, Joy Degruy (2005) *Post Traumatic Syndrome: America's Legacy of Enduring Injury and Healing*, Milwaukie, Oregon, Uptone Press

Lee, J. W. *Address to WHO staff* (2003) Geneva, World Health Organization

Lewis, Beresford (2007) Unpublished PhD Thesis, Birmingham University

Light, Alan (1998) *Tupac Shakur*, London: Plexus Publishing Limited.

McDowell, Josh and Hostetler, Bob (1994) *Right from Wrong – What you need to know to help youth make right choices*, London, Word Publishing

Lyseight, Oliver (1995) *Forward March – An Autobiography*, Birches Printers, Willenhall

Macintyre, Alasdair (1969) *Marxism and Christianity*, London, Gerald Duckworth & Co. Ltd

Majors, R. and Billson, J. (1992) *Cool Pose: The Dilemmas of Black Manhood in America*, New York, Lexington Books

Martin, David (2002) *Pentecostalism: The World Their Parish*, Oxford, Blackwell Publishers

Martin, Larry (ed.) (1999) *Azusa Street Sermons: William Seymour*, Missouri, Christian Life Books

Marx, Karl (1975) *Early Writings* (written in 1844, introduced by Lucio Colletti and translated by Rodney Livingstone and George Benton), Harmondsworth, Middlesex, Penguin Books

Maxwell, John C. (1998) *21 Irrefutable Laws of Leadership*, Nashville, Thomas Nelson Publishing

Maxwell, John C. (1999) *21 Indispensable Qualities of a Leader*, Nashville, Nelson Books

McGrath, Alister (1994) *Christian Theology: An Introduction*, Oxford, Blackwell Publishers

McGrath, Alistair (2004) *The Twilight of Atheism: The rise and fall of disbelief in the modern world*, London and Sydney, Random House

Mclean, C., Campbell, C., Cornish, F. (2003) 'African-Caribbean interactions with mental health services in the UK: experiences and expectations of exclusion as (re)productive of health inequalities', *Social Sciences and Medicine*, 56(3): pp.657–69

McMillan, M. (2001) *Growing Up is Hard to Do – Young people and sexual health*, Young people's health project, Lewisham

Mendez-Bowen, Deborah (2006) *Mediation Skills Workshop*, Institute for Dispute Resolution Limited

Michel, David (2000) *Telling the Story: Black Pentecostals in the Church of God*, Cleveland, Pathway Press

Milbank, John (1990) *Theology and Social Theory: Beyond secular reason*, Oxford, Blackwell Publishers

Mitchell J., and Weatherly D. (2000) 'Beyond church attendance: Religiosity and mental health among rural older adults', *Journal of Cross Cultural Gerontololog*, 15(1): pp.37–54

Mohabir, Philip (1988) *Building Bridges*, London, Hodder & Stoughton

Moltmann, Jürgen (1977) *The Church in the Power of the Spirit: A Contribution to Messianic Ecclesiology*, London, SCM Press

Moltmann, Jürgen (1967) *Theology of Hope*, London, SCM

National Statistics (2006), Table 4 (Population: by ethnic group and age, 2001) Great Britain, Crown Copyright

Neilson, A. (2008) *Child Prisons Are 'Hotbeds of Violence'*, A Howard League Publication, Cambridge, Blackwell Publishing Ltd

Newberger, Ken (2006) Conflict in my church www.resolvechurchconflict.com http://www.resolvechurchconflict.com

Newbold Jr., Robert T. (1980) *Conflict in the Black Church Christian* [Online] Library.com http://ctlibrary.com/le/1980/spring/8012099.html

Nweneka C.V. (2007) 'Sexual practices of church youths in the era of HIV/AIDS: playing the ostrich', *AIDS Care*.19(8): pp.966–9

Office of National Statistics (2003) *Ethnic group statistics: A guide for the collection and classification of ethnicity data*, London, Palgrave Macmillan

Office of National Statistics (2006) *Focus on Ethnicity and Religion*, London, Palgrave Macmillan

Osborne, J. W. (1997a) Race and Academic Disidentification, *Journal of Educational Psychology*, 89: pp.728–735

Pattilio-McCoy, M. (1998) 'Church Culture as a Strategy of Action in the Black Community', *American Sociological Review*, 63 (6) pp.767–784.

Pityana, N. Barney (1989) 'Towards a Black Theology for Britain', in Anthony Harvey (ed.) *Theology in the City: A theological response to 'Faith in the City'*, London, SPCK

Pruitt, Raymond M. (1981) *Fundamentals of the Faith*, Cleveland, Tennessee, White Wing Publishing House and Press

Raboteau, Albert J. (1999) *Canaan Land: A Religious History of African Americans*, Oxford University Press

Rankins, J., Wortham, J., Brown, L.L. (2007) 'Modifying soul food for the Dietary Approaches to Stop Hypertension diet (DASH) plan: Implications for metabolic syndrome (DASH of Soul)', *Ethnicity and Disease*. 17(3 Suppl 4):S4–12

Reddie, Anthony (ed.) (2002) 'Singing the Lord's Song in a Strange Land', *Black Theology in Britain: An International Journal*, London, Continuum Publishing

Reddie, Anthony G. (2003) *Nobodies to Somebodies: A practical theology for education and liberation,* Peterborough, Epworth Press

Reddie, A and Jagessar, Michael N. (2007) *Black Theology in Britain – A Reader,* London, Equinox Publishing Ltd

Richard S. Reddie (2007) *Abolition: The struggle to abolish slavery in the British Colonies,* Oxford, Lion Hudson

Reese, T. David and Clamp, Christina A. (2000): *Faith-Based Community Economic Development: Principles and Practices,* Federal Reserve Bank of Boston.

Religious Trends ,UK Christian Handbook, 2002/2003

Rhamie, J. and Hallam, S. (2002) 'An Investigation into African Caribbean Academic Success in the UK', *Race, Ethnicity and Education.* 5, (2)

Roberts, J. Deotis (1974) *A Black Political Theology*, Philadelphia, Westminster Press

Roberts, J. Deotis (1975) A Black Ecclesiology of Involvement, *Journal of Religious Thought,* (Spring-Summer)

Sanders, Bryan H. (2008) *Conflict Management Series,* Enrichment Journal, Pentecostal Ministry

Scazzero, Peter (2003) *The Emotionally Healthy Church*, Zondervan

Scheffler R.M., Brown T.T., Syme L., Kawachi I., Tolstykh I., Iribarren C. (2008) 'Community-level social capital and recurrence of acute coronary syndrome', *Social Science and Medicine*, Apr.66(7): pp.1603–13 (e-publication)

Scott, Cathy (2001) *The Notorious B.I.G – The Murder of Biggie Smalls*, London, Plexus Publishing

Scottdale, P. (1983) *When Caring Is Not Enough: Resolving conflicts through fair fighting,* Herald Press

Sedmak, Clemens (2007) *Doing Local Theology: A guide for artisans of a new humanity,* Maryknoll, Orbis Books

Sinha, S., Curtis, K., Jayakody, A., Viner, R., Roberts, H. (2007) '"People make assumptions about our communities": Sexual health amongst teenagers from Black and minority ethnic backgrounds in East London', *Ethnicity and Health,*12(5): pp.423–41

Smith A. (2002) *The New Ethnicity Classification in the Labour Force Survey*, Office of National Statistics

Smith, Iain Duncan (2006) *Breakdown Britain*, London, Social Justice Policy Group, Interim report on the State of the Nation

Smith, Io, with Green, Wendy (1989) *An Ebony Cross: Being Black in Britain Today*, London, Harper Collins

Spencer, M. (1991) 'Adolescent African American self esteem: suggestion for mentoring programme content', Conference Paper Series. Washington, Urban Institute

Sturge, Mark (2005) Look What the *Lord Has Done! An Exploration of Black Christian Faith in Britain*, Bletchley, Scripture Union

Sugirtharajah, R. S. (2002) *Postcolonial Criticism and Biblical Interpretation*, Oxford, Oxford University Press

Swann, Lord (1985) *Education for All: Final Report of the Committee of Inquiry into the Education of Children from Ethnic Minority Groups.* Cmnd 9453, London, HMSO

Synan, Vinson (1980) 'Introduction', in Bartleman, Frank *Azusa Street – Roots of Modern-day Pentecost,* New Jersey, Bridge Publishing

Szczepura A. (2005) 'Access to health care for Ethnic Minority populations', *Postgraduate Medical Journal*, 81(953): pp.141–7

Teenage Pregnancy Research Programme (2005) *Research briefing. Protective and risk factors for early sexual activity and contraception use amongst Black and Minority Ethnic adolescents in East London*, London, Department for Education and Skills and Department of Health

Thomas, Hugh (1998) *The Slave Trade: The History of the Atlantic Slave Trade, 1440–1870*, London, Papermac

Thomas, John C., (ed.) (2008) *Journal of Pentecostal Theology* 17:2, The Netherlands, BRILL

Thomas, J.M. and R.N. Blake (1996) 'Faith-based Community Development and African-American Neighbourhoods', in (eds) W.D. Keating, N. Krumholz, and P. Star Lawrence, *Revitalising Urban Neighbourhoods*, University Press of Kansas

Tillich, Paul (1957) *Dynamics of Faith*, New York, Harper and Row Publishers

Tinsley J., Jacobs M. (2006), 'Deprivation and ethnicity in England: a regional perspective' Office of National Statistics/Regional Trends Report No.39 http://www.statistics.gov.uk/articles/RegionalTrends/Article3RT39,pdf

Tocqueville, Alex de (1968) *Democracy in America*, London, Fontana

Tomlinson, S. (1977) 'Race and Education in Britain 1960–77: An Overview of the Literature', *Sage Race Relations Abstracts*, 2 (4)

Van Olphen, J, Schulz, A, Israel, B, Chatters, L, Klem, L, Parker, E, (2003) 'Religious involvement, social support, and health among African-American women on the east side of Detroit', *Journal of General Internal Medicine*, 18(7): pp.549–57

Viner, R. M., Haines, M. M., Taylor, S. J., Head, J., Booy, R., Stansfeld, S. (2006) 'Body mass, weight control behaviours, weight perception and emotional well being in a multiethnic sample of early adolescents', *International Journal of Obesity* (Lond) (10): pp.1514–21

Walker, Robin (2006) *When We Ruled*, London, Every Generation Media

Warren, Rick (1995) *Purpose Driven Church: Growth without compromising your message and Mission*, Grand Rapids, Zondervan

Watt, D., Sheriffe, G. and Majors, R. (1999) 'Mentoring Black Male Pupils', Unpublished manuscript, City College Manchester

Weber, Max (1992) *The Protestant Ethic and the Spirit of Capitalism*, London, Routledge

Weich, S., Nazroo, J., Sproston, K., McManus, S., Blanchard, M., Erens, B., (2004) 'Common mental disorders and ethnicity in England: the EMPIRIC study', *Psychological Medicine*, 34(8): pp.1543–51

Wilkinson, John (1993) *Church in Black and White*, Edinburgh, St Andrews Press

Williams, Stanley, T. (2004) *Redemption – From original gangster to Nobel Prize nominee*, Preston, Milo Books

Wilson, David and Rees, Gwyther (2006) *A study into black young people's experience of the youth justice system* in Just Justice Report, London, Children's Society

Zaninotto, P, Mindell, J., Hirani, V. (2007) 'Prevalence of cardiovascular risk factors among ethnic groups: Results from the Health Surveys for England', *Atherosclerosis*, 195(1):e48–e57